Please remember that this is a library book,
and that it belongs only temporarily to each
person who uses it. Be considerate. Do
not write in this, or any, library book.

THE GOLD COAST AND THE SLUM

The GOLD COAST AND THE SLUM

A SOCIOLOGICAL STUDY *of* CHICAGO'S NEAR NORTH SIDE

HARVEY WARREN ZORBAUGH

WITH AN INTRODUCTION BY HOWARD P. CHUDACOFF

THE UNIVERSITY OF CHICAGO PRESS

CHICAGO & LONDON

The University of Chicago Press, Chicago 60637
The University of Chicago Press, Ltd., London

International Standard Book Number: 0-226-98945-3
Library of Congress Catalog Card Number: 76-19218

TABLE OF CONTENTS

TABLE OF MAPS vi

INTRODUCTION, 1976 vii

INTRODUCTION. xvii

ACKNOWLEDGMENT xxi

    I. THE SHADOW OF THE SKYSCRAPER 1

    II. AN AREA IN TRANSITION 17

    III. THE GOLD COAST 46

    IV. THE WORLD OF FURNISHED ROOMS 69

    V. TOWERTOWN 87

    VI. THE RIALTO OF THE HALF-WORLD 105

    VII. THE SLUM 127

    VIII. LITTLE HELL 159

    IX. COMMUNITY INSTITUTIONS AND THE SOCIAL AGENCY . . 182

    X. THE LOWER NORTH COMMUNITY COUNCIL 200

    XI. THE CITY AND THE COMMUNITY 221

    XII. REFORM, REALISM, AND CITY LIFE 252

INDEX 281

TABLE OF MAPS

THE GOLD COAST 50
THE WORLD OF FURNISHED ROOMS 70
SUICIDES 83
A NIGHT CLUB GOES TO COURT 102
NON-SUPPORT CASES, COURT OF DOMESTIC RELATIONS . . . 129
THE POTTER'S FIELD 132
CRIME 157
POVERTY AND PHILANTHROPY 174
JUVENILE DELINQUENCY 176
THE GANG 178
THE CHURCH IN THE CHANGING COMMUNITY 184
BUSINESS MEN'S ASSOCIATIONS IN THE NEAR NORTH SIDE . . 191
THE LOWER NORTH COMMUNITY COUNCIL 219
THE ANATOMY OF THE CITY 230
NORTH SIDE RESIDENTS IN *Who's Who* 244

INTRODUCTION, 1976
Howard P. Chudacoff

A half century has passed since Robert E. Park and Ernest W. Burgess laid the groundwork for scientific study of modern urban life. Working with colleagues and students at the University of Chicago in the 1920s, these urban sociologists posited new theories about the development of cities, and they experimented with new methods of investigating forces that determined patterns of geographical and social organization. In the years that have passed since these efforts began, social scientists have revised many of the original concepts and refined much of the methodology. Yet the zest that Chicago sociologists had for their work is still refreshing, and much of their work remains useful.

Among scores of studies inspired by Park and Burgess's work Harvey W. Zorbaugh's *The Gold Coast and the Slum*, originally published by the University of Chicago Press in 1929, stands today as an important link between the Chicago school's fascination with community structure and current efforts by local groups to inspire neighborhood awareness. Sponsored by the University of Chicago's Local Community Research Committee, Zorbaugh's book presents a graphic analysis of social segregation within Chicago's Near North Side. Zorbaugh established himself with his mentors as being among the first to recognize explicitly that patterns of neighborhood life resulted from historical processes involved in the growth of the greater city. Moreover, he applied theoretical concepts of urban growth to a specific district and showed how a community was fragmented. His identifications of structural defects in community organization instruct and challenge modern reformers who want to improve old neighborhoods by preserving them. His sensitive descriptions survive as graphic historical documents about contrasting types of neighborhood life fifty years ago.

In 1932 a Chicago social worker observed, "The lower North Side has a beautiful front yard but a sorry-looking backyard." This area was the setting for *The Gold Coast and the Slum*. It was a district about a mile wide and a mile and a half long which in the 1920s included both extremes of the urban social spectrum. The "front yard," or "Gold Coast," contained the highest residential land values of any area in Chicago, more professional men, more persons listed in *Who's Who* and the *Social Register*, and more philanthropists. But behind the facade of fashionable apartments, hotels, and town houses that stretched along Lake Michigan lay the "sorry backyard," gray neighborhoods of rooming houses, honky-tonk dives, and immigrant tenements. Within the Near North Side area lived ninety thousand people—as many as inhabited the entire state of Nevada—of varied types: elites, artists, hoboes, Italians, Persians, blacks, and many more. Zorbaugh's task was to try to make some sense of this "nondescript" region and see if it had any potential for common interest and common action.

Zorbaugh sorted out the Near North Side by dividing it into geographical and social subdistricts. Chapters 3–8 present perceptive analyses of the characteristics and evolution of these places. The descriptive prose, among the most vivid written by students of the Chicago school, endures as a model for modern social analysts who depend more heavily on statistical finesse. Zorbaugh's literary skills, plus his presentation of individual cases, give the book a human quality necessary for social area analysis. As one contemporary reviewer remarked, Zorbaugh wrote "from the standpoint of a reporter rather than a scientist," but his technique enabled him to approach his topic more intimately than a direct empirical examination might have allowed.

Yet Zorbaugh's analysis raised problems because, of necessity, it was tangled in the issues of community, a concept that still nags social scientists. Most agree in the abstract that the term "community" connotes some form of shared interactions and sense of belonging within a geographically limited space. But controversies have resulted when someone has tried to apply the model to a specific case or, perhaps more frequently, when someone could not match reality with the model and therefore lamented the "breakdown" of community. Zorbaugh sided with the latter group; he found segregation and social disorganization in the Near North Side so pervasive that "there is scarcely an area that may be called a community" (p. 182).

On the other hand, his richly detailed descriptions reveal important forms of social organization that imply alternative types of community life. In his unsuccessful search for traditional agencies that would stabilize social behavior, such as family, clan, and church, Zorbaugh overlooked new urban institutions that assumed important functions. Several passages of *The Gold Coast and the Slum* mention how places such as barbershops, ethnic lodges, pawn shops, cafes, and coffee houses nurtured close human interactions and, by implication, replaced or reproduced older forms of community organization. Zorbaugh might have argued that these institutions were merely impersonal and artificial substitutes for older forms; yet, it seems clear that his concern with social disorganization deflected his attention from newer and different types of relationships. Moreover, Zorbaugh even documents a richness in the family life that he simultaneously identifies as being in a stage of dissolution. Although his chapter on "Little Hell," the Italian slum, laments the breakdown of social tranquility and control, he admits that in "Little Hell" family cohesiveness prevented serious disorganization, and he closes his narrative with a moving testimony from one of his documents on the district: "But after all I wonder if there is as much happiness on the Gold Coast as over in these basement rooms. When the father comes home at night, six or seven children run to meet him, and a warm supper is always ready; and summer nights—the streets—you would go a long way to hear the concertinas" (p. 181).

The virtues and drawbacks of Zorbaugh's study lie within the larger implications that his and similar analyses suggest. In the 1920s, the Chicago school of sociology made pioneering efforts to understand the forces of urban society by designing a new method for studying the city, a method that focused on the interactions between urban inhabitants and their environment. This approach was called "human ecology" because it paralleled similar investigations of the ways that plants and animals adjusted to their environments. Human ecology had attractions as a theory because it conceived of the city as an organism with complex, differentiated parts that somehow integrated into the larger urban society. The different parts were "natural areas," as Park called them, and they provided the locales for the most basic urban institutions and activities. Zorbaugh explained that these areas were the "unplanned, natural product of the city's growth," and he considered Chicago's Near North Side to be a typical example. The organic view of the city in the 1920s logically extended issues raised in the preceding Progressive years, and the concept of natural areas inspired closer, more systematic examinations of subregions (neighborhoods) and subgroups (ethnic, occupational, status, etc.). These examinations have informed urban planning and policy for the past five decades.

But two principal problems, one of vagueness and the other of emphasis, haunted works like Zorbaugh's that took an ecological approach. First, Chicago sociologists do not seem to have offered a clear definition of "natural areas." In plant ecology, natural areas were specific spatial units distinguished by their own peculiar characteristics. Human ecologists, however, blurred the translation to social situations. Thus, as critic Miller Alihan noted, it was not certain whether a "natural area" was a unit of geography, a grouping of buildings, a system of human relationships, or some combination of features. In some instances, the terms "natural area" and "neighborhood" were equivalent; on other occasions neighborhoods represented subunits of natural areas. Louis Wirth, another noted Chicago sociologist, wrote that land values determined boundaries of natural areas and then in the following sentence observed that rivers, streets, railroad tracks, and other physical barriers marked limits of natural areas. According to Wirth's first definition, Zorbaugh's Gold Coast, rooming-house district, and "Little Hell" qualify as natural areas; according to Wirth's second criterion and to Zorbaugh's own implications, the Near North Side is the principal natural area. Moreover, there was an unclear correspondence between natural areas and the series of concentric zones that Burgess postulated to typify the modern city's physical and spatial structure and that Zorbaugh applied to his own work. Thus although the areal emphasis seems to make sense intuitively, refined definitions are elusive.

Perhaps more importantly, the human ecologists' emphasis on environment raised questions about the role of human choice. That is, the ecological approach tended to view environmental factors as stimulants to behavior and change. This principle seemed reasonable when applied to biology, where environmentally produced competition effected a process of natural selection that then determined the survival and distribution of certain organisms. Human social systems, however, contain institutions which derive from conscious and rational choice as well as from nature. Park, Burgess, Zorbaugh, and the others undoubtedly recognized this distinction, but their emphasis on the principle of environmental determinism left the impression that the area was chiefly responsible for sifting and sorting people just as it did with plants and animals. Thus Zorbaugh asserts in a revealing footnote that "the modern city, industrial or commercial, like the plant or animal community, is largely an ecological product; that is, the rate and direction of the city's growth, the distribution of city features, the segregation of communities within the city, are by-products of the economic process—in which land values, rents, and wages are fixed—and the unintended result of competition" (p. 232).

Recent historical studies, particularly those of Sam Bass Warner, Jr., have confirmed that this theoretical statement has validity. Yet the concept ascribes an overly causative role to the environment and undervalues human volition. In a 1923 essay, Zorbaugh wrote "each natural area of the city tends to collect the particular individuals *predestined* to it" (italics added). Although Zorbaugh explained that these particular individuals gave each area its distinct cultural identity, his view of predestination or determinism implied a rigid process, particularly when applied to so-called disorganized areas. It then became possible to conclude that unstable areas attracted, and even produced, unstable people. Thus, in *The Gold Coast and the Slum*, the anonymous rooming-house district created restless and lonely people; unconventional Towertown encouraged egocentrics and neurotics; the poverty of the slum undermined social sanctions and group identity.

Again, such generalizations include some valid assumptions, but they overlook the dynamics and functions of the areas examined. The disorganized neighborhoods of Chicago's Near North Side contained residences that were least adaptive to the needs of urban families. Rather, the "World of Furnished Rooms," the "bohemia," the "Rialto," and even the slums offered small rental units and cheap, unfurnished tenement apartments that either filled the housing needs of unattached, familyless individuals or served as temporary expedients for young families hoping to find better dwellings elsewhere (though their hopes were not always realized). The areas, inevitably characterized by high mobility, fulfilled the important function of providing housing for migrants, old people, young singles, immigrant families, and persons on the edge of poverty. As sociologist Peter Rossi observed in *Why Families Move* (1955), "mobile areas are mobile because they provide housing for households in those life cycle stages which are particularly unstable" (p. 181). Although this mobility often prevents viable organizational life in a neighborhood, it often reflects a natural—and functional—exercise of human choice that secures the needed environment.

One area in Zorbaugh's survey, the Gold Coast, preserved some solidarity, if not stability. This region, with its wealth, leadership, and sense of aristocratic responsibility, seemed to hold the keys to the city's destiny. Zorbaugh hoped that the people who inhabited the Gold Coast would assume functions beyond those of mere "pageantry, display, and froth"; for only these people had roots deep enough to identify with the welfare of the entire city, and only they had resources and ability to improve civic and social life. Zorbaugh's hopes and admiration, coming at the end of the 1920s, a period when local initiative still was the canon of urban policy, sound outmoded in the wake of the New Deal, subsequent federal intervention in cities, and the exodus of affluent whites to the suburbs. And yet the need for able and visionary local leaders, who can identify with the entire metropolitan area as well as understand its diverse subareas, still presses modern society.

The Gold Coast and the Slum and works by other Chicago sociologists remain important today not only as historical documents of urban theory but also as catalysts for discussions of how order and social progress could be achieved within heterogeneous cities. If Zorbaugh and his colleagues did not fully explore the meaning and functions of community and mobility, modern policymakers have not always recognized the subtle complexities of urban life that the Chicago school stressed. These complexities change as cities grow and are transformed; but thanks to the work of the Chicago school, urban experts have become more sensitive to the process of change and the dynamics of city life.

Harvey Warren Zorbaugh was born in Cleveland, Ohio, September 20, 1896. He received an A.B. from Vanderbilt in 1922 and studied at the University of Chicago between 1923 and 1926 as a Laura Spelman Rockefeller Memorial fellow. He spent the rest of his career on the faculty of New York University where he became a leading specialist in the social adjustment of gifted children. During his study of Chicago's Near North Side, Zorbaugh noticed that leaders of gangs were extremely intelligent youths who apparently had become lawbreakers because no one had discovered or channeled their talents. After completing *The Gold Coast and the Slum*, he involved himself in a number of clinics, committees, conferences, and projects that addressed problems of gifted children. Zorbaugh also pioneered in educational and commercial television and was an outspoken opponent of race prejudice in public schools. He died January 21, 1965, at the age of sixty-eight.

INTRODUCTION

One of the pleasures of travel, says Von Ogden Vogt, is that of "discovering communities that are *descript* rather than nondescript." He mentions Oberammergau, Bangkok, Oxford, and adds "or any other place where there has been some sustained attempt to describe all things and set forth the common views in laws, customs, and all the arts of life from house building to worship." A descript community is "a place of unity and charm." A nondescript community is one that lacks these qualities. A nondescript community may be interesting, of course, but it will not be restful, and will not be satisfying merely as an object of contemplation.

The community with which this volume is concerned is nondescript; it is a place of unusual interest, but it has neither the unity nor the charm of a place in which the common view is set forth "in laws, customs, and all the arts of life." There are few customs that are common at once to the "Gold Coast" and to "Little Sicily," and there is certainly no common view which holds the cosmopolitan population of this whole region together in any common purpose. Furthermore, the laws which prevail are not a communal product, and there is no organized public opinion which supports and contributes to their enforcement. In fact, it is doubtful whether, in any proper sense of the word, the "Lower North Side" can be called a community at all. It is a region; one of the characteristic regions of a metropolitan city, remarkable for the number and kinds of people huddled and crowded together in physical proximity, without the opportunity and, apparently, with very little desire for the intimacies and the mutual understanding and comprehension which ordinarily insure a common view and make collective action possible. It is, however, just this "nondescript" situation, so lacking in "unity and charm," that gives this region its peculiar interest. It is nondescript because it is in process of evolution. It is typically an area of transition, the character of its populations and the problems which it presents are at once a reflection and a consequence of the conditions which this period of transition imposes.

What is true of the region is characteristic of most of the very different classes and kinds of people that inhabit it. From the Gold Coast on the lake front to Little Sicily on the river, they are all in transition. Everywhere the old order is passing, but the new order has not arrived. Everything is loose and free, but everything is problematic.

This is particularly true of the so-called rooming-house area, which occupies the center of the region. Into this area all the young and adventurous people, who come to the city to seek their fortunes, tend to drift. Presently they will find their places somewhere in the broad cadre of occupations which the great city offers them. In this way they will become incorporated into the permanent economic and social order about them. In the meantime they are at large, and in transition. In the rooming-house area there is apparently a larger number of young women than of young men. The Lower North Side is for young women in particular, a kind of Latin Quarter, where students of art and music find places to live in close proximity to the studios. It is this region that supports most of the little theaters, the smart book stores, and the bohemian and radical clubs. Here is Bohemia, which is itself a place of transition, a place in which life is adventurous, to be sure, but often very lonely.

Every great city has its bohemias and its hobohemias; its gold coast and little Sicilies; its rooming-house areas and its slums. In Chicago, and on the Lower North Side, they are in close physical proximity to one another. This gives one an interesting illustration of the situation in which the physical distances and the social distances do not coincide; a situation in which people who live side by side are not, and—because of the divergence of their interests and their heritages—cannot, even with the best of good will, become neighbors.

It is this situation which constitutes the specific problem and the central theme of this study. Our political system is founded upon the conviction that people who live in the same locality have common interests, and that they can therefore be relied upon to act together for their common welfare. This assumption, as it turns out, is not valid for large cities. The difficulty of maintaining in the city the intimate contacts which in the small town insured the existence of a common purpose and made concerted action possible is certainly very great. Particularly is this true of those parts of the city where people live in hotels or lodging houses, where few people own their homes and most people are transient dwellers. Under such circumstances, all the traditional forms of local government fail or break down altogether. The fact that there exists on the Lower North Side a community council which recognizes this problem and has sought to solve it, is itself an evidence of the conditions it seeks to remedy. It was, by the way, this community council and its problems which furnished the original motive for this study.

Perhaps I should add that this volume is not a solution; it is a definition of the problem merely. The statement which it offers has, at any rate, laid the foundation for further study and experiment. Furthermore, it offers an example of a kind of investigation of urban life which is at least comparable with the studies that anthropologists have made of the cultures of primitive peoples. It is upon studies of this general character, I am convinced, that we must base our programs for the reorganization of our own political and collective life.

ROBERT E. PARK

UNIVERSITY OF CHICAGO

ACKNOWLEDGMENT

The writer wishes to acknowledge his great indebtedness to Dr. Robert E. Park, under whose direction the research upon which this book is based was carried on, for his many critical and stimulating suggestions both as to methods of investigation and as to the interpretation of data. The writer is indebted to Dr. Robert E. Park and Dr. Ernest W. Burgess for the conception of the city about which this book is written, and to Dr. Ellsworth Faris for many suggestions as to the effect of the city upon human personality. The writer takes this occasion to thank the many friends and fellow-students of human behavior in the city who have generously placed at his disposal the results of their own research, among them Nels Anderson, Guy Brown, Ruth Shonle Cavan, Frances Donovan, Everett Hughes, Ernst Krueger, Franc L. McCluer, Ernest Mowrer, Walter Reckless, Clifford Shaw, Eyler Simpson, Frederic Thrasher, Louis Wirth, and Erle Young. The writer also wishes to thank the Chicago Historical Society for help in collecting material for "An Area in Transition"; Miss Florence Nesbitt, of the United Charities, for access to the case records of the Lower North District, and for many interesting sidelights on the life of the slum; Miss Helen A. Day, formerly head resident of Eli Bates House, for material on "Little Sicily"; Miss Frieda Foltz, of the Lower North Community Council, for material on the Council itself, as well as for material on the Near North Side at large, and for help in making many useful contacts; Miss Dora Allen for much interesting material on the slum, the "Rialto," and the "World of Furnished

xxi

Rooms"; Mrs. Charles Harrington Chadwick for material on slum life; the many persons who contributed material for the chapter "The Gold Coast," whose names are omitted at their request; and a host of other individuals and agencies on the Near North Side, and many students in the graduate school of the University of Chicago, for suggestions, access to materials, data, documents, and assistance in the actual investigation which has made possible this cross-section of the tidelands of city life. Finally, the writer wishes to thank the Local Community Research Committee of the University of Chicago for its assistance in the study, and Professor Paul Bixler for his careful reading and helpful criticism of the manuscript.

HARVEY WARREN ZORBAUGH

CHAPTER I

THE SHADOW OF THE SKYSCRAPER

.... It is a veritable Babel, in which some thirty or more tongues are spoken. .... Gunmen haunt its streets, and a murder is committed in them nearly every day in the year. It is smoke-ridden and disfigured by factories and railway yards, and many of its streets are ill-paved. Moreover, the people who throng them are more carelessly dressed than those in Fifth Avenue, and their voices not so well modulated as those of the inhabitants of Boston. Their manners, too, are of the kind the New Yorker defines as western.—CHATFIELD-TAYLOR, *Chicago*

The Chicago River, its waters stained by industry, flows back upon itself, branching to divide the city into the South Side, the North Side, and "the great West Side." In the river's southward bend lies the Loop, its skyline looming toward Lake Michigan. The Loop is the heart of Chicago, the knot in the steel arteries of elevated structure which pump in a ceaseless stream the three millions of population of the city into and out of its central business district. The canyon-like streets of the Loop rumble with the traffic of commerce. On its sidewalks throng people of every nation, pushing unseeingly past one another, into and out of office buildings, shops, theaters, hotels, and ultimately back to the north, south, and west "sides" from which they came. For miles over what once was prairie now sprawls in endless blocks the city.

The city's conquest of the prairie has proceeded stride for stride with the development of transportation. The outskirts of the city have always been about forty-five minutes from the heart of the Loop. In the days of the horse-drawn car they were not beyond Twenty-second Street on the South Side. With the coming of the cable car they were extended to the vicinity of Thirty-sixth Street. The electric car—surface and elevated—again extended the city's outskirts, this time well past Seventieth Street. How far "rapid transit" will take them, no one can predict.

Apace with the expansion of the city has gone the ascendancy of the Loop. Every development in transportation, drawing increasing throngs of people into the central business district, has tended to centralize there not only commerce and finance, but all the vital activities of the city's life. The development of communication has further tightened the Loop's grip on the life of the city. The telephone has at once enormously increased the area over which the central business district can exert control and centralized that control. The newspaper, through the medium of advertising, has firmly established the supremacy of the Loop and, through the news, focused the attention of the city upon the Loop. The skyscraper is the visible symbol of the Loop's domination of the city's life. The central business district of the old city—like that of modern London—with its six- and eight-story buildings, sprawled over an unwieldy area. But the skyscraper, thrusting the Loop skyward thirty, forty, fifty stories, has made possible an extraordinary centralization and articulation of the central business district of the modern city. Drawing thousands daily into the heart of the city, where the old type of building drew hundreds, the cluster of skyscrapers within the Loop has become the city's vortex.

As the Loop expands it literally submerges the areas about it with the traffic of its commerce. Business and industry encroach upon residential neighborhoods. As the roar of traffic swells, and the smoke of industry begrimes buildings, land values rise. The old population moves slowly out, to be replaced by a mobile, shifting, anonymous population bringing with it transitional forms of social life. Within the looming shadow of the skyscraper, in Chicago as in every great city, is found a zone of instability and change—the tidelands of city life.

A part of these tidelands, within ten minutes' walk of the Loop and the central business district, within five minutes by street car or bus, just across the Chicago River, lies the Near North Side, sometimes called "North Town." Within this area, a mile and a half long and scarcely a mile wide, bounded by lake Michigan on the east and by the Chicago River on the south and west, under the shadow of the Tribune Tower, a part of the inner city, live ninety thousand people, a population representing all the types and contrasts that lend to the great city its glamor and romance.

The first settlers of Chicago built upon the north bank of the Chicago River, and Chicago's first business house and first railroad were on Kinzie street. But early in Chicago's history destiny took its great commercial and industrial development southward, and for several decades the North Side was a residential district, well-to-do and fashionable. The story of early Chicago society centers about homes on Ohio, Erie, Cass, and Rush streets; and street after street of old stone fronts, curious streets some of them, still breathe an air of respectability reminiscent of earlier and better days and belying the slow conquest of the slum.

Here change has followed fast upon change. With the growth of the city commerce has encroached upon residential property, relentlessly pushing it northward or crowding it along the lake shore, until now the Near North Side is chequered with business streets. Into this area, where commerce is competing the conquest of the community, has crept the slum. Meantime great industries have sprung up along the river, and peoples speaking foreign tongues have come to labor in them. The slum has offered these alien peoples a place to live cheaply and to themselves; and wave upon wave of immigrants has swept over the area— Irish, Swedish, German, Italian, Persian, Greek, and Negro —forming colonies, staying for a while, then giving way to others. But each has left its impress and its stragglers, and today there live on the Near North Side twenty-nine or more nationalities, many of them with their Old World tongues and customs.

The city's streets can be read as can the geological record in the rock. The old stone fronts of the houses on the side streets; old residences along lower Rush and State, crowded between new business blocks, or with shops built along the street in front of them; a garage with "Riding Academy" in faded letters above its doors; the many old churches along La Salle and Dearborn streets; an office building growing out of a block of rooming-houses; "Deutsche Apotheke" on the window of a store in a neighborhood long since Italian— these are signs that record the changes brought about by the passing decades, changes still taking place today.

The Near North Side is an area of high light and shadow, of vivid contrasts—contrasts not only between the old and the new, between the native and the foreign, but between wealth and poverty, vice and respectability, the conventional and the bohemian, luxury and toil.

Variety is the spice of life, as depicted in the books of the Board of Assessors; autocracy and democracy mingle on the same pages;

aphorisms are borne out; and "art for art's sake" remains the slogan of the twentieth century.

On one page of North District Book 18, the record of the worldly holdings of James C. Ewell, artist, 4 Ohio Street, is set down as "Total personal property, $19." So-and-so, artists, are reported thruout the district with this notation: "Attic room, ill-furnished, many paintings: unable to estimate."

The art colony is located in this section, as is the colony of the rich and the nearly rich. And on the same page are the following three entries which span the stream of life:

Cyrus H. McCormick, 50 E. Huron St., $895,000; taxable assessment, $447,500.

Mary V. McCormick, 678 Rush St., $480,000; taxable assessment, $240,000.

And then—as another contrast—the following entry appears on record:

United States Senator Medill McCormick, guest at the Drake Hotel, $_____,000,000,000.[1]

At the corner of Division Street and the Lake Shore Drive stands a tall apartment building in which seventeen-room apartments rent at one thousand dollars a month. One mile west, near Division Street and the river, Italian families are living in squalid basement rooms for which they pay six dollars a month. The greatest wealth in Chicago is concentrated along the Lake Shore Drive, in what is called the "Gold Coast." Almost at its back door, in "Little Hell," is the greatest concentration of poverty in Chicago. Respectability, it would seem, is measured by rentals and land values![2]

The Near North Side is not merely an area of contrasts; it is an area of extremes. All the phenomena characteristic

[1] *Chicago Herald and Examiner*, July, 1923.

[2] United Charities of Chicago: *Sixty Years of Service.* In 1920–21 there were 90 contributors to the United Charities in less than a square mile on the Gold Coast, and 460 poverty cases in the square mile behind it.

of the city are clearly segregated and appear in exaggerated form. Not only are there extremes of wealth and poverty. The Near North Side has the highest residential land values in the city, and among the lowest; it has more professional men, more politicians, more suicides, more persons in *Who's Who*, than any other "community" in Chicago.[1]

The turgid stream of the Chicago River, which bounds the Near North Side on the south and the west, has played a prominent part in its history. A great deal of shipping once went up the river, and tugs, coal barges, tramp freighters, and occasional ore boats still whistle at its bridges and steam slowly around its bends. This shipping caused commerce and industry to locate along the river, and today wharves, lumber and coal yards, iron works, gas works, sheet metal works, light manufacturing plants and storage plants, wholesale houses for spices, furs, groceries, butter, and imported oils line both sides of the river for miles, and with the noise and smoke of the railroads make a great barrier that half encircles the Near North Side, renders the part of it along the river undesirable to live in, and slowly encroaches northward and eastward.

[1] Taking figures for five widely differing "communities" in Chicago, this fact is clearly brought out:

Community	Population	Who's Who	Physicians	Politicians	Poverty Cases	Suicides
Back of the Yards*.......	39,908	1	28	4	185	8
Bridgeport†.............	64,875	0	44	12	180	3
Lawndale‡.............	105,819	1	212	14	251	6
Woodlawn§.............	69,594	31	185	14	48	8
Near North.............	83,819	151	212	30	555	28

* Immigrant community back of the Stockyards.
† Polish "area of first settlement" on the Southwest Side.
‡ Jewish "area of second settlement" on the West Side.
§ South Side residential community, surrounding the University of Chicago, containing many professional men and women.

"North Town" is divided into east and west by State Street. East of State Street lies the Gold Coast, Chicago's most exclusive residential district, turning its face to the lake and its back upon what may lie west toward the river. West of State Street lies a nondescript area of furnished rooms: Clark Street, the Rialto of the half-world; "Little Sicily," the slum.

The Lake Shore Drive is the Mayfair of the Gold Coast. It runs north and south along Lake Michigan, with a wide parkway, bridle path, and promenade. On its western side rise the imposing stone mansions, with their green lawns and wrought-iron-grilled doorways, of Chicago's wealthy aristocracy and her industrial and financial kings. South of these is Streeterville a "restricted" district of tall apartments and hotels. Here are the Drake Hotel and the Lake Shore Drive hotel, Chicago's most exclusive. And here apartments rent for from three hundred fifty to a thousand dollars a month. Indeed, the Lake Shore Drive is a street more of wealth than of aristocracy; for in this midwest metropolis money counts for more than does family, and the aristocracy is largely that of the financially successful.

South of Oak Street the Lake Shore Drive, as it turns, becomes North Michigan Avenue, an avenue of fashionable hotels and restaurants, of smart clubs and shops. North Michigan Avenue is the Fifth Avenue of the Middle West; and already it looks forward to the day when Fifth Avenue will be the North Michigan Avenue of the East.

On a warm spring Sunday "Vanity Fair" glides along "the Drive" in motor cars of expensive mark, makes colorful the bridle-paths, or saunters up the promenade between "the Drake" and Lincoln Park. The tops of the tan motor busses are crowded with those who live farther out, going home from church—those of a different world who look at "Vanity Fair" with curious or envious eyes. Even here the element of contrast is not lacking, for a mother from back west, with a shawl over her head, waits for a pause in the stream of motors to lead her eager child across to the beach, while beside her stand a collarless man in a brown derby and his girl in Sunday gingham, from some rooming-house back on La Salle Street.

For a few blocks back of "the Drive"—on Belleview Place, East Division Street, Stone, Astor, Banks, and North State Parkway, streets less pretentious but equally aristocratic—live more than a third of the people in Chicago's social register, "of good family and not employed." Here are the families that lived on the once fashionable Prairie Avenue, and later Ashland Boulevard, on the South and West sides. These streets, with the Lake Shore Drive, constitute Chicago's much vaunted Gold Coast, a little world to itself, which the city, failing to dislodge, has grown around and passed by.

At the back door of the Gold Coast, on Dearborn, Clark, and La Salle streets, and on the side streets extending south to the business and industrial area, is a strange world, painfully plain by contrast, a world that lives in houses with neatly lettered cards in the window: "Furnished Rooms." In these houses, from midnight to dawn, sleep some twenty-five thousand people. But by day houses and streets are practically deserted. For early in the morning this population hurries from its houses and down its streets, boarding cars and busses, to work in the Loop. It is a childless area, an area of young men and young women, most of whom are single, though some are married, and others are living together unmarried. It is a world of constant comings and goings, of dull routine and little romance, a world of un-satisfied longings.

The Near North Side shades from light to shadow, and from shadow to dark. The Gold Coast gives way to the world of furnished rooms; and the rooming-house area, to the west again, imperceptibly becomes the slum. The common denominator of the slum is its submerged aspect and its de-tachment from the city as a whole. The slum is a bleak area of segregation of the sediment of society; an area of extreme poverty, tenements, ramshackle buildings, of evictions and evaded rents; an area of working mothers and children, of high rates of birth, infant mortality, illegitimacy, and death; an area of pawnshops and second-hand stores, of gangs, of "flops" where every bed is a vote. As distinguished from the vice area, the disintegrating neighborhood, the slum is an area which has reached the limit of decay and is on the verge of reorganization as missions, settlements, playparks, and business come in.

The Near North Side, west of Clark Street from North Avenue to the river, and east of Clark Street from Chicago Avenue to the river, we may describe as a slum, without fear of contradiction. For this area, cut off by the barrier of river and industry, and for years without adequate trans-portation, has long been a backwater in the life of the city, This slum district is drab and mean. In ten months the United Charities here had 460 relief cases. Poverty is ex-treme. Many families are living in one or two basement rooms for which they pay less than ten dollars a month. These rooms are stove heated, and wood is sold on the streets in bundles, and coal in small sacks. The majority of houses, back toward the river, are of wood, and not a few have windows broken out. Smoke, the odor from the gas works, and the smell of dirty alleys is in the air. Both rooms and lots are overcrowded. Back tenements, especially north of Division Street, are common.[1]

Life in the slum is strenuous and precarious. One reads in the paper of a mother on North Avenue giving away her baby that the rest of her children may live. Frequently babies are found in alleyways. A nurse at the Passavant Hospital on North La Salle tells of a dirty little gamin, brought in from Wells Street, whose toe had been bitten off by a rat while he slept. Many women from this neighborhood are in the maternity ward four times in three years. A girl, a waitress, living at the Albany Hotel on lower Rush Street, recently committed suicide leaving the brief note, "I am tired of everything. I have seen too much. That is all."[2]

Clark Street is the Rialto of the slum. Deteriorated store buildings, cheap dance halls and movies, cabarets and doubt-

[1] A five-room house on Hill Street, the rooms in which are $9 \times 12 \times 10$ feet high, has thirty occupants. Another nurse told the writer of being called on a case on Sedgewick Street and finding two couples living in one room. One couple worked days, the other nights; one couple went to bed when the other couple got up. Mrs. Louise De Kowen Bowen (*Growing Up with a City*), reminiscing of her United Charities experiences, tells of a woman who for three years existed on the food she procured from garbage cans and from the samples of department store demonstration counters. She adds:

"Sometimes fate seems to be relentless to the point of absurdity, as in one case I remember of an Italian family. . . . . The man was riding on a street car and was suddenly assaulted by an irate passenger. . . . . His nose was broken and he was badly disfigured. . . . . A few days later, on his way home from a dispensary where he had gone to have his wound dressed, he fell off a sidewalk and broke his leg. The mother gave birth to a child the same day. Another child died the following day, and the eldest girl, only fourteen years old, who had been sent out to look for work, was foully assaulted on the street." Such is the life of the slum!

[2] *Chicago Evening American*, December 21, 1923.

ful hotels, missions, "flops," pawnshops and second-hand stores, innumerable restaurants, soft-drink parlors and "fellowship" saloons, where men sit about and talk, and which are hangouts for criminal gangs that live back in the slum, fence at the pawnshops, and consort with the transient prostitutes so characteristic of the North Side—such is "the Street." It is an all-night street, a street upon which one meets all the varied types that go to make up the slum.

The slum harbors many sorts of people: the criminal, the radical, the bohemian, the migratory worker, the immigrant, the unsuccessful, the queer and unadjusted. The migratory worker is attracted by the cheap hotels on State, Clark, Wells, and the streets along the river. The criminal and underworld find anonymity in the transient life of the cheaper rooming-houses such as exist on North La Salle Street. The bohemian and the unsuccessful are attracted by cheap attic or basement rooms. The radical is sure of a sympathetic audience in Washington Square. The foreign colony, on the other hand, is found in the slum, not because the immigrant seeks the slum, nor because he makes a slum of the area in which he settles, but merely because he finds there cheap quarters in which to live, and relatively little opposition to his coming. From Sedgwick Street west to the river is a colony of some fifteen thousand Italians, familiarly known as "Little Hell." Here the immigrant has settled blocks by villages, bringing with him his language, his customs, and his traditions, many of which persist.

Other foreign groups have come into this area. North of "Little Sicily," between Wells and Milton streets, there is a large admixture of Poles with Americans, Irish, and Slavs. The Negro, too, is moving into this area and pushing on into

"Little Hell." There is a small colony of Greeks grouped about West Chicago Avenue, with its picturesque coffee houses on Clark Street. Finally, there has come in within the past few years a considerable colony of Persians, which has also settled in the vicinity of Chicago Avenue. The slum on the Near North Side is truly cosmopolitan.

In the slum, but not of it, is "Towertown," or "the village." South of Chicago Avenue, along east Erie, Ohio, Huron, and Superior streets, is a considerable colony of artists and of would-be artists. The artists have located here because old buildings can be cheaply converted into studios. The would-be artists have followed the artists. And the hangers-on of bohemia have come for atmosphere, and because the old residences in the district have stables. "The village" is full of picturesque people and resorts—tearooms with such names as the Wind Blew Inn, the Blue Mouse, and the Green Mask. And many interesting art stores, antique shops, and stalls with rare books are tucked away among the old buildings. All in all, the picturesque and unconventional life of "the village" is again in striking contrast to the formal and conventional life of the Gold Coast, a few short blocks to the north.

One has but to walk the streets of the Near North Side to sense the cultural isolation beneath these contrasts. Indeed, the color and picturesqueness of the city exists in the intimations of what lies behind the superficial contrasts of its life. How various are the thoughts of the individuals who throng up Michigan Avenue from the Loop at the close of the day—artists, shop girls, immigrants, inventors, men of affairs, women of fashion, waitresses, clerks, entertainers. How many are their vocational interests; how different are their ambitions. How vastly multiplied are the chances of life in a great city, as compared with those of the American towns and European peasant villages from which most of these individuals have come. What plans, plots, conspiracies, and dreams for taking advantage of these chances different individuals must harbor under their hats. Yet they have little in common beyond the fact that they jostle one another on the same street. Experience has taught them different languages. How far they are from understanding one another, or from being able to communicate save upon the most obvious material matters!

As one walks from the Drake Hotel and the Lake Shore Drive west along Oak Street, through the world of rooming-houses, into the slum and the streets of the Italian Colony one has a sense of distance as between the Gold Coast and Little Hell—distance that is not geographical but social. There are distances of language and custom. There are distances represented by wealth and the luster it adds to human existence. There are distances of horizon—the Gold Coast living throughout the world while Little Hell is still only slowly emerging out of its old Sicilian villages. There are distances represented by the Gold Coast's absorbing professional interests. It is one world that revolves about the Lake Shore Drive, with its mansions, clubs, and motors, its benefits and assemblies. It is another world that revolves about the Dill Pickle Club, the soap boxes of Washington Square, or the shop of Romano the Barber. And each little world is absorbed in its own affairs.

For the great majority of the people on the Gold Coast—excepting those few individuals who remember, or whose parents remember, the immigrant communities out of which they have succeeded in climbing—the district west of State Street exists only in the newspapers. And from the newspapers they learn nothing reassuring. The metropolitan press pictures this district as a bizarre world of gang wars, of exploding stills, of radical plots, of "lost" girls, of suicides, of bombings, of murder.

The resident of the Lake Shore Drive forms his conception of Little Sicily from such items as these:

"LITTLE ITALY" STORE WRECKED BY BOMB

For the eighth consecutive Sunday the North Side "Little Italy" was awakened by its usual "alarm clock." The "alarm clock" was a large black powder bomb. The detonation was heard throughout the colony. A part of the grocery store of Mrs. Beatrice Diengello was wrecked, and the eight families living in the adjoining tenement were rudely awakened.

TWO SHOT TO DEATH IN WHISKEY FEUD

Two bullet-ridden bodies were found yesterday near "Death Corner," Cambridge and Oak streets. Police investigation developed the theory that a feud among whiskey runners was responsible for the murders.

KIN'S SILENCE AGAIN HIDES ITALIAN SLAYER

The usual shrugging of shoulders answered detectives who are trying to clear up Chicago's latest Italian murder—that of Frank Mariata, a laborer, who was shot to death as he was leaving his flat, 462 West Division Street, yesterday morning. Three men were seen rushing from the building after the shooting, but relatives of the dead man claim they have no idea who the slayers are. Although three guns were found under Mariata's pillow, his wife insists he had no enemies.

FIFTY-THREE PER CENT OF CHICAGO'S KILLINGS OCCUR
IN LITTLE ITALY AND BLACK BELT

More than half of the violent deaths in Chicago in the first ninety days of this year occurred among Negroes or Italians, two groups constituting about 7 per cent of the population. The Italian blackhand zone is on the Near North Side, bounded by Erie, Dearborn, Division, and the river.

Similarly, the "Gold Coaster" concludes from his morning paper that the Persian colony is a place of feuds, flash-
ing knives, flying chairs, and shattering glass:

TWO COPS END WAR OF 200 PERSIANS: THREE MEN STABBED

Three men were stabbed, several badly beaten, and ten arrested
during a pitched battle between rival factions of Persians in a coffee
shop at 706 North Clark Street early yesterday evening. Police in
answering a riot call had to fight their way through more than two
hundred fighting men.

For several years there has been an unwritten law that no Syrian
Persian was allowed north of Huron Street on Clark Street. Five members of the race wandered into the coffee shop of Titian and Sayad
and sat down at a table to play cards. In a short time six Assyrian
Persians entered the place and saw them. They walked to the table,
it is said, and remarked that the Syrians had better get off the street.
At that the five Syrians started to fight.

In a moment other men in the place drew knives and advanced
on the battlers. Chairs were overturned and windows broken. The
fight led out to the street. Finally more than two hundred had taken
up the fight. Then someone sent in a riot call.

Beyond these newspaper reports, little is known of the
world west of State Street by the people of the Gold Coast.
Their affairs rarely take them into the river district. The
reports of social agencies are little read. It is a region remote.

But to the people who live west of State Street the Gold
Coast is immediate and real. It is one of the sights of the
town. They throng its streets in going down to the lake on
hot summer days. From the beach they gaze up at the
magnificent hotels and apartments of Streeterville, and at
the luxurious and forbidding mansions of the Lake Shore
Drive. They watch the streams of costly automobiles and
fashionably dressed men and women. The front pages of the
newspapers they read as they hang to straps on the street

cars in the evening are filled with pictures of the inhabitants of the Gold Coast, and with accounts of their comings and goings. It all enlists the imagination. Consequently the people from "back west" enormously idealize the Gold Coast's life. They imitate its styles and manners. The imagination of the shop girl, of the immigrant, of the hobo plays with these externals of its life. In the movie they see realistic pictures of "high society." These they take to be the inner, intimate life of which they see the externals along the Lake Shore Drive. As a result the social distance from Death Corner to the Drake Hotel is no less than the distance from the Casino Club to Bughouse Square.

The isolation of the populations crowded together within these few hundred blocks, the superficiality and externality of their contacts, the social distances that separate them, their absorption in the affairs of their own little worlds— these, and not mere size and numbers, constitute the social problem of the inner city. The community, represented by the town or peasant village where everyone knows everyone else clear down to the ground, is gone. Over large areas of the city "community" is little more than a geographical expression. Yet the old tradition of control persists despite changed conditions of life. The inevitable result is cultural disorganization.

CHAPTER II

AN AREA IN TRANSITION

This teeming, shifting area, with its striking high-lights and deep shadows—the Near North Side of today—is to be understood only in its past relation to the growth of the greater city. Its early history, consecutive movements of population, the encroachment of commerce and industry as the city crossed the river and sprawled northward, have all left their impress and have contributed to the establishment of these social distances within this "community" in the inner city.

Within the memory of men still living on the North Side, Indians camped along the river where now great factories smoke and thousands of vehicles clamor at the bridges. Indeed, it is only a little over a hundred years ago, as tradition has it, since a black man from San Domingo, bearing the ornate name of Jean Baptiste Point de Saible, built the first log cabin of what was to be early Chicago, on the north bank of the river, at a spot long marked by the abutments of the old Rush street bridge. This cabin was later acquired by John Kinzie, the first American and the first real settler, who brought his family on in 1804. Kinzie's cabin became the center of a little settlement near the stockade of the long-vanished Fort Dearborn.

After the War of 1812 a village grew up between the northern and southern branches of the river and the lake. With the dredging of the harbor, in 1833, the village became a town. Wharves were built along both banks of the river. Chicago's first packing house was built at this time. Immigrants from the East came crowding in, and by 1837, the year in which Chicago was incorporated as a city, it had become a community of several thousand, and had pushed northward to North Avenue and Lincoln Park. It was expected that Kinzie Street would be *the* business street of the new city, and Chicago's first railroad, the Galena & Chicago Union Railroad, was brought down the center of Kinzie Street in 1847. The lumber business was then locating along the river, and things were in a state of boom.

But Chicago was still a frontier town. In 1845 there were but 5,000 persons between Chicago and the Pacific.

On the northwest corner of Michigan Avenue and Lake Street was a very large, vacant field, which was usually filled with camping parties; whole communities migrating from the East to the West. It was a common sight to see a long line of prairie-schooners drive into this field, with cows tied behind the wagons. There they would unload for the night. There was always mystery and charm about their evening campfires. . . . .

The greatest excitement was the arrival of the weekly boat from Buffalo. . . . . These boats brought many supplies, and our only news from the outside world. In those days the great West Side, as we know it now, did not exist; and even the North Side seemed like a separate town because there were only one or two bridges connecting the two sides of the town. . . . .[1]

THE SIXTIES

In the decade and a half previous to the Civil War the city grew rapidly, and by 1860 there were 29,922 persons living north of the river. During the years between 1850 and 1860 nearly half of Chicago's increase in population was by foreign immigration; as it was, also, between 1860 and 1870. And while previous to 1860 the population of the North Side was mainly native American, the first statistics avail-

[1] C. Kirkland, *Chicago Yesterdays*, pp. 42–43.

able on the national composition of Chicago's population by
wards, those for 1866, show that there were then a considerable number of Irish and Germans living in the North
Division.[1] The Irish, the first of five waves of immigration
that were to sweep over the Near North Side, began coming
in during the late fifties, a part of the great immigration from
Ireland in 1848; and the Germans began coming in soon
after the Irish.

The commercial importance of the North Branch continued to grow. The tanning and meat-packing industries
were locating along it; the lumber business was rapidly increasing; warehouses were building; and in 1857 Chicago's
first iron industry, the North Chicago Rolling Mills, located
on its banks. Later, as railroads came into the city, a number of machine shops were built on Clark, Wells, State, Erie,
Kinzie, and Division streets, and on Chicago and North
avenues, thus binding the North Side more closely to the
activities of the city as a whole.[2] And between 1859 and
1864 horse-drawn trams began to run out Clark, Wells, and
Larrabee streets, and across Chicago Avenue and Division

[1] See *Smoke Abatement and Electrification of Railway Terminals in
Chicago* (Report of the Chicago Association of Commerce Commission,
Chicago, 1913); and *Chicago: Historical and Statistical Sketch of the Garden
City* (Chicago, 1868), p. 16, according to which the composition of the popula-
tion of the North Division was, in 1866:

Ward	American	German	Irish	Swedish	Other Nation-alities
14	6,197	6,568	831	298	271
15	10,044	4,222	2,984	1,920	1,200
16	9,066	2,283	2,652	916	1,964
Total	25,307	13,073	6,467	3,134	3,435

[2] Andreas, *History of Chicago*, II, 60–61.

Street.[1] Meanwhile some little retail business was springing up on the streets near the river.

The tendency to the segregation of population on the basis of race, nationality, and economic status, which is an inevitable accompaniment of the growth of the city, was becoming evident at this early date. The more well-to-do and fashionable native element, and the Irish and German immigrant elements, as well as the laboring population and a small element of riff-raff and transients, were beginning to live in groups to themselves and to characterize certain streets and sections of the North Side.

The Near North Side has always been a more or less fashionable residence district, though it was not until 1900 that the Lake Shore Drive became *the* place to live. In the sixties the fashionable and aristocratic residence section of Chicago on the North Side was in the district from Chicago Avenue south to Michigan Street, and from Clark Street east to Cass Street. Residences on Ohio, Ontario, Erie, Superior, Rush, Cass, Pine, Dearborn, and North State streets appear frequently in the "society column" of the sixties. It was on these streets that the leading families of the early settlers and the early aristocracy lived. And they, with South Michigan Avenue, were the "modish" streets of the day. One of this early aristocracy writes:

The North Side was "home," and a lovely, homelike place it was. The large grounds and beautiful shade-trees about so many residences gave a sense of space, rest, flowers, sunshine and shadows, that hardly belongs nowadays to the idea of a city. There was great friendliness, and much simple, charming living.

Over between Clark, Illinois, Dearborn, and Indiana streets stood the old North Side Market, where the men of the families often took

[1] *Ibid.*, II, 119–21.

their market-baskets in the morning, while the "virtuous woman" stayed at home "and looked well to the ways of her household."

Another institution of our day was the custom of sitting on the front steps, though even then there were those who rather scorned that democratic meeting place. But for those of us who did not rejoice in porches and large grounds, they had their joys. . . . . In fact, it was even possible for unconventional people like ourselves to carry out chairs and sit on the board platforms built across the ditches that ran along each side of the street, and on which carriages drove up to the sidewalks.

Of course there were "high teas," when our mothers and fathers were regaled with "pound to a pound" preserves, chicken salad, escalloped oysters, pound-cake, fruit-cake, and all other cakes known to womankind; and where they played old-fashioned whist and chess. . . . . Parties usually began about half-past seven or eight o'clock, and "the ball broke" generally about eleven or twelve o'clock; where there was no dancing it ended at ten or eleven o'clock.

Of course there was no "organized charity," as we know it now-adays, but there was much of that now despised "basket charity," when friendships were formed between rich and poor.[1]

Between Clark Street and Wells Street, south of Chicago Avenue, was a neighborhood of storekeepers and merchants; while west of Wells lived the laboring people. In this area there were a number of laborers' boarding-houses and cheap saloons. At this time there was nothing but a sandy waste between Cass Street and the lake.[2] And there was an un-savory population on the sand flats at the mouth of the river and immediately along its banks, known as "Shanty-town," and ruled over by the "Queen of the Sands." A memorable event of the decade was the raid on the "Sands" led by "Long John" Wentworth, then mayor, when the

[1] C. Kirkland, *Chicago Yesterdays*, pp. 122, 124, 139, 140–41, 60–61.

[2] Document 1, interview with Robert Fergus, editor of the "Fergus Historical Series."

police razed its brothels amid the mingled cheers and hisses of the populace.[1]

The Irish had settled along the river, to the south and west. The settlement extended as far east as State, immediately along the river, but the most of the Irish lived between Kinzie and Erie, in the vicinity of old Market Street. This river settlement along the North Branch was known as "Kilgubbin," or oftener, perhaps, as "the Patch"; and any woman who seemed a little loud was at once put down as "comin' from the Patch." The Irish were then mostly laborers, not having been in America long enough to have exploited their flare for politics. They were already displaying their love of a fight, however, and a solidly Irish regiment was recruited from Kilgubbin during the Civil War.[2]

Kilgubbin was in reality a squatters' village, and contained within it a lawless element. In an article printed in the *Chicago Times*, in August, 1865, some account is given of Kilgubbin and its population:

At the head of the list of the squatter villages of Chicago stands "Kilgubbin," the largest settlement within its limits. It has a varied history, having been the terror of constables, sheriffs and policemen. . . . . It numbered several years ago many thousand inhabitants, of all ages and habits, besides large droves of geese, goslings, pigs, and rats. It was a safe retreat for criminals, policemen not venturing to invade its precincts, or even cross the border, without having a strong reserve force.[3]

The Germans, on the other hand, were truck gardeners rather than laborers. Very few went into business, though there were three breweries owned by Germans where the

---

[1] H. C. Chatfield-Taylor, *Chicago*, p. 103.   [2] Document 1.
[3] Quoted by J. S. Currey, *Chicago: Its History and Its Builders*, p. 177.

pumping station now stands. But the majority of the Germans lived north of Chicago Avenue and east of Clark Street, in cottages on small farms or gardens, and did truck farming. There were German families scattered along Clark. La Salle, and Wells streets, however. And the German element for a time found the center of its social activities in the vicinity of the German Theater, at the corner of Wells and Indiana streets. This theater, supported by a German musical society, offered "the first purely musical entertainment ever presented in Chicago," and for years continued to present dramatic sketches in the German language.

The city limits extended at this time, 1860–70, to North Avenue. But until after the fire the area north of Division Street, and even north of Chicago Avenue to the west, was practically "country."

FROM FIRE TO FAIR

The great conflagration of 1871, which marked a crisis in the history of the city, completely wiped out the North Side. Shortly before the fire the iron and packing industries had begun to remove from the North Branch south and west to the outskirts of the city. The other industries were destroyed by the fire. Of the total area burned, by far the greater portion lay north of the river; and the district immediately along its banks suffered the greatest loss, the great lumber yards serving to accelerate the spread of the fire. The residential areas suffered as severely as did the river district. Most of the residences and many of the business structures were of wood, and were reduced to ashes. Indeed, only two dwellings were saved: the home of Mahlon F. Ogden, and the house of an Irish policeman whose cider barrels provided a fire extinguisher. The water tower is the only monument of the fire today. Because of the conflagration the only "sights" connected with early Chicago are the sites—all the rest has been obliterated. And in 1871 the entire North Side lay in heaps of smoldering ash, or blackened Gothic-like ruins, church after church standing gutted and grim.

The first reconstruction took place in the center of the city, and all efforts were bended toward rebuilding the business district. "For over a year after the fire, the North Side gave no evidence of recuperation; but the building 'boom' finally crossed the river, and business blocks took the place of vacant lots along North Clark Street, and fine residences began to spring up on La Salle, Dearborn, and cross streets."[1] Indeed, when rebuilding did start on the North Side it progressed rapidly. There was a great growth in business, and by 1881 business property was worth five hundred to six hundred dollars a front foot. Old hotels, theaters, and schools were rebuilt, as well as new ones built. And the old wooden residences were replaced by more substantial and pretentious ones of brick and stone.

In 1871 the population of the North Division was 77,758 and its area 2,533 acres. By 1884, when we find the next statistics on the national composition of the population by wards, the population of the North Division had increased to 128,490.[2] The German element had by this time greatly increased; there continued to be a fair proportion of the Irish; and the Swedish, who had begun to come in just previous to the fire, had become a considerable factor in the

[1] Andreas, *History of Chicago*, III, 448.

[2] *Ibid.*, II, 702. *Chicago Daily News Almanac and Yearbook* (1920), p. 918.

life of the Near North Side.[1] Indeed, the Germans were the
dominant nationality in the Eighteenth Ward; while the
Swedish were the largest national group in the Seventeenth
Ward, where the Irish were a close second. The southern
European groups had not yet begun to come into the city in
any considerable numbers, and there were few on the Near
North Side. Yet the North Side had begun to share with
the city as a whole a quite cosmopolitan character.

Industries continued to multiply along the river. By
1884 the North Branch was already being invaded by the
retail trade. At that time there were about five hundred
steamers and sailing vessels employed in the lumber traffic
in Chicago, a large number of them plying the waters of the
North Branch. Shortly before the Fair there was an incoming of light industries along the river, and the Northwestern
Railroad laid its tracks along the North Branch. Because
of the smoke from the railroad and factories the region in
the vicinity of the river was known as Smoky Hollow, and
already was becoming the barrier that was to play an important part in the history of the Near North Side. Meantime, additional street railroad lines had been built along
State, Division, and Wells. Lower Wells, Clark, and State

[1] The national composition of the population of the North Division was,
in 1884:

	*Ward 16	Ward 17	Ward 18
American	4,080	1,992	11,931
Danish	407	672	800
German	21,818	6,035	7,536
Irish	1,667	8,555	4,281
Italian	54	481	104
Norwegian	317	953	242
Swedish	1,077	10,742	1,237
Other nationalities	1,009	2,112	1,768

* From the *School Census of the City of Chicago*, 1884 Wards 16,
17, and 18 then comprised the area which in 1920 comprised the
southern half of Wards 21 and 22.

streets, and transfer points, were showing a considerable growth in business.

By the time of the eighties the groups that characterized various areas on the Near North Side had become more clearly defined than they had been in the sixties. For a decade and more after the fire, Lower Michigan Avenue, Prairie Avenue, and Ashland Avenue shared with the North Side the character of fashionable residential districts. But the area along the lake shore between the Virginia Hotel and Lincoln Park was already becoming the center of the city's social life. La Salle Street and North Dearborn Parkway were preferred streets in the eighties. A few residences were being built on Pine Street, now North Michigan Avenue, and many on North State Street. What is now the Lake Shore Drive, however, was still a barren, wind-swept waste.

In the late eighties the Near North Side began to be characterized, too, by what were at the time beautiful and fashionable family hotels. We read in a contemporary guide to the sights of Chicago: "The residence part of the city, particularly on the North and South sides, is thickly dotted with first-class family hotels. . . . . The two most magnificent are the Virginia, 78 Rush Street, and the Metropole, at Michigan Avenue and Twenty-third Street. These two houses cannot be surpassed for style and elegance, and are patronized exclusively by people of means."[1] The Revere and the Clarendon were also popular as family hotels on the North Side. The Revere was "the largest, finest, and best equipped hotel in the North Division," and the Clarendon "the permanent home of a number of prominent families."[2]

[1] *Chicago by Day and by Night*, p. 33.

[2] Andreas, *History of Chicago*, III, 359–60.

The Regis, and a little later the Walton, the Newberry, and the Plaza were other "family hotels" the names of whose guests appeared in the *Blue Book* of the day.[1]

The social life of the eighties remained simple, as compared with that of today. But already there were making their appearance trends which were prophetic of a new social world:

About this time there crept in a hitherto unknown factor in interior furnishings—a terrible something called "art." The Centennial Exposition at Philadelphia, in 1876, gave this a fatal impetus. "Eastlake," with its ebonized, flimsy furniture, its fragile gilt chairs, became the fad. A little later William Morris darkened and blighted our homes by inspiring brown and green wall-papers, adorned with geometric figures, and put on, in fearsome, longitudinal sections called dadoes, picture-screens and friezes. Also there were diseased moments in the search for the new and original when gilt milking-stools and chopping-bowls adorned drawing-rooms; when bunches of dried cattails stood in up-ended sewer-tilings in the most elegant houses; when chair-legs were gartered with big ribbon bows; when cheese-cloth was considered chic stuff for drawing-room curtains; when not to have a spinning-wheel by the fire-place was to proclaim yourself a *parvenu*.

At the same time, however, society was really taking form and shape. Ladies' luncheons and formal dinner parties (at which the hour was set as late as seven o'clock) became popular forms of entertainment. The "hired girl" became the "maid." She was induced to wear long white aprons, white collars and cuffs, and to permit a frilled cap to be perched upon her head. A few people even had butlers, though I think these were usually drawn from the colored race. I remember, however, that Mrs. W. W. K. Nixon, then living at No. 156 Rush Street, had a white butler, one Edward, who was the pride of the neighborhood.[2]

The moral distance between today and yesterday may be judged from the remark of a society matron of the eighties, who, when asked whether she was going to see

[1] Document 1, Interview with Robert Fergus.
[2] C. Kirkland, *Chicago Yesterdays*, pp. 258–59.

Bernhardt, replied, "I do not consider that anyone who would go to see Bernhardt play would be a fit guest at my dinner table!" And by the shocked indignation of certain sanctimonious citizens at the sight of the "fast young men" of the day driving trotting horses with flowing manes along the shady streets to "sulkies" and "sidebat" buggies.

The vicinity of North Clark Street, even in the late eighties and early nineties, was declining as a residential district and was becoming the region of bright lights and night life which was later to earn it the sobriquet of the "Little White Way." The Clark Street Theater and the Windsor Theater affected a sensational type of play, specimens of the wild and woolly border drama being usually presented for the edification of their mercurial patrons.[1] And along the street were numerous saloons, dance and music halls, dime museums, and the like.

One of the famous resorts of the day, on the west side of Clark Street, a few doors north of Division, was Engel's Music Hall Café.

Enter Engel's at any time between eight and nine in the evening, after having paid the modest admission fee of ten cents, and you will find the large hall, with its imposing array of polished tables and rows of seats, rather sparsely filled. By ten o'clock, however, there is a perceptible increase in the attendance, and the white-aproned waiters are kept busy hurrying to and fro.

The curtain rises and a pert soubrette with a very gaudy complexion and abbreviated skirts trips to the footlights and sings a song of true love, or something equally interesting. Meanwhile more drinks are ordered by everybody, and general hilarity prevails.

The last hour is usually devoted to an opera in one act, a burlesque of the follies of the day, or anything else that will give an opportunity for the singing of "catchy" songs, the execution of intricate dances, and, above and beyond all, the lavish display of feminine charms.

[1] *Chicago by Day and by Night*, pp. 39–40.

It is a pleasant custom of the place for young men of means, possessed of more money than sense, to purchase bouquets, which are carried up and down aisles on trays by attractive flower-girls, and cast the same upon the stage at their especial favorites. When a more than usually attractive damsel sings an unusually taking song, the boards upon which she treads are often fairly deluged with flowers, and the degree of grace with which she stoops to pick them up enhances in just that ratio the warmth of the applause.

Another feature of Engel's, and many find it an agreeable one, is the stage boxes. These boxes are located above the stage and behind the curtain, being arranged in such a way that persons seated therein may view all that is going on forward on the stage itself and still remain invisible to the audience. With prominent citizens, or other people who like to keep their attendance at the music hall a secret, this is an advantage not to be denied.[1]

And the after-the-show revels in the café, to the tune of the gay if shrill laughter of "Papa" Engel's coryphées and the popping of corks of champagne bottles, were the talk of the town.

North Clark Street had its more exclusive entertainments. "The halls along North Clark Street, notably North Side Turner Hall, advertise masquerades and plain dances the year around, some of which are very select. The finest masquerades of all, however, are given at the Germania Club, on North Clark Street, near Division. Admission is solely by invitation, and one must possess an acquaintance with some member of the club in order to secure entrance, and even then it is very difficult."

The district from Wells to the river was already assuming the character of the slum. And it was into a slum area that

[1] *Chicago by Day and by Night*, p. 55. The saloon which until a few years ago occupied the southwest corner of Clark and Division streets was a favorite dropping-off place, of nights, of homeward bound "Gold Coasters," and was known on the Gold Coast as "the North Side branch of the Chicago Club."

the Swedes, the third great foreign group to sweep over the
Near North Side, had come. The first Swedish immigrants
to Chicago had come in 1846. The Swedish immigrants were
exceedingly poor. In 1855 Swedish and Norwegian paupers
cost the city $6,000, and over one hundred of them were
buried at public expense. The Swedes settled first in the
area bounded by Indiana, Erie, Orleans, and the river. This
district was locally known on the North Side as Swede
Town. Later they moved northward along the north and
south streets west of Wells—principally along Market,
Sedgwick, Townsend, Bremer, and Wesson streets—mingling with the Irish. Chicago Avenue became the "Swede
Broadway." The Swedish colony was hard hit by the fire.
Of the 50,000 destitute, 10,000 were Swedish. But the Swedish district soon rebuilt, expanding northward as it did so.
In the eighties there were over a hundred Swedish lodges,
benevolent societies, singing societies, theaters, and similar
organizations in Chicago. There were also eight large Swedish daily or weekly papers. Most of these were located in or
near the North Side colony, which contained three-quarters
of the city's total Swedish population.[1]

The district west along the river continued to be an
Irish settlement. The fire had practically wiped out the
original Irish settlement. As the houses were largely unin-
sured, and the new fire regulations called for more expensive
structures, many of the Irish were unable to rebuild in the
old district, and moved north of Chicago Avenue into "Forty
Acres," then a prairie without streets, in the vicinity of the
old "Gas House," and built cheap two- and three-room
shacks, spreading along the river to North Avenue. The
main body of the Irish still lived below Chicago Avenue,

[1] E. W. Alson, *History of the Swedes in Illinois*, I, 301-12.

however, and the area bounded by Wells and the river was largely Irish despite a large admixture of Swedish. The name "Kilgubbin" had passed, to be replaced by that of "Little Hell."

The Irish were the dominant political power in the old Seventeenth Ward, as they were indeed in the entire North Side, and elections were exciting affairs. Little Hell was the scene of a battle every election day, and more than one of these battles ended fatally for some unfortunate politician or gangster. The following story from the *Chicago Tribune*, on the occasion of the death of "Sinator Moike," gives a picturesque sketch of the politics of the day:

Mike gravitated naturally into politics the hour he shifted short "pants" for long ones; and he was busy with politics, more or less, until the day he died. What Mike did not know about the ins and outs of ward politics in the days of rough and tumble work in the old Seventeenth Ward, the bosses of which fathered the activities of the notorious "Market Street Gang," could not be taught.

If ever a man had intimate association with the wild and woolly crew of ward heelers of the old school, it was "th' Sinator." It was his great glory to get into a muss with an east wind Democrat, and in those days, when the town was wide open, Democrats in the ward were as clouds of locusts, compared with the Republican handful. He had a masterful bunch to fight, and when the opposing gangs came together a Donnybrook fair was a crossroads prayer-meeting compared with it.

Old Market Street and other thoroughfares, parallel and crosswise, had many saloons, and each saloon had its water trough in front; when bands of political opponents clashed or luckless voters did not cast their pasted ballots right, these troughs were filled with the offenders, or such of them as were not beaten up, to show them the error of their ways.

Then there was great glorification in the district, which included a section of the city stretching from Davidson's stone-yard at the river and Market Street—now Orleans—to Goose Island, that delectable tract known as "Little Hell" in the good old days of no gas, no water, no police, and the king of which was a take and dare old land buccaneer named Jimmy O'Neil, whose habit it was to trail his coat behind him and invite the denizens of the place to tread on it.

By the time of the Fair, Chicago was a large and a metropolitan city, with a population of 1,099,850.

The far North Side, the far South Side, and the "great West Side" were beginning to take shape. Already the Near North Side was becoming an area of the inner city; and in 1886 occurred the last of these romantic episodes in the history of the North Side which are more of the frontier than of the city. On a July afternoon, in a terrific storm on Lake Michigan, a little craft was driven ashore a short distance north of the Chicago River. And when the storm died down, the captain of the vessel, George Wellington Streeter, waded ashore and claimed the lake front by right of discovery. Streeter called his claimed land the "District of Lake Michigan," had it formally organized, with legal ceremony, and sold lots in it to such hardy characters as were willing to gamble on so dubious a title. Through years of litigation, dragging into this twentieth century, Captain Streeter defended his squatter sovereignty with a true rifle. "For several years, for the guerilla warfare was lengthy, the doctors were busy picking shot out of men engaged in the Streeter War." At last Streeter killed a man, and was sentenced to the penitentiary. The war was over. The city engulfed the last squatter domain, and Streeterville became a district of fashionable apartments. The Near North Side, with the greater city, had reached maturity.

THE TWENTIETH CENTURY

The late nineties and the early nineteen hundreds witnessed several movements that were greatly to alter the

Near North Side, to alter both its physical appearance and the nature of its social life. These movements were the expansion of business and industry across the river and up the streets of the Near North Side; the coming of the immigrant from Southern and Eastern Europe; the deterioration of the old residential area and the incoming of a transient population, accompanied by various pathological social phenomena; and the development of the fashionable shopping, apartment, and residential district along North Michigan Avenue and the Lake Shore Drive.

From the rebuilding of the North Side after the fire until the late nineties the Near North Side came increasingly to be considered as a desirable residential area. But we have already noted the incoming of industry, beginning just before the Fair, which gave the southwest portion of the Near North Side the name "Smoky Hollow." The wholesale and terminal business along the river and the streets immediately north also grew rapidly. Its extent is attested by the fact that "the seven east-and-west streets immediately north and south of the Rush Street bridge carried 38 per cent more traffic across Michigan Avenue, to and from the railway freight terminals on the lake-front and the warehouses on the west point, than enters London at its seven principal points of entrance"; and that "Rush Street bridge was one of the most crowded in the world," carrying "16 per cent more traffic than London Bridge."[1]

This growth of industry along the river, and the flow of east-and-west traffic involved in the terminal business, plus the fact of inadequate transportation served as a great barrier which for years influenced the nature of the growth

[1] *Chicago: The Great Central Market*, p. 148.

of the Near North Side.[1] It slowed the march of the central business district, allowing the Gold Coast to become firmly intrenched along the lake, limiting the commercial development of the central streets of the Near North Side to business of a local nature, and isolating the slum district along the river, allowing it to stagnate for years.

Into this slum district along the river, and in the vicinity of this industrial area, which had been first Irish and then Swedish, had been known as Kilgubbin, as Little Hell, and lastly as Smoky Hollow, began to come, in the late nineties, the Italian—the Italian from the southern island of Sicily. He came in small numbers at first. But with the opening years of the twentieth century came a Sicilian wave, part of the great Italian immigration of 1903–4, and the Sicilian began to take possession of the Irish and Swedish community between Sedgwick Street and the industrial belt along the river. This wave reached its crest about 1906.

While the Irish and Swedish had gotten on well as neighbors, neither could or would live peaceably with the Sicilian. There was considerable friction, especially among the children of the two races. The play parks were the scenes of many a "battle" when the Irish boys would attempt to run out the Italian, and alley garbage cans were stripped of their covers which served as shields in these encounters. As the Italians continued to penetrate the neighborhood, how-

[1] The Michigan Boulevard link bridge was not erected until 1918, and it was only shortly before that the Franklin-Orleans bridge was built. "The Rush Street bridge carried 77 per cent of all the commercial vehicles entering the Loop district from the North side of the city. The four other bridges— the farthest being only four blocks distant—carried the remainder. This enormous traffic, aggravated in summer by the opening of the bridges to pass deep-draft lake vessels, supplemented by the heavy cross traffic caused a confusion that beggared description" (*Chicago: The Great Central Market*, p. 148).

ever, by the very force of their numbers, the Swedish and Irish, many of them of the second generation and fairly prosperous, began to move away. The Swedish moved slowly north, until they now center about Belmont Avenue and along North Clark Street to Diversey; and the Irish moved first to the vicinity of Webster, and then, as the Italians followed, they went along Center to Devon, and are now scattered about Sheffield, Edgewater, and Rogers Park; so that today the few Swedish and Irish who remain on the Near North Side are those who were too poor to take part in this exodus, or who have clung to their old homes for sentimental reasons. The southern European immigration has engulfed the west district, turning it into a strangely hybrid bit of America and Sicily, and is now pushing north into the German district along North Avenue.

Meantime business was slowly moving out the central streets of the Near North Side, from State to Wells, with Clark Street as its axis. The business on these streets consisted of small retail stores of various sorts, catering to the local population—to the more well-to-do families to the east, and to the slum families to the west. Clark Street itself was fast becoming a street of cheap hotels, second-hand stores, restaurants, and theaters.

With the incoming of business and industry, and with the penetration of the southern European, with his "outlandish" ways, his strange tongue, and his lower standard of living, the Near North Side became progressively less desirable as a residential district. The encroachment of business was a greater factor than the Italian immigration. But both contributed to lower the desirability and prestige of the old fashionable residential area north of the Virginia Hotel, and one by one the residences in the vicinity of Chicago Avenue, and north along State, Dearborn, and La Salle, were deserted as families moved east into the neighborhood of "the drive," or north along Sheridan Road.

Practically all the old residences that remain in this neighborhood have been turned into rooming-houses, men's hotels, restaurants, beauty parlors, shops, and the like; and many have been torn down to make way for modern stores and wholesale houses. Others, however, have been converted into studios. It is in this vicinity that Towertown, Chicago's bohemia, has grown up, seeking the anonymity afforded by the physical change taking place in the neighborhood. State Street north to Goethe, and Division, Dearborn, La Salle, and Wells streets, have suffered a like fate. While there are still "marble-fronts" and brick mansions with mansard roofs to recall that these were favorite residential streets until the decade of the Fair, and while a few old families still cling to them, the little black and white card "Rooms for Rent" on the door or in the window of house after house bears mute testimony to the changed status of this area.

The change in character of the population, which began on the western side of the district, progressed eastward. The rooming-house brought in a population of lower economic status, with a large transient element and including many foreign groups.[1] And by the close of the first decade of the twentieth century the area south of Oak Street and west of State Street had greatly deteriorated. With this deterioration had come a vast amount of disorganization.

The report of the Chicago Vice Commission tells the story of this deterioration and disorganization in vivid

[1] In 1910 the total population of the Twenty-first and Twenty-second wards was 96,930. Of this total, 22,586 were native white, born of native

fashion. The whole of the once fashionable residential district had become honeycombed with houses of prostitution,
saloons, dance halls, cabarets, call flats, massage parlors, and
all kinds of dives. The old hotels had gone down with the
surrounding neighborhood: the Revere had become a
theatrical hangout of questionable reputation, and the
Clarendon, the Regis, and others had long since all but
forfeited the last vestige of respectability.

Clark Street was the center of this disorganization, with its bright
lights, backroom saloons, and hotels. Among its notorious dives was
McGovern's old "Liberty," which has recently reopened as "Spark
Plug Inn." Along lower La Salle and Wells were cheaper houses, with
brightly lighted red windows, in which the girls wore the loudest of
colored kimonos and negligees, and affected the vilest of perfumes.
East of Clark Street were places more pretentious. On the north side
of West Erie, just off State Street, was a big house that boasted of its
high-class trade, and in front of which used to be parked every night
big limousines from out along the North Shore and Evanston. Solicita-

---

parents; 28,878 were foreign-born white; 1,235 were Negro; and 44,231 were
native white, of foreign parents.

The principal foreign-born groups were:

	Ward 21	Ward 22
Canadian........................	1,264	249
English.........................	1,083	229
German.........................	3,695	5,201
Greek..........................	575	169
Hungarian......................	311	1,283
Irish...........................	2,331	1,128
Italian.........................	461	8,216
Persian.........................	122	37
Polish..........................	304	570
Swedish........................	2,130	3,980

The Poles are included, though few, to call attention to the fact that the
Polish wave that swept over the northwest side never crossed the river onto
the Lower North Side, being effectively cut off by the barrier of river and
industry; and the Persians are included to point out that the Persian immigration had not yet begun in any considerable number (*United States
Census*, 1910).

tion was common on all these streets. A man walking north on Rush at night would be approached a dozen times between the river and Division. The Near North Side was not one of the so-called "restricted" districts. But it had a large population of prostitutes, criminals, dope-fiends, pan-handlers, and riff-raff of all sorts, and just before the war had become a favorite stamping ground for the street meetings of the Midnight Mission.[1]

Into the Near North Side, just after the war, came two more racial groups, the Negro and the Persian. Both had been coming in in a straggling fashion since 1900, but it was not until after the war that either group came in in any considerable numbers.

The Negro, part of the post-war migration from the South, an unskilled group of the lowest economic status, naturally crowded into the slum, along Franklin, Orleans, Townsend, and certain blocks on Wells Street. As the Irish, Swedish, and Germans had left the west district when the Sicilian came in, so now the Sicilian is beginning to give before the pressure of the Negro invasion, and is moving out, chiefly west, along Grand and Chicago avenues, though in small numbers south into Englewood.

The Persian, in contrast with the Negro, was an immigrant of a higher economic status, thrifty and intelligent, often with considerable education and a trade, and occasionally with a profession. A few Persians came to Chicago in the early 1900's, and the oldest child in the colony is now fifteen. But the real immigration began after the war, under pressure of religious persecution in Asia Minor. Most of them live in the vicinity from Oak Street south to Chicago Avenue and Huron, and between La Salle and Rush streets. The colony now numbers perhaps 4,000 persons.

[1] Document 2.

This encroachment of business, this invasion by foreign groups and by a transient population with its accompaniments of vice and crime, has but accelerated the exodus of the *beau monde* from the old residential district which began with the dawn of the twentieth century. As we have noted, this exodus was in two directions: east to Lake Shore Drive, and north along Sheridan Road.

In the days before the fire, Chicago had been socially a united city. But between fire and fair, West Washington Street and Ashland Avenue, Prairie Avenue and the shady boulevards of the South Side, passed as fashionable residential districts, and the social world turned north as the families from these old streets "migrated" one by one to the region lying between the Virginia Hotel and Lincoln Park, this portion of the North Side being now the abode of most of the families which were eminent in the days before the fire, as well as of those whose wealth is surpassing.[1]

Until the Fair, Dearborn, La Salle, and Wells streets were favorable residential streets in this North Side world of fashion and wealth. But in the decade after the Fair the tide of fashion turned eastward; and shortly after 1900 the newly completed Lake Shore Drive became *the* street of the *beau monde*. As the city pressed into the old residential streets, family after family deserted their ancestral homes to build new ones, either on "the drive" itself, or on the side streets running off it between Bellevue Place and Lincoln Park. "The Lake Shore Drive and its adjoining streets have now become our Mayfair." Perhaps no other city in the world has witnessed the concentration of its fashionable world in so restricted an area. As family after family has built its palatial home in this district, or has moved into its

[1] H. C. Chatfield-Taylor, *Chicago*, pp. 97–98.

magnificent apartments, as its clubs and hotels and shops have become the center about which revolves the entire city's social life, as the Lake Shore Drive has come to represent more wealth than any other street in the world save Fifth Avenue, this district has come to be known as the Gold Coast.

The *Tribune* acclaimed the opening of the Drake Hotel, at Oak Street and "the drive," as

. . . . a social event in the better sense, a landmark in the life of the community. Its location fixes a new social focus, around which will grow a small new city of theatres, clubs and fashionable shops. It will be, in fact, the center of the new age of fashion, and the *belles* and *beaux* of a generation will pass in review before its mirrors. Many of the social events which men and women look back upon will be held here—great balls and the endless procession of dances, teas, wedding receptions, and coming-out parties. . . . .

Celebrities of all high varieties will pass in and out its doors—statesmen and famous soldiers, captains of finance and industry, poets who flutter and dovecotes of culture, novelists and preachers at whose feet sit the breathless aspiring, ladies of fashion and actresses adored, princes viewing mankind and diplomats grave and debonair. In a word, the Drake should be a mirror of the time as great hostelries have been in every age and land and clime; as the Grand Pacific, to speak only of our own brief past, mirrored the Chicago of the 70's and 80's, and the Auditorium of the 90's.

The loop will remain the core, the towering central range of our business structure. But the great avenue will be the parade where such ceremonial life as our democracy indulges in will chiefly center, where the peacock, Fashion, preens in the sun of his own esteem, where pleasure is pursued and sometimes caught, where what glitter and gay gesture our hard working society of the mid-continent may indulge in may be shared and seen.[1]

The indications are, however, that within a decade even the Lake Shore Drive will have altered in character, "a generation being the longest period throughout which a Chicago

[1] *Chicago Daily Tribune*, November 30, 1920.

street has been able to maintain its supremacy. Already a small colony of fashionables has been established north of Lincoln Park," and "it seems likely that the exclusive quarter of the next generation will be this newly made portion of the lake shore" along Sheridan Road.[1]

Before 1916 the Lake Shore Drive had been isolated from the northward push of the city. But with the completion of the Michigan Boulevard link bridge the city surged north along North Michigan Avenue. A romance in land values followed; and stimulated by this development and the opening of the Franklin-Orleans bridge, the march of business out the central streets of the Near North Side and along the river in the west district was quickened.

North Michigan Avenue itself is developing into a fashionable shopping street, with tall office buildings near the river, and with clubs, smart restaurants, and hotels. East of Michigan Avenue is developing, south of Chicago Avenue, a district of wholesaling. A number of large advertising firms have also erected buildings here. And north of Chicago Avenue is Streeterville, a restricted area of fashionable apartments and hotels. The Michigan Avenue development is clearly a part of the expansion of the central business district and is backed by a strong businessmen's association definitely linking it with the Loop. Already it has pushed north to Oak Street, where the Drake Hotel marks its outpost. Only a zoning ordinance has checked it here. Meanwhile business pushing out State Street, and the rooming-house area creeping east from Clark Street, hold the Gold Coast in siege. It would seem that the city but awaits the expiration of the restriction clause in the zoning ordinance to sweep on and engulf the Gold Coast.

A development of a different nature is taking place along

[1] H. C. Chatfield-Taylor, *Chicago*, p. 106.

the central streets of the Near North Side, about Clark Street. These streets saw the first business development on the North Side, but have been overshadowed by the recent Michigan Avenue boom. The business along these streets is of such a nature as caters to the slum and transient populations: cheap hotels and theaters, pawnshops and second-hand stores, innumerable white-tile restaurants, barber shops, grocery stores, meat markets, and the like, with occasional office buildings south of Chicago Avenue. Into the cheap hotels, lodging-houses, and furnished rooms of the area about Chicago Avenue have come a large group of transients, and several small foreign groups, including the Greek and the Persian. Practically the whole area about Clark Street, from Rush and State streets to Wells Street, and east even of Michigan Avenue to the south, has been entirely taken over by rooming-houses. Real estate men of this district prophesy that because it has the electric transportation Clark Street will eventually surpass North Michigan Avenue. But this is unlikely, as the street connecting the fashionable residence district with the central business district has in every city more than held its own.[1] There is no doubt, however, that business will eventually succeed the rooming-house and the slum in this central district of the Near North Side.

Still different in character is the development taking place in the southwest district, in the vicinity of the north bend of the river. It comprises light manufacturing plants and wholesaling houses. Since the trackage in this district is limited, its development will be chiefly of such business as

[1] Witness Fifth Avenue, like North Michigan Avenue, with only motor bus transportation. See McMichael and Bingham, *City Growth and Land Values*, p. 92.

does not require trackage, such as printing plants. There is already a movement of printing plants in this direction, and many small manufacturing plants and large storage houses and garages have recently been built in this district. Until now industry has taken over the slum as far north as Chicago Avenue, and is yearly pushing eastward into the slum from the river. The Sicilian population is slowly giving ground, and the old buildings in the district are rapidly deteriorating. Into this situation the Negroes are coming in ever increasing numbers.[1]

One element runs through practically the whole of the Near North Side of today: it is the element of change and flow. The life of the Near North Side is all flux and movement. Its population has a large "fly-by-night" group, and a great proportion of it is constantly shifting. Moreover, the Near North Side is the thoroughfare for the hundreds of thousands living on the far north and the northwest sides. Approximately 200,000,000 people pass along North Michigan Avenue in a year. The traffic at North Michigan Avenue and the link bridge exceeds that at Fifth Avenue and Forty-second Street, reaching a maximum of 4,360 vehicles during the rush hour.[2] And North Clark Street, with State and Wells streets, is the center of street railroad traffic between

---

[1] The population of the Near North Side, excepting Streeterville and the Gold Coast, decreased 20–35 per cent between 1910 and 1920, as business took over old residential streets—and this in spite of the local increase in the rooming area.

[2] *Chicago Tribune*, August 12, 1923. The hourly traffic at North Michigan and the bridge, averaged for the period from 7 A.M. until midnight, is 3,118 vehicles, as against an hourly average of 2,300 vehicles at Fifth Avenue and Forty-second Street. An average of 53,014 vehicles cross the boulevard bridge a day, as against 18,387 vehicles crossing London Bridge, and a against 27,131 vehicles crossing Brooklyn Bridge (*Chicago: The Great Central Market*, p. 149).

the Loop and the far North Side. The Clark Street line carries, itself, thousands of people daily, and many of these transfer at points on the Near North Side. Perhaps the best index of the reality of this mobility is the ever present taxi stand and the United Cigar store on corner after corner.[1] Meanwhile there is constant agitation for the widening of La Salle Street, Clark Street, and the Lake Shore Drive, that this traffic may be increased. This traffic has an obvious correlation with the encroachment of business upon the residential areas of the Near North Side, and it has social consequences which will become evident as we analyze in more detail the life of various groups living on the Near North Side.

The Near North Side is today, then, a teeming area in the heart of a great city of three million souls. Within this area, a mile and a half from south to north, and scarcely a mile wide, live ninety thousand people—a population as large as that of the state of Nevada.[2] Just outside the central business district it is being rapidly invaded by business and industry. Save for the Gold Coast clinging to the lake shore, it is a disorganized area, a slum area. North of the encroaching industry and commerce, and west from the Gold Coast to La Salle Street, is a vast area of furnished rooms, housing some 26,000 people. Through the center of this area runs Clark Street, a street of bright lights and vice, the Rialto of the half-world. About Clark Street and Chicago Avenue are colonies of Greeks and Persians, and a little east of them is "the village." In the vicinity of Wells Street is a cosmo-

[1] The United Cigar stores are located by the "clocking" of the pedestrian traffic.

[2] The 1920 census gave the population of the Near North Side (by census tracts) as 91,009.

politan area, an interpenetration of all manner of people from the Old World, especially of Poles and Hungarians. West again, from Sedgwick to the river, and north to Clybourne, is Little Sicily, pushing the rear guard of the old German population north across North Avenue. And into the heart of Little Sicily comes the Negro.

The population of the Near North Side today includes twenty-eight specified foreign nationalities, the Negro, and the category "all other countries," in addition to the native-born population. Fifty-five per cent of the Twenty-first Ward, and 81 per cent of the population of the Twenty-second Ward, is foreign.[1] The Near North Side is a cross-section of the larger Chicago of which Chatfield-Taylor wrote. Yet its streets, teeming with life, thronging with strange people, resounding with outlandish tongues, and the noises of industry and commerce, are pervaded with the glamor and romance of the forward march of the greater city. This glamor and romance, however, exists in the social distances that, while they make the city a mosaic of little cultural worlds intriguing to the journalist, the artist, and the adventurer, make it impossible for these same little worlds to comprehend one another, and so atomize the life of the city.

[1] In "foreign" are included foreign-born, or native-born of parents both of whom were foreign-born. An additional 8 per cent of the Twenty-first Ward and 9 per cent of the Twenty-second Ward are of mixed parentage.

The principal groups in the composition of the population of these wards are:

Ward 21*		Ward 22*	
American	37.85	American	11.98
German	11.15	Austrian	7.42
Irish	6.88	German	18.95
Italian	6.20	Hungarian	17.00
Swedish	6.98	Italian	25.70

* From *Report of the Industrial Department of the Chicago Association of Commerce*, prepared in 1923, and based upon the United States Census for 1920.

CHAPTER III

THE GOLD COAST

The "Gold Coast," extending along the North Shore from East Chestnut Street to Lincoln Park, and west to Nort State Parkway, is the home of the leaders of Chicago's "Four Hundred."

The Four Hundred are those who have "arrived." They form a self-conscious group. They have mores of their own—"good form" and the amenities of life are of enormous importance in their lives. To violate the social code is a vastly greater sin than to violate the Ten Commandments. A gentleman may drink, he may gamble, but under no circumstances may he appear at an afternoon tea in a morning coat, or at dinner without an evening jacket. How elaborate is this social code is attested by the bulk of Emily Post's *Blue Book of Etiquette*, a codification for the yearning "common," for those not to the manner born. The Four Hundred have their own papers, *Clubfellow* and *Town Topics;* the daily newspapers devote columns to their comings and goings; they have their own clubs, such as the Onwentsia and the Casino; their own summer colonies at Lake Forest, Hubbard Woods, and half a dozen other places. They live in a totally different world from that of the rest of the great city of which they are a part. Within this world they lead a life of kaleidoscopic activity, centering about the fashionable hotels along the Drive, fashionable resorts, "pet charities," the golf club, and the bridle path, to say nothing of the bridge and dinner table, with occasional trips to La Salle Street. And of the prerogatives of this world they are jealous.[1]

Such is "society" at a first superficial glimpse. Such is the Gold Coast. For in Chicago all that is aloof and exclusive, all that bears the mark of *l'haute société*, is crowded

[1] Document 3. The documents upon which this chapter is based were written, without exception, by residents along the Gold Coast. Consequently they represent friendly insights and half-amused self-analysis, rather than jealous intolerance For sufficient reasons, the documents are anonymously presented here.

along the strip of "drive" between the Drake Hotel and Lincoln Park, or along the quiet, aristocratic streets immediately behind it. Here is the greatest concentration of wealth in Chicago. Here live a large number of those who have achieved distinction in industry, science, and the arts. Here are Chicago's most fashionable hotels and clubs. Here live two thousand of the six thousand persons whose names are in the social register of Chicago and its suburbs, and these two thousand include in their number those who are recognized as the leaders of "society."

But if we look more deeply into the life that goes on within these luxurious hostelries, these "exclusive" clubs, these stately and forbidding mansions, the picture is less clear. For what, after all, is "society"? At the question social leaders and society editors shake their heads, look bewildered, smile helplessly.

A generation ago the question would have been promptly answered: "Social position is a matter of family, breeding, aristocracy." The old "society" was a caste—very nearly, indeed, a clan. The old "assemblies" were almost a hereditary institution. The dowagers of the older families were the heads of the clan and the arbiters of social destiny. An invitation to the assemblies was a proved title of social rank. If one was received at the assemblies, one was received everywhere in "society."

But the growth of the city with its monetary standards and its economic organization, its startling mobility, and its very force of numbers was to change the nature of "society" just as it was to change every other phase of social life. The old "society," based on hereditary social position, has passed, to be replaced by a "society" of cliques and sets, of wealth and display, and, above all, of youth.

There is no society in Chicago as there used to be. Instead, there are numbers of small groups. One little group is dancing its head off, another is drinking its head off and hunting, and still another is madly playing bridge. Everyone is doing things madly and at a great pace. It is the pace which makes the small groups in the place of the older, broader, more dignified society. The little groups come together at "assemblies." But they don't mix—they divide into the same little groups of a dozen or two members, and dance together as if there weren't any other people in the ballroom. They don't wish to run the risk of new people, to talk to someone they don't particularly like, to dance with someone who doesn't dance well. They even try to duck the receiving line.

Society has no leaders such as it used to have—gracious, charming, genuinely hospitable older women. These women were real leaders. One must be on their lists to be recognized as belonging to society. They could invite whom they chose—an eccentric or a dandy, on occasion—and the fact that this person was invited to this house insured his courteous recognition by all. That is the real test of leadership. This leadership may still exist in Europe, and in some cities in this country, but not in the Chicago of today. Chicago society is in the hands of young people—cliques of very rich young people. The leadership is often in several cliques, or in one season one clique will be on top, and another season may find another in power. The pace is so fast, competition is so keen, that in practically all the smart cliques there is no one left of the type who is there because of good family, personal charm, and culture. These people must live up to the standards of the day—dress smartly, attend smart functions, entertain smartly and often—or they will be forgotten; and it doesn't take long to forget.

The society of today is topsy-turvy. No doubt it is due to the growth of the city. Great fortunes and great wealth have led to ostentation and display. The city is so large that society can no longer hold together. The faster pace of the city has put youth on the social throne.[1]

[1] Documents 4 and 5. One of these documents was contributed by a woman who is a member of one of Chicago's oldest and most aristocratic families; the other by a man very popular in the society of today, and much sought after as a leader of social functions and charity entertainments. Their comments might almost have been lifted bodily from Mrs. John King Van Rensselaer's *The Social Ladder*, a history of society in New York.

This change in the nature of "society," which has come with the city's growth, can be phrased in a sentence: "One no longer is born to social position; one achieves social position by playing the 'social game.'" And this is as true of the "society" of London or of New York as it is of the "society" of Chicago.[1] In every great city hereditary and traditional social barriers are breaking down. "Society," in the old sense, is being replaced by the "social game," and in the Chicago of today one must constantly "play the game" to maintain that envied distinction known as social position.

THE SOCIAL GAME

The "social game" is a constant competition among those who are "in" for distinction and pre-eminence; a constant struggle upon the part of those who are not "in" to break into the circles of those who are. Perhaps as good a criterion as there is of social position, which is the goal in the "social game," is the *Social Register*, a thin blue book which one can own only by virtue of having one's name in, containing a complete list of Chicago's socially acceptable, with their universities, their clubs, their marriages, their connections, and their deaths. To have one's name in the *Social Register* "one must not be 'employed'; one must make application; and one must be above reproach."[2]

[1] Mrs. John King Van Rensselaer, *loc. cit.*, and Document 6.

[2] Document 3. For an interesting account of the mysteries of the *Social Register* see Norman S. Hall, "The Ins and Outs of American Society," *Liberty*, February 13, 1926. One of the amazing things about the *Social Register* is the utterly unquestioning acceptance which society accords to its verdicts. While talking with several of the acknowledged leaders of Chicago society one afternoon the writer asked what was the criterion of social position. It was agreed that acceptance by the *Social Register* was perhaps the safest criterion. Yet no one had the faintest idea who selected the names for the *Social Register*, or upon what basis they were included.

The *Social Register*, however, but sets the seal of approval upon those who have already arrived. It but certifies that they are already members of certain clubs, are seen at certain social functions, are on certain invitation lists.

There are certain events of the season to which *the* people are invited. The big events of the season are the Bachelors and Benedicts, late in November; the Some Bachelors; the First Assembly; the Twelfth Night Party; and the Second Assembly, the middle of January, by which time the season is pretty well over. The Assemblies get a few younger married people, but mostly the older people—no debs —and are a terrible bore.

There are, besides, the Service Club Play—a mixture of prominent people and people unheard of; the Junior League Play and Party— after Easter, when people are back in town before going away for the summer; the opera; and certain charity affairs—the Paderewski concert for the Children's Home, and the Chauve Souris for Eli Bates— where it counts to be seen on the main floor or in the boxes.

Then there are certain more general things to be in on—the Women's Exchange lunchroom, for one. Society women go there in committees, wait on tables, work hard for two or three hours. It's the "smart" thing to do; that's the psychology of it—it's "exclusive."

You can't refuse the invitations of the social season; if you do, you are dropped. Generally speaking, you're in if you're invited, and you're out if you're not.

Then, too, there are certain clubs, and the like, to which one *must* belong. You *immediately* place a man by his clubs. *The* clubs are the Casino and the Saddle and Cycle. The Onwentsia, Shore Acres, the Racquet, and Indian Hill are also good. Of the women's clubs, only the Friday Club is exclusive enough to mean much.

Churches mean nothing—people for the most part simply don't go. Certain of them are more or less "fashionable," though, and if one does go it is to St. James, St. Chrysostom's, or to the Fourth Presbyterian.

If one lives at a hotel, it must be at the new Lake Shore Drive Hotel, which is *the* hotel of the day, or at the Ambassador, the old "Mayflower of the Gold Coast."[1]

[1] Document 6.

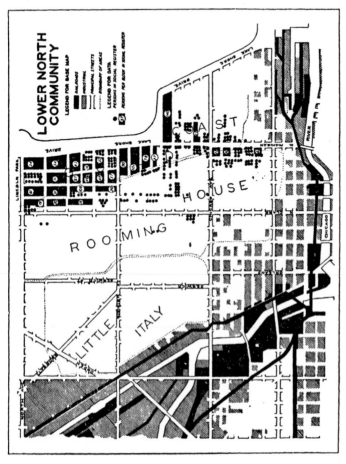

THE GOLD COAST.—Chicago's society is concentrated along the strip of lake shore north of "Streeterville," with a scattering on LaSalle, lower Rush, Huron, Superior, Ohio, and Cass, streets, fashionable a generation ago. This map, compared with those of the "World of Furnished Rooms" and "Little Sicily," brings out strikingly the segregation characteristic of the life of the great city. In this and succeeding maps the solid black areas indicate that the dots—here representing the residences of persons whose names appear in the *Social Register* (1923)—cluster too thickly to be individually represented.

It is about these clubs and hotels, these "events" of the season—assemblies, balls, the opera *première*, and the Easter parade—that the formal pageant of "society" moves. Invitations to assemblies and to membership in "smart" clubs are necessary plays in the social game. To some, indeed, they are coveted prizes. But within this pageant the "game" goes on for higher stakes: invitations to certain box parties at the opera, certain "dinners of 100" at the Casino, a dinner and dance at the Saddle and Cycle, to meet the Prince of Wales, at which "the heirs to the city's social throne are chosen"; eventual inclusion in the number of those who are recognized as swaying the destinies of the Four Hundred.

The means by which members of the Four Hundred become the arbiters of the social world, get into the top dozen, are many and varied. One accomplishes it by managing a world's fair and taking a prominent part in notable civic movements, whereupon she is taken up by the newspapers, and made—for the order in which and frequency with which names appear in the society column is a fairly accurate index of social influence. Another sponsors and heads the Casino Club; another is a patron of art; still others rise through money and lavish spending. Occasionally the sponsoring of some notable charity is the means of getting to the top.[1]

Without the exclusive citadels of the Four Hundred is always a throng seeking to push its way in. The "social game" has created a new social type—the "climber." The wiles of the "climber" are many and devious. The most obvious step up is a brilliant marriage; but this route is open only to men.[2] The majority of climbers seek to buy their way into society—not openly, to be sure, but tactfully and insidiously, in the name of charity. Many "climb," too, by

[1] Document 3.

[2] It is seldom, indeed, that the wives of men who marry "beneath" them achieve social success.

clever stage management—taking up a titled foreign *émigré,*
the writer of a best seller, or the latest sensation at the opera
and making him the rage for a season.[1] The ability to con-
trive a brillant *salon,* with a celebrity or two, and a few of
"just the right people" as drawing cards has accomplished
more than one social triumph. Finally, there are occasional
knight errants of "society," like the celebrated Ward Mc-
Allister of a generation ago, who achieve success by sheer
force of personality.[2] Whatever route the climber elects to
travel, a long and carefully planned campaign is required.

For example, Mrs. John Jones has social ambitions. She is the
wife of a man who has made his fortune in the Northwest in lumber.
She moves her family to Chicago. By applying, can she get her name
in the *Social Register?* No one in the family is employed. The family
name is above reproach—after all, a certain romance attaches to lumber. But no—she first has to be accepted socially. She must, as it is
vulgarly put, "climb." Now there are, of the six thousand who have
their names in the *Social Register,* some two hundred, or perhaps
three hundred, who form the "top layer"; and of these three hundred
there are a dozen who are the "élite." Mrs. Jones's problem is to secure an invitation to dinner in one or more of the homes, of the "top
layer" surely; of the "élite" if possible. But Mrs. Jones cannot accomplish this by inviting them first to her home; her invitation would
go pointedly unanswered.

One Mrs. Jones, from an eastern manufacturing city, took apartments at one of the fashionable Drive hotels. Her little girl got acquainted about the hotel with the little girls of mothers whose names
appear in the *Social Register.* Then she gave her little girl a birthday
party to which these other little girls were invited. Their mothers
then felt under obligation to her. She was invited to a tea, to a dance,
and finally to a dinner. Then she had arrived. An invitation to a political meeting or a wedding means nothing—but opportunities. An
invitation to tea is a first step. Then follow a dance, a luncheon, and

---

[1] Document 3; e.g., the social adventures of "Topsy and Eva."

[2] *See* Mrs. John King Van Rensselaer, *The Social Ladder,* pp. 205 ff.

finally a dinner, which is equivalent to a certificate of social acceptance—and the smaller the dinner, the more enviable the certificate.

More commonly, however, the ambitious climb by the "pet charity" route. For each of the socially prominent has her "pet" charity,
or her pet political or social movement. Mrs. Van Derfelt has at her
home an afternoon meeting of the Democratic Women's Committee.
Mrs. Jones is at the meeting. Afterward she goes up to Mrs. Van Derfelt: "Oh, Mrs. Van Derfelt, I've just heard about your interest in
the Home for Crippled Children, and what a wonderful work it is
doing. May I not contribute a little something?" Mrs. Van Derfelt
then feels more or less obliged to invite Mrs. Jones to tea. The game
goes on. And if Mrs. Jones plays her cards well, next year her name
will be seen in the *Social Register*.

Still another wile of the climber is that of sending her children
to a fashionable school, where they get acquainted with the children
of the Four Hundred. Through the children the parents meet, and
the first step is taken.[1]

The successful "climber" is an artist in self-advertise-
ment, in getting and keeping her name in the society columns, in associating herself with just the "right" people
and just the "right" things.[2]

The "social game," whether that of getting in, or of staying in, requires a continual planning, maneuvering, recipro-
cation of invitations, effort to "keep in the swim." For in
the "society" of today one must constantly keep up the
pace, or one is dropped. One's position is never so asssured
that one can afford to relax one's efforts—unless one is content to live in the memories of past successes.

[1] Document 3.

[2] *See* Document 7: A Mrs. _____, whom you and I both know, never
misses a trick; she gets a position on a committee of a fashionable club, or
on the same board of trustees with Mrs. _____, and you see it in the Dowagers' Column the next day; she sees everyone at the box parties: "I'm just
sure I saw you in Mrs. McCormick's box last night." A Mrs. _____ has
her picture taken with a group of settlement children, and the picture appears the next day as Mrs. _____'s "box party," though actually she didn't
take the children.

B and her husband, A, are members of the smartest group in Chicago society, the types of members who work early and late to keep their positions. Their entrée came through the fact that both belonged to families who were in the society of an earlier generation, and through attendance at private schools which accepted only the children of the fashionable world or those well recommended. This insured invitations, during childhood and youth, to the parties given for children in fashionable homes, and meant a more or less familiar acquaintance with the society of their generation.

But as the A's had an income that was relatively small, it was a real struggle to keep this position after their marriage and the setting up of their own establishment. In fact, they had finally to give up the effort of keeping a house or apartment, as the cost of maintaining it at the standard of their set was too great, and they resigned themselves to a suite in the most exclusive hotel in the neighborhood.

Their real "hold" came through an unusual gaiety and zest which both possessed. B is unusually spirited, and enlivens any gathering of which she is a part. This is her reputation, and she lives up to it unflinchingly. No comedy actor on the public stage could be more merciless with himself. I have seen her quite exhausted and dispirited, even bitter, after some dinner or dance at which she has been "the life of the party."

A takes a delightfully genuine pleasure in social life—somewhat unusual and readily felt. He is a popular leader of dances and other entertainments. His tall, handsome figure, graceful gestures, and gay smile bring out all the high spirits latent in a gathering. "I always drink one good glass of champagne before this sort of thing, and stay in bed the next day," he explains, admitting that the effort and late hours "take it out of me."

This zest and gaiety, and a ready willingness to do services for their friends—from helping to choose the latest ball gown to arranging flowers at a funeral—are the assets which make their success despite a small income. They dress with great care—always something very smart and exclusive and a little ahead of the popular style. They entertain in the same way, at carefully thought out intervals, and spend an immense amount of time and energy in making the entertainment very smart and novel. They are very painstaking about their lists of guests—no risks taken there, only the recognized smart people, with perhaps an opera singer, just the right stage star, or a literary light; dinners, a dinner and dance, a very snappy tea at the Casino for some much-sought person, a small gathering at the hotel.[1]

The leaves of a society woman's calendar for a month vividly portray this constant round of activities that make up the social game:

Hairdresser—once or twice a week.
Manicure—once or twice a week.
Massage—once a week.
Dressmaker.
Shopping—every few days.
Ballet class, to preserve the figure—once a week.
French class, group of six, at a friend's home—once a week.
Lectures—Bridges' series of six (time to attend only three) at the Playhouse, and the Fortnightly Club.
Club meetings—two clubs, each meeting monthly, at the Fortnightly; non-uplift; papers by members, and luncheon or tea.

For the most part, life on the Gold Coast is an affair of constant display. For one must constantly keep it up, reciprocate invitations and gifts to one's charities by invitations to others and gifts to other charities, in order to keep in. And the game becomes so complex that it may demand the entire time of a social secretary. One of Chicago's wealthiest "married maidens" has, for example, a calling list of two thousand names, filling two indexes, which contain merely the names of those to whom she owes obligations, or with whom she must keep in touch to keep in the game. She has to have a secretary to handle her correspondence, to plan her dances and receptions, to send out invitation, acknowledge other invitations, and keep track of her social obligations. Indeed, the requirements of the game are such that there have sprung up women whose profession is

[1] Document 8.

that of compiling lists of eligible bachelors, of children, their ages and birthdays, of the movements of families, of marriages, of divorces, of getting out invitation lists and managing dances, dinners, receptions, and the like.

An interesting index in the files of the social secretary is that of the "five hundred dancing men." They are eligible young bachelors whose names are in the *Register;* who dance and play bridge uncommonly well; who can talk, and who play golf or tennis passably. This list is at the service of the matron who wishes to give a big dance, a house party, or such.

Then there are the "hall room boys." They are young men from other cities, of good connections, usually university graduates, employed by prominent firms in the city, living in fashionable bachelor apartments or rooming-houses—not yet in the Chicago *Social Register*, but living in hopes. These outside men are welcome with the daughters of the Four Hundred, who play them off against the "dancing men" just as the girls on "Main Street" play off the new boy against the town boys. They are extra men, much invited about, and often one of them is the lion of the season. Their names, too, will be found in the files of the social secretary.

She may be able, also, to put the *parvenu* of social ambitions in touch with one of the "little brothers to the rich," young society bachelors, of limited means, who for a "professional consideration" will undertake to launch the most unpromising candidate in the social swim.[1]

Such is the social game as it is played along the Gold Coast. In its essence it is a struggle for status and prestige, for position and influence. It involves an art of publicity, of display, and lavish spending, resulting in a glorification of the person to be found nowhere else in the life of the city. Some play the game from pure vanity; some play it because they are born to it, and because it is "the thing to do." Women make it a profession to advance the fortunes of their husbands. Adventurers play it for gold. Others play

[1] Document 3.

the game for power, or because they are idle, or for the sheer love of excitement. But from whatever motive the game may be played, it resolves itself into a passion for recognition that becomes the center about which life is organized. And the social game, the passion for recognition, is the dominant interest in the lives of at least a third of that group known as "society."[1]

THE SOCIAL RITUAL

About the social game has grown up a vast amount of ritual, conventional ways of doing things, that serves to set off the aristocracy from the "common." And social control in "society" is largely effected through this ritual. To the "climber," to the person who is not sure of his position, the social ritual is the Ten Commandments. The mores of the larger group may be violated with impunity—if they are violated by "the" people, and if their violation is not too flagrantly flaunted. But there are conventions in the social ritual to violate which is to invite exile. A great deal even of the ritual may be ignored, however, by the few whose social position is unquestioned—if those few possess that indefinable something, that indispensable combination of assurance and discrimination known as *savoir faire.*

A society woman writes half-humorously, half-seriously, of this ritual:

Unless you have a sound social position, do not live north of North Avenue or west of North State Street, and be careful of your choice of blocks. If you must live at a hotel live at the Drake, the Blackstone, the Lake Shore Drive, the Ambassador, or the Pearson. Variations from this list are not unusual, but demand discretion. A disapproved neighborhood or hotel goes to prove that you are undesirable.

[1] Document 9.

Service is a solemn matter if one attempts it. It is proper, now, for young people to entertain without servants. But if there are servants, certain forms are absolutely required. The maid is neat and noiseless, and after five is in black. The face of man or maid is quite expressionless. A servant must open the door when guests or callers arrive. The table must be properly set. The table cloth is unpopular; a center light is *de trop;* candlelight, without shades, is required. The maid must know the service-plate game; it would be unpardonable if one's maid removed more than one plate at a time.

"Well-groomed" is the summing up of an unbreakable commandment. The perfectly coiffed or barbered hair, dustless and spotless clothes, exquisite slipper or speckless spat ("bankers always wear spats"). Women's nails *must* be polished; men's *may* be. One bath a day (or two) is in the ritual. Underclothes, in the past ten years, have assumed a new importance. Formerly one should be clean, but one might indulge in personal taste or follow personal comfort. But today the Sicilian mother is proud to show seven skirts on her child; the woman of fashion is embarrassed if she is caught wearing anything more under her gown than might be bundled into a large coat pocket. For a time pink silk crêpe was unescapable. It could have little flowers, but not too many: "M——sent me a rose crêpe chemise with a lot of colored flowers on it—harlot underclothes—I sent it to the White Elephant rummage sale." If her doctor orders wool—even knee-length and short-sleeved—she struggles to hide it from her dressmaker, from her week-end hostess. If unsuccessful, she tries to explain; but no explanation avails if she continues the habit. "She is the sort of person who wears woolen underclothes!"

Clothes must be in the prevailing exclusive mode, but not the extreme of popular fashion. "Of course one doesn't wear green slippers or shoes in the daytime, as they do up around Wilson Avenue." When the shopgirl moves up to the new style, that style is abandoned. "It is almost impossible, these days, to have exclusive clothes. The mob, from New York to Kansas, copies everything so quickly!" The woman of *l'haute société* does not wear evening slippers on the street, nor evening-cut neck, sleeves, or material in the daytime. Style in the smart set must be followed from tip to toe. The wrong gloves, the wrong line, the wrong slipper spoils the impression one strives to create. "She does not know how really to be smart." Useless to try to list the up-to-date—change is too rapid. "Where did you get your mink coat, my dear? You should move up to Wilson Avenue; you look like a kept woman." Exhibitionism in clothes seems more prevalent on "Boule Miche" than on the "Gold Coast." This, however, may be accounted for by the difference in the group one seeks to impress. The "Boul Miche" seeks to impress the world at large; the "Gold Coast" wishes to impress the followers of a more exclusive and fastidious mode.

Personal cards and notepaper, invitations, are matters which demand absolute conformity to the approved styles. Never make a call; if you do call, it proves that you came from Spikesville, Kansas, or any other place which is running a quarter of a century behind the times. Never go out after the first act at the opera; wait until after the second act. It is unsafe to carry a package or an umbrella. An artist was invited to an afternoon musicale at one of the exclusive "Gold Coast" homes. It was raining, and she arrived with a wet umbrella. She passed the man at the awning entry, ascended the carpeted stairs, and came to the family servant who guarded the door. She held out her wet umbrella. He looked at it unresponsively, but made no move to take it. A person who would carry an umbrella could not have been invited.

It is unfortunate to go to functions via the street car or the Yellow Cab. Some garages advertise cars which look exactly like private cars, and which may be used on social occasions. Most of the people you know could not be taken to the opera in a Yellow Cab. It is superfluous to state that you could not take anybody anywhere on a street car, not even in the daytime.

Apologies, hand-shakings, introductions, should be used with great caution. You may apologize if you are late, but not if the fish is burned, or the maid's hair awry, or you have worn gloves when you should not have done so. If you are young, or go in the younger set, you can occasionally say "damn," or "hell," or "Oh, my God!" "Shut your damned face!" has been known to pass. But "I'm pleased to meet you" would be practically fatal. *Nil admirari*, unless surprise, admiration, or comment is expected. If you must notice the details or special features of a room or costume, do it without the possibility of being detected. Curiosity is the height of bad breeding.

You may stand on your head in the drawing-room at a small or a large party, if you do it in the right way, at the right moment; you may crawl along the floor on your hands and knees; you may put your elbows on the table. If you are young enough, you may have a nine-year-old tussle with a perfectly strange young man who looks the apothesis of the Y.M.C.A., and he may wind a handkerchief around your neck, and drag you about, and kiss you. All this may happen at the smartest of parties, and, if your *savoir faire* is perfect, you will not be criticized. But if you hold your spoon or fork wrong, you will never have another invitation to that house. Strangely enough, a person who could use a toothpick has never had even a first invitation. There is something about a person who could use a toothpick which you can tell, even though you have never had a moment of table intercourse.

If you make a mistake, it is quite plain that you have done so, and explanation or deceit is unsafe. The best way out is to take the attitude that it is of no concern—rather amusing; right, or altogether negligible, because *you* did it. "Whatever I do is *right* because *I* did it," was the repeated admonition of a well-known social leader to her young daughter. "I came over on the street car," you state, with a little laugh, or with an air of complete composure, giving the impression that you are the sort of person who can do what she likes—that you are above criticism. A friend of mine was visiting at one of the most exclusive country homes in the most exclusive of summer colonies. After an afternoon at a polo match she returned to the house with two young men before her hostess' return. A stiff serving man brought in a splendid and elaborately appointed tea table, and other tables, announcing that the hostess had 'phoned that she would not return to tea. My friend had never had tea this way; she was perfectly certain she would not serve it properly, and for a moment was frozen. This was absolutely unforgivable—she would disgrace herself and her hostess. She turned to the butler. "Will you serve the tea, Houghton?" Then she laughed. "Or won't you serve it, Mr. C.? Tea is something I never play with. Somehow it has never interested me, and I should be sure to make a wrong move. Horribly unfeminine, I admit." Then she proceeded with the conversation, holding her air of complete confidence.

The manner habitual must be self-possessed; there must be an air of well-being and success. Graciousness in readily adjusted degrees, which at one degree warms and at another cools the recipient, is indispensable. An air of complete self-confidence, of easy assurance, with an occasional glint of *hauteur*, is requisite to social success.[1]

The social ritual, with the attitudes which cluster about it, serves at once as a mark to identify the members of the Four Hundred, as a means of intercourse among them, and as a barrier between them and the rest of the world. The behavior patterns which are embodied in the ritual, which may be summed up in the words "good form" and *savoir faire*, backed up by the ruthless competition of the social game, constitute the main force for social control in "society." But more than this, the ritual lends to "society" an ease, a dignity, and a charm which are the despair of many a "climber" and the envy of many not "born to the manner."

POLITICS AND PHILANTHROPY

The social game is but one side of the life of the Gold Coast. True, it is the more spectacular side. And it sets the tempo of social life. No one who moves in society can quite escape it. But political and civic movements are not always fads. Not all charities are "pet" charities. There is a genuine and serious side to the life of the Gold Coast.

Since the war, playing the social game is not so *terribly* important as it was before. Everyone still wants to be "in," of course, but many are getting off into something else, too. It's not the thing to do just to be a social butterfly any more. And many social leaders are *really* busy women; nor is it just a matter of teas. Social recognition is increasingly secured through political, civic, and philanthropic work.[2]

These days society attempts to demand that its members be peo-

[1] Document 10.
[2] Document 6.

ple who add some achievement, some successful work or accomplishment to position and wealth. There are many persons in society who do not come up to this, of course, but they are considered "nit-wits" by the more serious and conservative social groups.[1]

There is a concentration of real leadership on the Gold Coast. Not only is there a concentration of wealth, but there is a concentration of contributors to civic and social organizations (see map, facing p. 174). There is a concentration of specialized ability and achievement (see map, facing p. 244). And a study of the boards of directors and trustees of the civic and social organizations of the city revealed the fact that there is, as well, along the Gold Coast a concentration of active leadership.

Many prominent society women—and men—have a sense of an obligation that culture, wealth, and leisure owe to "the less fortunate." They actively support churches, charity organizations, social settlements, nurseries and dispensaries, reform movements in politics, city plan commissions, the "city beautiful," and movements for the democratization of art and the opera. This support is often genuine and sincere. Without it, none of these civic enterprises could exist.

There are clubs, like the Friday Club, which take a serious interest in the arts and literature, in modern movements of thought, where serious papers are read and discussed. One suspects this is not taken *too* seriously, however. A member of the Friday Club remarked, with a note of embarrassment in her voice, "One can't be civic *all* the time, you know!" The remark is interesting, for it shows that one is expected to be civic *some* of the time. One is frowned upon, a little, in more conservative circles if one does not

[1] Documents 4 and 5.

take a part in the larger civic and social movements of the day.

THE GOLD COAST AS A COMMUNITY

The Gold Coast has a common background of experience and tradition. True, with very few exceptions, the families of Chicago when traced back a generation or two are found to come from diverse and not too aristocratic origins. But as we have seen, the exigencies of the social game demand that "society" live in certain neighborhoods, attend certain finishing schools or universities, belong to certain clubs, patronize certain of the arts, serve on the boards of trustees of certain social and civic organizations, hold certain political prejudices, and, above all, conform to a common ritual. Consequently "society" comes to have a more or less common body of experience and tradition, of attitudes and conventions.

Moreover, "society" is class conscious. "I believe in aristocracy," writes a society woman; "there is something about leisure, luxury, travel, and an acquaintance with the arts which makes for a kind of superiority in the individual who has had these advantages."[1] In the consciousness of this superiority "society" holds itself aloof from all that might be termed "common."

The solidarity of this group is probably as dense as that of any known group. It is largely based on material interests. It results from a consciousness of notable wealth, success, social position. It is conscious of expressing itself in a certain manner of life, a luxurious standard which demands an accepted and costly "style" in material details. The group is conscious of a common distinction in personal appearance and manners, of common pursuits which are followed in approved places usually inaccessible to other groups.[2]

Society feels itself above all other groups. It is quite sincere and simple in this, and the consciousness gives it a certain sense of respon-

[1] Document 11.   [2] Cf. Veblen, *The Theory of the Leisure Class.*

sibility. It must preserve its standard of life, its etiquette, its polish—both for itself and in duty to civilization. In order to do this it must have no intimate contact, no equal footing, with other groups. Necessary contact with other groups is always safeguarded by holding clearly and constantly in mind the superiority of society and the impossibility of an equal footing. The child in school and in play is carefully guarded from other groups of children.[1]

But not only has "society" a common body of experience and tradition, and a degree of self-consciousness as against other groups. Beyond this, "society" in Chicago is highly localized, being concentrated in that strip along the Lake Shore Drive from Streeterville to Lincoln Park, which is known as the Gold Coast, a strip scarcely a mile in length, and not over two blocks in depth. Here are *the* streets, *the* families, *the* hotels, *the* clubs, their segregation strikingly emphasized by the encircling area of furnished rooms.

In the present generation the center of social life in Chicago has always been along the "Gold Coast." I have not been to the South Side twice in the past five years, and seldom in that time have I been north of Lincoln Park. People in this neighborhood refuse, as a matter of fact, all invitations to tea or dinner on the South Side, or north of Lincoln Park—unless they come from some *notably* influential person, or from an *intimate* friend. People from the rest of the city all come to affairs on the "Gold Coast," however. Indeed, long before the last of the old families moved to the "Gold Coast" they found that to have anyone at their affairs they must give them at the Casino, or at some other "Gold Coast" club. Chicago has a remarkably localized and integrated social life—as compared with New York, for instance. The last of the old families have long since moved to the "Gold Coast." The South Shore and the district along Sheridan Road north of Diversey[2] are different social worlds. I don't know anyone north, and only a cousin along the South Shore—and she might as well be in St. Louis or New York so far as her belonging to my social world is concerned.[3]

[1] Document 12.

[2] That fringe of Lincoln Park known as Lincoln Park West is merely an integral part of the Gold Coast.

[3] Document 6.

The Gold Coast, then, with this localization of "society" with its self-consciousness and common tradition, would seem to be a community. The fights waged by the Gold Coast to keep busses off North State Parkway, to keep apartments off Astor Street, and shops off the Lake Shore Drive, to prevent the widening of the Drive, to do away with the Oak Street beach, demonstrate the possibility of common action along the Gold Coast. But analysis reveals less of community here than at first appears.

To begin with, the "solidarity" of the Gold Coast is not based upon residence along the "Coast." Rather, residence on the Gold Coast is the result of the competitive segregation of the social game. There are remnants of the old neighborliness based on local residence. A few of the old residents call the old street-car conductors by such affectionate names as "Polly Black Sheep" and "Tooty." But these things are interesting only because they *are* remnants. The local life they go back to is a thing long past.

We have seen that the "society" of today is a thing of sets and cliques. And the life of the Gold Coast resolves itself largely into that of these smaller groups, while these groups are based upon common ages, or whims, or passing interests rather than upon common residence.

The Gold Coast is broken up into smaller groups. There is a Division Street crowd, for instance, composed of older girls, bachelors, and live young-marrieds. It has a sort of small town atmosphere, with its gossip and parties. Half the affairs I go to are on Division Street. One slang phrase, or peculiarity in dress, will go through thi: whole set at a time. But it is in no sense a *neighborhood* affair—numbers of houses are skipped; and *who* lives in those houses we *never* will know.[1]

Along the Gold Coast, as elsewhere in the city, one does not know one's neighbors. At a tea on the Gold Coast,

[1] Document 6.

when the subject of neighborliness came up, there was a chorus of "No, we don't know our neighbors."[1] One woman who lives on the Lake Shore Drive said that she did not know the woman who lived next to her, though they had lived side by side for over twenty-five years. Another woman, living on North State Parkway, told of seeing smoke coming out of a house across the street, and of telephoning all about the neighborhood in a vain attempt to discover who lived in it. The men interviewed make the same point.[2] One declares that he knows no one within a block in any direction of where he lives. Another says:

There is no neighborliness among those who live on the North Side. I live in a twenty-apartment hotel, and of the others who live in it I have a speaking acquaintance with but five, and know but one. I do not think there is any local attachment or feeling on the part of those who live there—naturally there would not be. People live on the Lake Shore Drive simply because it is the most expensive place in the city to live.

The rapid increase in the number of apartments and hotels along the Gold Coast is tending to accentuate this. For one thing, the very nature of apartment and hotel life makes for secondary contacts; and moreover the hotel and apartment are being increasingly used by the *nouveau riche* and the "climber" as a means of acquiring prestige through residence along the Gold Coast.[3]

[1] Document 13.

[2] Documents 15 and 16.

[3] Two interesting and spontaneous efforts at neighborhood organization of an informal sort came to untimely ends. The Virginia Hotel a few years ago decided to give Saturday night dances for its guests. The dances were a great success, so far as number went: but it was discovered that no one from the hotel itself was attending.

More recently a woman on Bellevue Place invited some of her neighbors,

A questionnaire endeavoring to discover the attitude of the person toward the locality in which he lived was sent to the residents of Astor Street. It revealed the fact that many of them did not think of the Gold Coast as a community, or of its streets as neighborhoods.[1] The majority of them stated that of their interests—social, political, religious, philanthropic, professional, intellectual, and artistic —only their "social" interests were centered along the Gold Coast. And we have seen that "social" interests mean playing the social game, not neighborly contacts. Moreover, the questionnaires revealed that without exception these people spend from three to five months of every year outside the city. All of them have their "summer places." Many of them travel abroad, or go to eastern, western, and southern resorts for parts of the year. The following cases are perhaps fairly typical of the movements of Gold Coast families:

A—Has an apartment on North State Parkway. Goes in May to Lake Forest. In August to a camp in the North. Back to Lake Forest for the autumn. The past two years has spent part of the winter abroad.

B—Gave up apartment in June; moved to Lake Forest. In October moved to the Drake. Went in February to Palm Beach. Back to the Drake in April. In May went to Lake Forest. Went in August to Dark Harbor, Maine.

---

whom she happened to know, to dinner. During the dinner the idea of occasional Bellevue Place parties was conceived. But they never matured. People were too busy; didn't know about Mrs. So-and-So; were indifferent, or interested elsewhere.

[1] To the question, "Do you think of the vicinity of the Lake Shore Drive as a neighborhood or as a community?" one man replied, "I am considerably mystified as to what the questionnaire is driving at. Of course, when asked whether I think of the locality where I live as a neighborhood or ͫͭ I feel like saying, 'I give it up, Mr. Bones—What is the answer'" (Questionnaire replies filed with the Local Community Research Committee of the University of Chicago).

C—Spent winter in Santa Barbara. To Europe in May. A few weeks in the autumn at the Drake.[1]

The fact is that much even of the "social" life of the people who live on the Gold Coast centers about the fashionable suburbs of Chicago, or about fashionable summering and wintering places scattered over the country. The social season lasts but four months. Then there is an exodus to warmer climates. A few weeks may be spent in Chicago around Easter time. Then everyone leaves for the summer.[2]

The Gold Coast, then, can scarcely be called a community. It is simply the fashionable place for the location of one's town house, an abode for the social season. The interests of a majority of the people who live along the Gold Coast are scattered. There are no neighborhoods; people associate as members of smart cliques rather than as neighbors. A great many of the people "living" in the vicinity of the "Drive" spend much of their time in other places. Others are not members of "society" itself. And the solidarity of those who are of "society" is a solidarity that is of caste rather than of contiguity. Yet the Gold Coast is perhaps as nearly a community as is any local group, not foreign, to be found within the inner city.

[1] Document 14.

[2] Document 6.

CHAPTER IV

THE WORLD OF FURNISHED ROOMS

Back of the ostentatious apartments, hotels, and homes of the Lake Shore Drive, and the quiet, shady streets of the Gold Coast lies an area of streets that have a painful sameness, with their old, soot-begrimed stone houses, their none-too-clean alleys, their shabby air of respectability. In the window of house after house along these streets one sees a black and white card with the words "Rooms To Rent." For this is the world of furnished rooms, a world of strangely unconventional customs and people, one of the most characteristic of the worlds that go to make up the life of the great city.[1]

This nondescript world, like every rooming-house district, has a long and checkered history.

The typical rooming-house is never built for the purpose; it is always an adaptation of a former private residence, a residence which has seen better days. At first, in its history as a rooming-house, it may be a very high-class rooming-house. Then, as the fashionable residence district moves farther and farther uptown, and as business comes closer and closer, the grade of the institution declines until it may become eventually nothing but a "bums' hotel" or a disorderly house.[2]

We have seen, in reading the history of the Near North Side, that after the fire this was a wealthy and fashionable residence district. But as business crossed the river and came

[1] This rooming-house district of the Near North Side is one of three such districts in Chicago. Similarly, on the South and West sides there are areas of furnished rooms, wedging their way along the focal lines of transportation, from the apartment areas into the slum and the business district. Rooming-house districts will be found similarly situated in every large city.

[2] Trotter, *The Housing of Non-Family Women in Chicago*, p. 5.

north it became less and less desirable as a place to live. Gradually the fashionable families moved out of their old homes. Less well-to-do, transient, and alien groups came in. As the city has marched northward, however, land values and rentals have been slowly rising, until now the families who would be willing to live in this district cannot pay the rentals asked. As a result the large old residences have been turned into rooming-houses—another chapter in the natural history of the city.

This lodging- and rooming-house district of the Near North Side lies between the Gold Coast on the east and Wells Street on the west, and extends northward from Grand Avenue and the business district to North Avenue. South of Chicago Avenue the district merges with the slum; its rooming- and lodging-houses sheltering the laborer, the hobo, the rooming-house family, the studios of the bohemian, the criminal, and all sorts of shipwrecked humanity, while some of its small hotels have a large number of theatrical people—and others the transient prostitute. The whole of the district is criss-crossed with business streets. The area north of Chicago Avenue, however, save for Clark Street, is not a slum area. And it is in this area, with its better-class rooming-houses in which live, for the most part, young and unmarried men and women, that we are interested in the present chapter.

An analysis of the *Illinois Lodging House Register* reveals the fact that there are 1,139 rooming- and lodging-houses on the Near North Side, and that in these houses 23,007 people are living in furnished rooms of one kind and another. Ninety blocks in the better rooming area north of Chicago Avenue were studied intensively, by means of a house-to-house census. This study revealed the additional facts that

The World of Furnished Rooms.—The addresses of proprietors of rooming and lodging houses (from the *Illinois Lodging House Register*, 1924, after Anderson). The Near North Side rooming-house area is one of three zones of mobile, anonymous life that follow focal lines of transportation from the Loop into the heart of the North, South, and West sides.

71 per cent of all the houses in this district keep roomers; and that of the people who live in these rooms, 52 per cent are single men, 10 per cent are single women, and 38 per cent are couples, "married," supposedly with "benefit of clergy."[1] The rooming-house area is a childless area.[2] Yet most of its population is in the productive ages of life, between twenty and thirty-five.[3]

The rooming-house is typically a large, old-fashioned residence, though many apartments are converted into rooming-houses as well.[4] And the population living in these rooming-houses is typically what the labor leader refers to as the "white collar" group—men and women filling various clerical positions—accountants, stenographers, and the like, office workers of various sorts. There are also students from the many music schools of the Near North Side. Most of them are living on a narrow margin, and here they can live cheaply, near enough to the Loop to walk to and from their work if they wish.[5]

The constant comings and goings of its inhabitants is the most striking and significant characteristic of this world of

[1] The schedules of this rooming census are filed with the Committee on Social Research of the University of Chicago.

[2] School census, 1920. The small number of children in this area is in striking contrast to the number in the slum area to the south and west; even to the number on the Gold Coast.

[3] This age grouping is based on the opinion of social workers, and on the findings of A. B. Wolfe, *The Lodging-House Problem in Boston.*

[4] Part of the story of the rooming-house is told in the fact that these great old residences can never be converted into tenements. See Breckinridge and Abbott, "Chicago's Housing Problem," *American Journal of Sociology,* XVI, 295–96.

[5] An accompaniment of the rooming-house is the cheap cafeteria and restaurant, scores of which are found along Clark and State streets, and Chicago Avenue, Division Street, and North Avenue.

furnished rooms. This whole population turns over every four months.[1] There are always cards in the windows, advertising the fact that rooms are vacant,[2] but these cards rarely have to stay up over a day, as people are constantly walking the streets looking for rooms. The keepers of the rooming-houses change almost as rapidly as the roomers themselves. At least half of the keepers of these houses have been at their present addresses six months or less.[3]

Most people on La Salle street are forever moving. The landlords move because they think they will do better in another house or on another street. I think many landlords might have been gamblers or inventors—they see visions, or are of the temperament which is always looking for a new stroke of luck. The tenants also keep moving, because they hope for something better in another house or on another street. They are always looking for a place more like home, or more comfortable, or cheaper.[4]

So the scenes shift and change in the drama of the rooming-house world—change with a cinema-like rapidity.

THE ROOMING-HOUSE

The rooming-house is not to be confused with the boarding-house.

[1] Census of Rooming Houses (see above). Of course there are people who have lived in the same room for years. But there are hundreds of others who live in a given house but a month, a week, or even a day. See Documents 14 and 15.

[2] As of November 1, 1923, 30 per cent of the houses in the district had cards in the windows. Census of Rooming Houses (see above).

[3] *Illinois Lodging House Register.* With respect to length of residence, 117 consecutive registrations for the Lower North Side were distributed as follows:

o–1 Mo.	1–3 Mo.	3 Mo.–6 Mo.	6 Mo.–1 Yr.	1–5 Yr.	5 Yr. and More
9	9	26	25	35	13

[4] Document 14: Interview with a resident of a rooming-house on La Salle Street.

The characteristics of the old-time boarding-house are too well known to need recounting here. With all its shortcomings, it will be admitted that there was in it something of the home element. Boarders knew each other; they met at table two or three times a day, and lingered a few moments in conversation after dinner in the evening. In summer they gathered on the front steps and piazzas, and in the winter often played euchre and whist in the landlady's parlor. Congenial temperaments had a chance to find each other. There was a public parlor where guests were received, and, in a reputable boarding-house at least, a girl would not have thought of taking a gentleman caller to her own room. The landlady of a good boarding-house took something of a personal interest, even if remote, in her boarders, and they often found themselves becoming a part of the family, even against their wills. There was a certain personal element in the relations between individuals; no one could be isolated and certainly shut up to himself.[1]

Here, at least, was a nucleus of opinion, set of personal relationships, which tended to define social situations. But the boarding-house has passed out of existence in the modern city. The rise of rents, the mechanization of life, and sharper definition of economic function resulting in the development of the café and restaurant business has reduced the former keeper of the boarding-house to the simpler employment of "taking lodgers." Not a dozen boarding-houses were found in this Near North Side district.

The rooming-house which has replaced the boarding-house is a very different sort of place to live. It has no dining-room, no parlor, no common meeting place. Few acquaintanceships spring up in a rooming-house.

One gets to know few people in a rooming-house. All told, in the year and a half I lived there, I didn't come to know over twenty well enough to speak to them. And there must have been nearly three hundred people in and out in that time—for there are constant comings and goings; someone is always moving out; there is always an ad in the paper, and a sign in the window. But rooms are never vacant

[1] A. B. Wolfe, *The Lodging-House Problem in Boston*, I, 46–47.

more than a few hours. There seems always to be someone walking the streets looking for a room, and someone is always moving in. People change so fast, and one is in so little—being at work all day, and out every evening as likely as not—that there is little chance to get acquainted if one wished. But one doesn't wish—there is a universal barrier of distrust in this rooming-house world. At first I couldn't comprehend it; but later I was to come to.[1]

The keeper of the rooming-house has no personal contact with, or interest in, his roomers. He is satisfied to collect his rents and to make a living. It is an entirely commercial consideration with him. Consequently the average keeper of a rooming-house is not too particular about who rooms in his house, or what goes on in it, as long as the other roomers are not disturbed.

Trotter, in her study of the housing of non-family women in Chicago, comments:

The question about entertaining men guests brought forth interesting varieties of standards. . . . . A number stated that the privilege of entertaining in a girl's room would be allowed on condition the door was left open. Some said, "Yes, if two girls are entertaining." Others stated limitation of hours at 10 P.M. and 10:30 P.M. One man who showed the house and gave privileges of entertaining in rooms said, "We don't care what they do, just so they are quiet after 12 o'clock." To the question "Are men callers permitted in rooms?" the answer most often received from those who granted the privilege was "Yes, if girls are nice." One woman said, "Yes, but I don't have nothing but first-class carryings on." Almost half of the 300 places visited granted this privilege.[2]

A woman who was asked by one of the census workers how many married couples there were in her house said: "I don't know—I don't ask. I want to rent my rooms."

[1] Document 15: the life-story of a "charity girl." This "barrier of distrust" was run against by those taking the census of rooming-houses. Faces peered from windows; doors were opened a crack and often slammed; questions were met with suspicious glances, and non-committal replies.

[2] Trotter, *The Housing of Non-Family Women in Chicago*, p. 11.

The rooming-house is a place of anonymous relationships. One knows no one, and is known by no one. One comes and goes as one wishes, does very much as one pleases, and as long as one disturbs no one else, no questions are asked. How complete this anonymity may be is shown in the following document:

> I had occasion to inquire for a man living in a rooming-house. He had roomed there about a week. There was no 'phone in the place, so I had to call at his address. I went there about 7:30. After I had rung the bell for some time, a woman about forty-five answered the door. She wore a house apron, and was evidently the landlady. I asked for Mr. X. She said "Who?" I repeated the name. She shook her head, and said that she didn't know anyone of that name. I looked at the address in my notebook, to see if I had the address correct. I told her that this was the address he had given, and went on to describe him. She knew of two men in the house who might answer to his description. I then told her that he did a lot of work on the typewriter in his room. Then she knew whom I meant. She told me to go to the third floor front and see if he was there. He was not in. I knocked at several other rooms, but no one knew anything about him. When I got downstairs the lady had disappeared, and I could not leave a message.
>
> I came back a week later, and the same woman came to the door. I asked if Mr. X. was in. She said he had moved yesterday. I asked if she knew where he went, but she did not know. She said that he left when his week was up. He had left a note for her, saying he had to leave. I asked her if he might not have left a forwarding address for his mail. She said that he did not, that he never got any mail.[1]

Such complete anonymity could be found nowhere but in the city of today, and nowhere in the city save in the rooming-house.

The peculiar social relationships of the world of furnished rooms are reflected in the behavior of the people who live in this world. Nothing could bring this out more clearly and

[1] Document 16.

significantly than the story which follows, the life-story of a "charity girl."

Emporia, Kansas, was my home until I was twenty-two. My father had a small business there. He was an upright, God-fearing man. . . . . He taught us to obey the Ten Commandments, to go to church on Sunday, to do all the things the "respectable" do in a small, gossiping place.

We were a large family but father managed to save enough to send me, the oldest, to a small college in the state. And from the time I was a little girl I had music lessons. It is about these music lessons that the story of my life revolves.

I was always looked upon as something of a prodigy about the town. At ten I played at Chopin and Bach. I played my little pieces at church recitals, at firemen's benefits, when mother entertained the Ladies' Aid Society, and at our high school graduating exercises. I was told that I had talent, "wonderful feeling for the soul of the masters," that I ought to go to New York, or abroad, where I could have competent instruction; that some day I would be a concert star.

Through my four years of college this ambition slumbered, but never died. And the day I got my diploma I wrote home that instead of going back to Emporia to marry a "Babbitt" and live on "Main Street," I was going to Chicago to study music. I went home for a stormy week. Father was amazed that I should suggest living alone in Chicago, and sternly forbade my going, saying that if I did he would send me no money—indeed, he had little to send. Mother said little, but when I left she put into my hand fifty dollars which she had been saving for a new dress. All told, when my ticket was bought, I had less than one hundred dollars on which to begin the conquest of a career.

Never shall I forget the time of the night that I arrived at the Northwestern Station, my purse clutched tightly in one hand, and my bag in the other, shaking my head at redcaps, confused and dazzled by the glare of the lights—but my heart singing, my ambition aflame it was the gate to the promised land. I went to the Travelers' Aid Bureau and inquired how to get to the Y.W.C.A. I walked uptown, carrying my bag, too excited to be tired. I still remember the romantic appeal the sluggish blackness of the river made, gleaming in the lights of the great electric signs. How differently it was to look two short years later!

The first few weeks went by like magic. It was all so strange and maddeningly stimulating to my small-town soul. The "Y" was a pleasant enough place to live—not at all the institutional sort of place I had expected it to be. But even in these first weeks I began to know what loneliness is. Most of my evenings were spent sitting in corners of the sitting-room, watching the old girls playing the piano and victrola, or entertaining their beaux. I got acquainted with a few other newcomers—a girl from Indiana who came to study, like myself, a girl who came from Alabama to get work as stenographer, and four or five others, from small towns in Illinois. All but myself seemed to have acquaintances or connections of some sort in Chicago. And sometimes, when I felt too unbearably lonely, I would go back to the big station in the evening, at the time when the train I came on would be coming in, and watch the faces in the crowd for a face from Emporia.

It was at the "Y" that I had my first acquaintance with that most pitiable figure of the rooming-house world—the old and unmarried woman who works. They were conspicuous in either the cafeteria or the upstairs sitting-room, because of their loneliness—eating lunch at a solitary table, sitting by themselves knitting, with shabby and unbecoming clothes, care-worn faces, and toil-worn hands. I was to learn later some of the tragedies their mute lips harbored.

After six weeks at the "Y" I moved to the Near North Side, to be nearer my music school. And during the next few months I lived at a dozen rooming-houses and homes for girls. The boarding-homes were more comfortable and pleasant, but I was working all day and taking lessons at night. I was out late, and this conflicted with their rules. I soon found a rooming-house was the only place I could live. But it was hard to find a rooming-house where I wanted to live. The rooms I could afford were in gloomy old houses on La Salle Street, bleak and bare, and so large that usually I had to share them with one or two other girls. The beds were hard, and often vermin-infested. The landladies were queer-looking and dowdy, tight-lipped and suspicious of eye, ignorant and coarse. They rarely took any other interest in you than to see that you paid your week in advance. The men and women living in the house were mostly a tough lot. There were goings on that shocked me then—though I would pay scant attention to them now.

My first year is a nightmare as I look back upon it. In order to keep clothes on my back and to pay for my lessons I had to work seven days in the week. My college education had fitted me for nothing. I tried one thing after another—salesgirl at Marshall Field's, milliner's helper, running a simple machine in a garment factory, ushering at a movie, and finally waiting at a "white tile" restaurant. Somehow I never held any of the positions very long.

The days were long and exhausting—up at six, a bath, a cup of coffee on a "sterno" stove, tidy my room a bit, and in the Loop by seven-thirty or eight. Then a long steady grind until five; a mile walk out to my rooming-house; supper in a nearby restaurant—and a plain supper at that; the evening devoted to my lesson or practicing; back to my room at ten-thirty or eleven, often too tired to undress until I had slept an hour or so.

I had come to the city in June. By Christmas my loneliness amounted almost to desperation. I had made no friends—a girl brought up on the Commandments doesn't make friends in rooming-houses or as a waitress very readily. I didn't talk the same language as the girls I worked with. At the theater or the restaurant men often came up to me and said things in a way that made me blush, though often I had no idea what they meant, unsophisticated little fool that I was. Mother was ill, and letters from home came less and less frequently. Shortly after Christmas she died, and the last tie that bound me to Emporia was gone. I was "on my own," and very nearly "on my uppers" as well. But I still had my ambition—I would some day be a great *artiste*, and all this loneliness and hardship would be forgotten. . . . .

In February, I think it was, I met a girl from Tennessee at the music school, with whom I became quite friendly. Within a few weeks we decided to get a room together, and we moved over to a house on Dearborn, just north of Division. The house consists of several large old residences thrown together. It has perhaps forty rooms, and there have been as many as seventy roomers in it at one time. It is cleaner than the run of rooming-houses, and quieter, and the man and the woman who run it are decent enough. But you would never mistake it for anything else than a rooming-house. Somehow, one gets to loathe that card in the window—"Rooms"! And the life and people were not much different from those on La Salle Street.

One gets to know few people in a rooming-house, for there are constant comings and goings, and there is little chance to get acquainted if one wished. But one doesn't wish. . . . . There were occasional little dramas—as when a baby was found in the alley, and when the woman in "the third floor back" took poison after a quarrel with her husband, or when police came to arrest a man who had eloped from Pittsburg with his wife's sister, and a new trio of roomers robbed most of the "guests" on the second floor; there were these occasional little dramas when the halls and bathrooms were the scenes of a few minutes' hurried and curious gossip. But the next day these same people would hurry past each other on the stairs without speaking.

As the months went by, my lessons cost more and more; I had to work shorter hours to get in my practice; our room was costing more; and I found myself always a week or so behind. It was a humiliating experience to have to cajole the landlady into giving me credit—humiliating to a girl who had been brought up to believe it wrong to have debts. But I got so that I could invent a reason for putting it off as brazenly as the "gold digget" in the next room.

[A year of this had gone by, when one day her music teacher told her there was no hope of her ever realizing her ambitions.] I turned dazedly from the piano . . . . I scarcely heard him. I picked up my music and tossed it into a waste-basket in the corner; and then I walked out of the room.

It was late afternoon, and I walked the streets, neither noticing nor caring where, until late that night I ended up along the embankment in Lincoln Park, and sat down exhausted, on the stone wall by the lake. My head was a bit clearer by now, and I began to take stock of myself. . . . .

The ambition for which I had sacrificed, which had kept me alive and going, was dead. There was nothing to hold me to home and family. Mother was dead. No one ever wrote. And my oldest brother, in Chicago a few months before, had told me that father never allowed my name to be mentioned about the house, save to use me as a horrible example of the wilful daughter gone wrong—he once referred to me as a street-walker. Those words kept repeating themselves in my mind—"street-walker, street-walker!" And a great bitterness burned in my heart, turning to ashes every love, every tie, every ideal that had held me at home.

Then I began to look at my life in Chicago. What was there in it, after all? My music was gone. I had neither family nor friends. In

Emporia there would at least have been neighborhood clubs or the church. But here there was neither. Oh, for someone or something to belong to!

My room-mate had been going to Sunday night services at the Fourth Presbyterian Church, over on the Lake Shore Drive. She told them about me, and one day some pastor's assistant's assistant came to call on me. I went one night after that. I was greeted with ostentatious and half-hearted civility. It was all so impersonal. . . . . I never went back; and no other church ever took an interest in me. The only other group I had had anything to do with, outside of my work, had been a social agency from which I had tried to get a little help in the spring. They treated me as impersonally as though I had been a rag doll. There was ringing of buzzers, long documents with endless questionings to be filled out—and not a human touch in it all.

The city is like that. In all my work there had been the same lack of any personal touch. In all this city of three million souls I knew no one, cared for no one, was cared for by no one. In a popular science story in the evening newspaper a few days before I had read how the universe is composed of millions of stars whirling about. I looked up at the sky. I was just like that—an atom whirled about with three million other atoms, day after day, month after month, year after year.

What *did* I have? I had no clothes, no shows, no leisure—none of the things all girls are supposed to love. My health was breaking under the strain. I was in debt. The answer was, Nothing—absolutely nothing! And there stretched ahead of me long years of nothing, until I married an honest but poor clerk or salesman and tried to make ends meet for a brood of hungry mouths, or until I became one of those broken-down, old working women that I had patronizingly pitied that first week at the Y.W.C.A.

Of course, there were two ways out: I might slip into the lake, there, and end it all. But somehow I didn't think seriously of that. Or I might do as some of the girls in the house, become a "gold digger," play life for what there was in it, pay with what there was in me. The idea half-sickened me, yet I played with it for a while—for so long that I drew up startled at the unknown possibilities that lurked within me, cold at the thought that there was neither person nor thing to hold me back.

I never went back to music school. I had been working as a wait-ress of late, ... and I kept on with it. But the days and nights were empty now—and at last I knew to the full what loneliness could be. One night a nice boy came into the restaurant—it was one of the larger downtown restaurants—and sat down at my table. He talked to me, as they all did; told me he was from a small town in Oklahoma, that he'd made money, and had come to see the big city. He was friendly, and ended by asking me to a show. I accepted, and we went to a cabaret afterward. In a spirit of reckless bravado, to show the small-town boy I was a city-wise woman, I smoked my first cigarette and took my first drink.

There's no use in making a story of it. He had an engaging smile, and was in search of adventure. I was unutterably lonely—and tired. He said that he loved me, and I was willing not to question too closely. I left the rooming-house, and we took a little flat out near Rogers Park. For a month I played at being respectable, got acquainted with young wives in other apartments, had lovely clothes, lazy hours, ate at the best restaurants, saw the best shows, shopped in smart shops, drove my own car. Then, one day, B. came home and told me he was going back to Oklahoma, and that I wasn't going with him. I said little; I had known it must come, of course, though I had hoped it wouldn't come so soon. There was a generous check. And I moved back into the rooming-house.

No, I felt no remorse. Life had cheated me. There was no one to care. Why slave and work when I might have the things I wanted? And not the least of these was the intimate touch and glance of a man—even if it were half make-believe. Someone to talk intimately with, someone to come home to, someone to ask where you've been—these, too, are things one can't live without.

Not every man or woman who lives in the world of fur-nished rooms is so articulate as this "charity girl." But most of their stories, however common-place they may seem in the telling, reveal the same isolation, loneliness and tend-ency to personal disorganization.[1]

[1] Document 15: the life-story of a "charity girl."

THE ROOMING-HOUSE AS A SOCIAL WORLD

The conditions of life in the world of furnished rooms are the direct antithesis of all we are accustomed to think of as normal in society. The exaggerated mobility and astonishing anonymity of this world have significant implications for the life of the community. Where people are constantly coming and going; where they live at best but a few months in a given place; where no one knows anyone else in his own house, to say nothing of his own block[1] (children are the real neighbors, and it is a childless world); where there are no groups of any sort—where all these things are true it is obvious that there can be no community tradition or common definition of situations, no public opinion, no informal social control. As a result, the rooming-house world is a world of political indifference,[2] of laxity of conventional standards, of personal and social disorganization.

The rooming-house world is in no sense a social world, a set of group relationships through which the person's wishes are realized. In this situation of mobility and anonymity, rather, social distances are set up, and the person is isolated. His social contacts are more or less completely cut off. His wishes are thwarted; he finds in the rooming-house neither security, response, nor recognition. His physical impulses are curbed. He is restless, and he is lonely.

The charity girl, in her foregoing story, exclaims "There was no one to care! Why should I slave and work, when I might have the things I wanted? And not the least of these was the intimate touch and glance of a man—even if it were

[1] As one woman put it, when asked if she knew her next-door neighbors, "No; it don't pay to know your neighbors on La Salle Street" (Census of Rooming Houses).

[2] A precinct captain in a rooming-house precinct said it was useless to try to get the people from rooming-houses to go to the polls (Document 17).

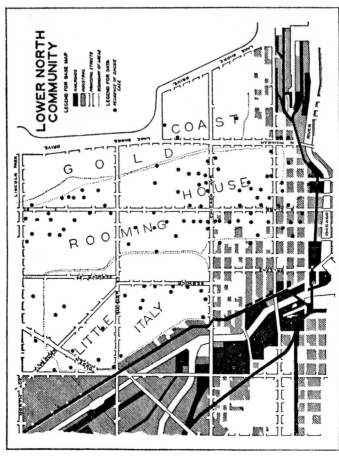

SUICIDES.—Suicide often seems the only escape from the isolation of rooming-house life. Suicide tends to concentrate in rooming-house areas, as this map of the addresses of Near North Side residents who committed suicide within a four-year period indicates (data, after Earle and Cavan, from the coroner's reports for 1919–22).

only half make-believe; someone to talk intimately with, someone to come home to, someone to ask where you've been; these, too, are things one can't live without." A man who lived in a North Side rooming-house wrote: "I found myself totally alone. There were evenings when I went out of my way to buy a paper, or an article at a drug store—just for the sake of talking a few minutes with someone." He goes on:

Worse, if possible, than the loneliness was the sex hunger. I had had a regular and satisfying sex experience with my wife. I began to grow restless without it. I thought of marriage—but the only girls I had met were office stenographers I never would have considered marrying. The constant stimulation of the city began to tell, adding tremendously to this sexual restlessness, lights, well-dressed women, billboards advertising shows.

It got so posters showing women in négligée or women's silk-clad legs excited me unbearably. Many times I followed an attractive woman for blocks, with no thought of accosting her, but to watch the movements of her body. Though my office work was over at four, I frequently put off coming home until four-thirty or five, so I could get in the rush hour crowd on the street cars and feel myself crushed against the warm body of some woman. A girl in the next house used to undress without pulling down her shade, and I literally spent hours watching her. I had fantasies of sexual intercourse with every attractive woman I saw on the street.[1]

The emotional tensions of thwarted wishes force the person to act somehow in this situation. His behavior may take one of three directions: He may find himself unable to cope with the situation, and attempt to withdraw from it. This withdrawal frequently takes the form of suicide. There was a bridge over the lagoon in Lincoln Park, in the heart of the North Side rooming-house district, which was nick-named Suicide Bridge because of the number of people who

[1] Document 18.

threw themselves from it into the lagoon. Because of its
sinister reputation the city tore it down. The map facing
page 83 showing the distribution of suicides on the Near
North Side indicates how frequently this seems the only
way out to the persons of the rooming-house world.

Or, again, the person may build up an ideal or dream
world in which are satisfied the wishes that find no realization in the harsher life without.

There were two girls in a room across the hall who worked as
shopgirls in the Loop. They came from some town in southern Illinois.
They weren't good-looking—and, besides, like myself, they had had
good homes, so they were lonesome. They used to go often to the
movies, and sometimes to a dance, but the celluloid heroes proved
more satisfying to these plain but heart-hungry children than did the
neglect of the dance hall "sheiks." Other evenings they spent reading
True Romance, Experience, True Story Magazine, and other such
magazines devoted to stories of the adventures of girls in the city. One
of them kept an intermittent diary, filled with stories—fictitious, I
always was sure—of street flirtations and adventure. We used to spend
evenings writing letters to Doris Blake, asking what a young girl should
do if a man she liked but didn't love tried to kiss her. It was all a make-
believe, a peopling our workaday world with adventure and heroes.

Upstairs was an old maid, who was somebody's secretary, who
still wore nipped-in corsets, and a curl hanging at the side of her head.
She had a picture of a handsome man on her dresser, in a big frame,
before which she used to powder and primp. She told a different story
about him to everybody in the house who would listen. She was the
only talkative person I ever found in the house.[1]

Or perhaps a substitution is made, and the person finds
satisfaction for his thwarted wishes in symbols which represent old associations, or lavishes his affection on a dog or a
parrot.

Her almost complete isolation brought her to a point where the
few whom she saw occasionally feared for her sanity. Then something

[1] Document 15: the life-story of a charity girl.

happened which she said later saved her life. One day a well-dressed man, holding a parrot in his hands, rushed up to her and pushed the bird into her arms, saying earnestly, "Take care of it." He disappeared before she could remonstrate. She 'phoned at once to police headquarters, asking to be relieved of the bird. Meantime she put the bird in a box and tried to forget it. After some time a voice said, "Hello!" The greeting was repeated at intervals. She went on with her work. Presently a boy came to relieve her of her charge. "I think," she said, "that I will keep it myself if no one puts in a claim for it."

She lavished attention, thenceforth, on the parrot. She bought it the best cage she could find, cared for it according to the best parrot lore, and returned home after work to give it food and exercise. It ate its supper with her, perched outside the cage on a basket handle, being fed now and then from her spoon. In the morning it flew to the side of the cage to greet her, and talked to her while she dressed. When she came home after work it was filled with joy; if she lay down to rest and moaned a little with weariness, the parrot made sad, sympathetic sounds. Anyone with whom it was left was asked to say certain words of greeting to it morning and night. It was her child. She sacrificed herself for it. "You can't imagine," she would say, "what it means to have Polly in my room—it makes all the difference. . . . ."

There are thirty-seven things on the wall, mostly pictures, among them a photograph of her grandfather's old stone house, the picture showing the country in which she had lived; a cheap print of a child in its nightgown descending the stairs; a colored print of a man and woman sitting in the firelight; some family pictures. There is a newspaper cartoon of a homeless man on Thanksgiving Day, shabby and alone at a cheap restaurant, seeing a vision of a pleasant family group about a generously laden table. There are thirty-nine articles on the bureau, two small stands, and a melodion—including a tiny doll and a tiny cradle. I have urged her to cast away nine-tenths of these things, in the interest of her time budget, to make cleaning simpler. "I have to have these things," she responds, "you have your home and family and friends and leisure and everything—you can't possibly understand." She plays hymns and the old songs of the countryside on the melodion—"Darling, I am growing old!" The parrot tries to sing after her.[1]

[1] Document 19.

More frequently, though, the person accommodates himself to the life of the rooming-house world, as did the "charity girl." Old associations and ties are cut. Under the strain of isolation, with no group associations or public opinion to hold one, living in complete anonymity, old standards disintegrate, and life is reduced to a more nearly individual basis. The person has to live, and comes to live in ways strange to the conventional world.

> I get along fairly well, now. I am no longer lonely. I am surprised to find that I can actually enjoy the girls I pick up at public dance halls, at restaurants, along the lake front, in the park. I know a great many of them now—many of them pretty and clever, and good companions for a night. I no longer go with prostitutes. I soon found that was unnecessary. For the city is full of women who are just as lonely as I was, or who draw on their sex as I would on my bank to pay for the kind of clothes they want to wear, the kinds of shows they want to see. Then, too, there are the "emancipated" women, who don't want to marry, who are not "gold diggers," but who feel the need of a man and a normal sex life.[1]

Such is the world of furnished rooms—a mobile, anonymous, individual world, a world of thwarted wishes, of unsatisfied longings, of constant restlessness; a world in which people, in the effort to live, are building up a body of ideas that free them from a conventional tradition that has become fixed, hard, and oppressive; a world in which individuation, so typical of the life of the city, is carried to the extreme of personal and social disorganization. People behave in strange and incalculable ways; quick and intimate relationships spring up in the most casual way, and dissolve as quickly and as casually. Behavior is impulsive rather than social. It is a world of atomized individuals, of spiritual nomads.

[1] Document 18.

CHAPTER V
TOWERTOWN

As one rides up North Michigan Avenue atop a bus one pauses for a moment at Chicago Avenue. Across the street rises an anomalous structure in grey stone, too ornate to be gaunt—the old Chicago water tower, the sole relic to be found on the North Side of Chicago before the fire. To the north looms the skyline of Streeterville and the Gold Coast. But to the west and south lies a nondescript area of business buildings and rooming-houses, where the "world of furnished rooms" merges with the district of cheap lodging-houses and the slum. If one gets off the bus at the water tower and rambles the streets within a half-mile radius of it one discovers, however, tucked away in dilapidated buildings, quaint restaurants, interesting art shops and book stalls, tearooms, stables and garrets with flower boxes, alley dwellings, cards in windows bearing the legend "Studio for Rent." For this is the "village," Chicago's Latin Quarter, dubbed by the newspapers "Towertown" because it lies about the foot of the water tower. Ironically enough, the last remaining landmark of the sternly moral, overgrown village that was Chicago before the fire becomes the symbol of the bizarre and eccentric divergencies of behavior which are the color of bohemia.

"THE KINGDOM OF BOHEMIA"

In Chicago, as elsewhere, the "village" has a flavor of art. Before the war, in the heydey of the "village," painters of some distinction tenanted its studios. Original and creative writers from time to time walked its streets—Sherwood

Anderson, Floyd Dell, Ben Hecht, Carl Sandburg, Edgar Lee Masters, and Alfred Kreymborg among them—engaging personalities who, while loudly denouncing and renouncing commercialism, were quite as eager for money as other literary aspirants.

With one breath they pledged themselves to poverty—though not, surely, to chastity or obedience!—and denounced such well-heeled poets as Kipling and Shakespeare as harlots of the marts. With the next they bargained with such editors as ventured to buy their wares, like Potash tackling One-eye Fligenbaum. But from this lamentable trafficking Kreymborg held aloof, a genuine Parnassian. He composed his bad poetry and worse novels on a diet of *schnecken* and synthetic coffee, and paid for that meager fare by teaching Babbitts chess.[1]

Kreymborg was the true type of the bohemian literati. Many young men and young women live like him today, in the back rooms of Towertown, working in bookshops or on newspapers by day and over the typewriter by night, picking up a precarious living, selling an occasional verse or book review, attending Harriet Monroe's "poetry evenings" at the Petit Gourmet, adding a few pages each night to the "great American novel." But since the war Towertown has degenerated, so far as art is concerned, into a second-rate bohemia. Successful art has looked beyond the approval of Towertown to the wider recognition of Greenwich Village and the Latin Quarter, or to the publishers' offices of Fifth Avenue and Broadway and the bounty of "philistia." The "artists" who remain, writers or painters, are for the most part obscure adherents of bizarre schools and "isms" of color or of verse.

On an alley off La Salle Street is a typical bohemian studio which has become the rendezvous of Towertown's struggling painters.

[1] H. L. Mencken, *Prejudices, Fifth Series*, "Greenwich Village."

W—— once taught in the Chicago Academy of Fine Arts. But he felt that conventional art forms were stifling his individuality. So he threw up his teaching and took a room in an old building opposite the Dill Pickle Club. He supported himself by odd jobs of commercial painting and began to paint as he chose, to seek "self-expression." He held continual open house in his "studio," and it soon became a rendezvous for a lot of serious but impecunious painters as well as for many of the literati. Hecht, Bodenheim, Edna St. Vincent Millay, Helen West Heller and others were found there many evenings. It was the center of the real artistic bohemia. There would be much talk until the small hours of the morning, when tea would be served. Then a fire burned all W——'s paintings and belongings, and he moved to his present alley location. Open house—it is part of the ritual of bohemia—still makes of his studio a rendezvous for the impecunious and struggling artists and near artists of Towertown. W—— looks upon himself as the prophet of a new art, the little group takes itself quite seriously, the all-night discussions continue—indeed, W——'s child has learned to sleep no matter how many overcoats are thrown across his bed. Occasionally one of the more successful painters, who for the most part hold aloof from the bohemian life, is drawn into the little group. Professional and business men of means who have a dilettante interest in art and in bohemia, and who enjoy posing as patrons of art, have also been drawn into the group, as have a few students and "intellectuals."

There is considerable solidarity in the little group, though old members are constantly dropping out of sight and new members are constantly drifting in. If an artist gets into difficulties his friends give a benefit for him, or raffle off his worthless canvasses, or appeal to one of the "patrons" on his behalf.

It was in W——'s "studio" that the idea of the Chicago No Jury Exhibit was conceived. Every year a No Jury Ball is given to finance the No Jury Exhibit, and to help out needy No Jury artists who can't get the patrons that "Lorado Taft and his gang of fakers have on their strings." The expenses usually eat up all the receipts, but it is a carnival occasion, and any "patron" or "friend" who did not buy tickets or help to underwrite the expenses would be considered cheap indeed.[1]

[1] Document 19.

In the "studios" of Towertown the artist who earns a comfortable living by painting conventional portraits and landscapes is likely to be looked upon as prostituting his talent—and yet the prospect of eviction and hunger sometimes makes it necessary to descend to the painting of hosiery and lingerie advertisements.

Towertown has, too, a student flavor, for on the Near North Side live many of the students of the Art Institute, and of the North Side's many schools of music, opera, dancing, and dramatic art. At the corner of Dearborn Parkway and Goethe Street stands the commodious Three Arts Club, a home for Near North Side art students, erected by society patrons of the arts. The majority of these students, however, live in furnished rooms in Towertown, eking out an existence as ushers in the theaters, "supers" at the opera, singing for women's clubs, dancing at movie palaces, or modeling. They mingle with bohemia at its studio parties and many evanescent little theaters—the Jack and Jill Players, the Impertinent Players, the Studio Players, Neo Arlimusc, and a score of others which are scattered about the "village."

Towertown, like bohemia everywhere, has its tinge of radicalism. Be it in Chicago, New York, or Paris, bohemia has always welcomed the radical as one of its own. Over tearoom tables, or in the Dill Pickle Club or Ye Black Cat Club, or at the Radical Book Shop, one will hear Towertown's radicals and "intelligentsia" airing their ideas on capital, or government, or sex. It is largely a radicalism of "wobblies" and poseurs. On a warm summer evening one may find a crowd of anarchists, socialists, proletarians, communists, syndicalists, I.W.W.'s, and curious loiterers gathered about two soap boxes from which the "social ambassador" (of the faculty of the "hobo college") and the "proletarian queen" guy at each other. Like as not the affair breaks up in a street row. Or on a winter evening, at the Dill Pickle Club, one may find assembled the "intellectuals," rebellious but sterile souls whose radicalism runs to long hair, eccentric dress, lilies, obscenity, or a Freudian interpretation of dreams.

The Towertown of today, however, is largely made up of individuals who have sought in its unconventionality and anonymity—sometimes under the guise of art, sometimes not—escape from the conventions and repressions of the small town or the outlying and more stable communities of the city. Some of these individuals have a genuine hunger for new experience, a desire to experiment with life. They run the tearooms and art shops and book stalls of the "village," or work in the Loop by day and frequent its studios and restaurants by night. Perhaps, like Collie, they keep a little red notebook with a list of the things they have always wanted to do, and strike them off as one experiment in living after another is completed. Most of these experimenters are young women. For Towertown, like Greenwich Village, is predominantly a woman's bohemia. In Paris the "Quarter" is a bohemia of young men students. In London bohemia belongs to the man about town, to the older artists—cultivated, clever—who like the adventure of the night life of the city. But of late years, in New York and Chicago, with changing mores and the emancipation of the younger generation of American women, Greenwich Village and Towertown have become women's bohemias. It is the young women who open most of the studios, run most of the tea-rooms and restaurants, most of the little art shops and book stalls, manage the exhibits and little theaters, dominate the

life of the bohemias of American cities. And in Towertown
the women are, on the whole, noticeably superior to the men.

But these genuine experimenters with life are few.
Most of Towertown's present population are egocentric
poseurs, neurotics, rebels against the conventions of Main
Street or the gossip of the foreign community, seekers of
atmosphere, dabblers in the occult, dilettantes in the arts,
or parties to drab lapses from a moral code which the city
has not yet destroyed. On the occasion of the suicide of
Wanda Stopa, who had sought in Towertown escape from
the life of Little Poland, Genevieve Forbes vividly por-
trayed the studio life of the "village" of today:

BABEL OF BUNK AND SEX—THAT'S SHAM BOHEMIA

Studio.—The working room of a painter, sculptor, or, by extension, one engaged in any more or less artistic employment (Webster's
dictionary).

And it's the elastic "more or less" that gives your real artist
pause.

For it is this amateur flair for pseudo-studio life that is sending
more than one Wanda Stopa from Poland, Czechoslovakia, or from
Sleepy Hollow three steps down or four flights up to a studio apartment in the "near Bohemia" of the near north side. It is sending them
to incense and psychoanalysis; to old-fashioned plumbing and new-
fashioned talking; to "freedom" and to dirt.

It was about five years ago, the historian of Chicago's Latin
quarter will tell you, that these amateur intelligentsia began to splash
a bit of red paint over a rickety stair and call it a studio. To sprawl
scraggly letters of a flip phrase across a shingle and make a tea shop.
To drape gauze scantily about the girls and name it an aesthetic cult
of intellectual liberty.

This influx, the same historian will explain, coincides pretty well
with the rise of the futuristic in art and letters. The old days of rigor-
ous apprenticeship were going. Anybody could be an artist or a poet.

And pretty nearly everybody was.

Some of them weren't even sincere in their own desires to be "artistic." Many began to exploit what they couldn't do, rather than what they could. And they flocked over to the near north side, to be with the group of serious minded artistic folk who had amiably and quietly congregated there.

The newcomers insisted upon plenty of scenery.

And they still keep up that tradition. Lots of paint and plenty of funny Russo-French teapots, battered candle sticks. Exotic drawings, a few "daring" books, and not too many brooms or dust pans. They live in tiny rooms, sharing kitchens and baths with other "artistic" tenants.

Nobody locks doors; it's so unfriendly. And trailing kimonos add to the picture.

A few blocks away, prim landladies are refusing to permit their girl guests to entertain men visitors in their bedrooms. But the studio is a bedroom as well as a reception hall. The bed, covered over with a brilliantly colored scarf and piled high with pillows, a bit dusty, is there.

And so are the men callers.

They sit about in the dimly lighted room and talk about life. They scoff at repressions; they speak loftily of "live your own life." Phrases of self-conscious daring tumble from the lips of young girls "asking advice." Free love, marriage a "scrap of paper"; "those who really understand"; "living, not existing." The whirligig of words revolves perpetually.

And it's all very modern and enlightened, they argue.

Physically, the life isn't so modern. The living-room may be more colorful than in a suburban bungalow; but the bathroom is likely to be darker and danker. Dirty dishes, perhaps, are piled high in the tub that doubles as a dishpan. The morning egg is fried in the midst of toilet articles and tooth paste.

It's the same in many of the nearby tea shops. Candle wax dripped in lumps all over the bare and dirty floor; penciled nudes, poorly done, about the walls; cracked panes of window glass—all give the place "atmosphere." There are no table-cloths, but if there were there is indication that they might show a Volstead bump.

And the same talk of sex.

Nobody quite dares to puncture the balloon. They all keep on seeking the thrill they think they're going to get. They haven't the courage of a Chicago woman whose diary was recently made public. In commenting on the discourse of a lion of the village colony, at a recent studio party, she said: "Interesting, but not especially intelligible."

But she didn't say it "out in meeting." For she would have been thought more guilty than Wanda Stopa, who not so long ago attempted to shoot this woman of the diary. At that meeting, one of the group, and she is widely known in Chicago, murmured to the speaker, as he voiced a twisted idea:

"It's so limitless it makes me shiver."

And the village accepted her for its own.

The following pages from the diary of a Near North Side student give perhaps a more intimate picture of the unconventional and bizarre life and personalities which move about the studios and tearooms of Towertown:

October 10. Went with F—— to M——'s rooms on East Chestnut. [M—— is business manager of the poetry magazine.] M—— took us to a studio a few doors away. It is in a ramshackle two-story frame building, reached by a rotten board walk and a precarious back stairway. We entered a little kitchen which was furnished with a low table, a one-burner oil stove, and a single chair. The walls were bare, the yellow plaster cracked and falling. In it two young men and a girl—one man fair, with careless dress and long hair; the other dark, with normally cut hair, a small moustache, and a marked southern accent. He is of a good southern family, says M——, of literary tastes, and feels he is "sowing his wild oats" in Towertown. The girl was vivacious, with dark eyes and hair. She had evidently been cooking their supper. She soon left. As she did so, she caressed T——, the dark chap, and said, "Perhaps they'd like to see my studio, too? But you boys don't know where I live, do you? Well, it's over the garage in the alley, two blocks up."

We went into the next room—the most bizarre room I have ever been in. It was hung in violent batiks—the four walls—and the ceiling draped to the center. The total effect was that of a booth on the midway. The only furnishings were two pallets on the floor. The walls were hung with deafening futuristic paintings, in glistening color

effects, the work of R—— the blond boy. (M—— says he paints
these things, then holds them this way and that until he finds in them
a faint likeness to something or other, mostly an imaginary likeness,
and then gives them names.)

We sat around on the floor and smoked, R—— with his hair
hanging over his face, and talked. T—— was eloquent in his eulogy
of the "professional bohemian," whom he defines as one who gets by
without working, picking up a bit here and a bit there. He will live
off one friend after another, sell a few pencils, do a little commercial
work if he is an artist, or get a part-time job in the Loop, pick up a
little through little theater plays, and the like. Then when times are
lean, he "hitches" his way to New York. Everyone is glad to see him.
He works the "village" in the same way for a few months, and then
comes back to Chicago. R—— told some amusing tales about B——.
He went to New York, looked up a friend, showed him both hands
bandaged, and said he'd been caught riding "blind baggage" and had
burned his hands against the fire-box. His friend took him in. It
went on for weeks. B's hands didn't get well; he couldn't work; and
his friend got tired of keeping him. Then one day he happened into
B——'s room and found him with the bandages off, busily playing
solitaire!

There was much glib talk of modern poets and schools, most of
which have never been heard of outside of studios and "village"
magazines. They talked of one another's work, each professing a pro-
found contempt for that of all the others. R—— said that if he were
an editor he would have none of T——'s. Oh yes, Harriet Monroe
would take it; but *he* wouldn't. R—— prides himself upon being a
"professional bohemian," and goes in for the long hair-cut and the
Bill Jones' blue denim and corduroys. He was recently hailed into
court by his landlady, who couldn't understand anyone's "not having
beds and chairs, and wearing long hair!"

November 11. Met W—— at six and walked down State to Pearson. Dark, and a fine rain falling. Turned into W. Pearson. Met
C—— hugging a lamp-post. The lighted windows of 19 West shone
mistily at the end of the dark street. No one downstairs—a couple of
men sitting upstairs smoking and playing chess.

V—— came in, fairly sober after being pretty well "lit" for four
days. She is a model—one dollar an hour, nude. M—— of the *Journal*,

drifted in ten minutes later, and we ordered dinner. M—— entertained us with stories of newspaper life from Greenwich Village to Melbourne and the Cape. Clever man, has lived an intense, interesting life; leans to poor puns and lewd stories.

Later, E——B—— and "Larry" joined us. E—— B—— is a clever, pretty, dark little thing, an ex-wobbly, who during the war visited the wobblies in prison, but who now addresses locals and distributes literature for the American Federation. "Larry" was another model, and dumb. E—— B——'s brother-in-law dropped in. A handsome, dark sheik who has lost one job after another, and now is living off his friends in the village, the girls mainly, in the grand manner of the "professional" bohemian.

A group of "homos" from the South Side also came in. They drank tea and talked loudly of labor. One was a beautiful boy with red hair and a dead white skin. He was a blousemaker. Another was named "Alonzo." He claims to be a Spaniard, but the village suspects him of being an octoroon, and will have nothing to do with him. The waitress was a pretty little Russian. She was enchanting a group of college boys who had been to the Dill Pickle and were slumming. About eleven-thirty the crowd from Keedy Studios came in—a group of little theater enthusiasts desperately trying to be bohemian.

The whole village was out, almost. F—— K——, who holds the international suicide-attempt record, a "dopey," and who recently picked out the doorstep of the Dill Pickle for her attempt, did not come in, however, and we were all disappointed.[1]

As one watches these types merge and mingle in the restaurants and studios of Towertown, one is struck by the fact that in Towertown nearly everyone plays a rôle, wears a masque. "Self-expression" is the avowed goal of "village" life. And where talent is lacking, self-expression runs to the playing of rôles and the wearing of masques, sometimes of the most bizarre sort. F—— K—— goes about the streets of Towertown the picture of cynicism and despondency, and periodically takes poison—always being careful not to take too much, and that she shall have an audience for her

[1] Document 20.

"suicide." "Durfie" writes the story of her life—it is the conventional pattern of the wayward girl, and everything "Durfie"is not. Then she contracts tuberculosis, assumes the rôle of the "pale spectre of death with hectic cheek," and extracts every ounce of drama from dying. These, however, are the pathological extremes one finds among Towertown's masques. The villager is usually content with assuming an eccentricity in dress or manner, an indifference to opinion that is far from real, a contempt for Rodin, Debussy, or Shakespeare, or a pose as the prophet of some new movement in drama, poetry, music, or painting. Once the rôle is adopted, or perchance thrust upon one, the whole "village" plays up to it, and a personality is crystallized.

The Neo Arlimusc recently held an exhibit for "Chicago's primitive artist." This primitive artist is P——, a conventional, small business man of sixty-two, who a year ago suddenly began to paint. He had been a clothing peddler in the ghetto, had earned a very mediocre living, but had managed to save a little and had retired. One day the old man dropped some papers from his pocket on which a friend saw some sketches. The old man was much embarrassed, but the friend insisted on taking them to W——, who exclaimed, "This man is a genius, a primitive artist!" P—— had never had a lesson in his life, and paints very crudely. With this encouragement P—— began to paint more crudely than ever. Then it was arranged to give P—— an exhibit. Only his own things were hung. They had an art critic from the University who came and discussed P——'s primitive technique, and a psychiatrist who probed back into P——'s primitive unconscious for the explanation of his turning to painting at so late an age. De K—— got up, and pointing to some Jewish sweatshop scenes painted on old cardboard, exclaimed: "See that? The artist's expression will out! Poverty stricken, he seizes on the only medium available." Then P—— was sent off to New York, where Greenwich Village hailed him as the exponent of a new art form. Under this definition by the group, P—— has ceased to be the timid clothing peddler, sketching and secreting his sketches, having constantly to be reassured he is an artist and has a place in the world, and has accepted the rôle created for him as the creator of a new and primitive art, and continues to paint more and more crudely.[1]

Behind these masques which the "villagers" present to one another and to the world one usually discovers the egocentric, the poseur, the neurotic, or the "originality" of an unimaginative nature. Occasionally, however, one finds behind these masques young persons who are struggling to live out their own lives, to remake the world a bit more after the fashion of their dreams—young persons who have come from north and west and south, from farm and village and suburb, to this mobile, isolated, anonymous area of a great city where they imagine they may live their dreams. It is these occasional dreams behind the masque, and the enthusiasms, intimacies, disillusionments that are a part of the living out of these dreams, that lend the "village," despite its tawdry tinsel, a certain charm, make of it what O. Henry termed "the Land of Illusion," "the Kingdom of Bohemia."

"FREE LOVE"

Transient but intense personal contacts are characteristic of this "bohemian" life of "studio" and "tearoom." Combined with the unconventional tradition of the "village," its philosophy of individualism, and the anonymity which its streets afford, these contacts give rise to unconventional types of sex relationship. Moreover, Towertown's debates on free love and its reputation for promiscuity, coupled with its unconventionality and anonymity, attract to its studios many individuals who are not bohemians, but who seek in Towertown escape from the repressive conventions of the larger community. Many of them become

[1] Document 21.

hangers-on of bohemia, but others isolate themselves in its midst.

Disregard of sex conventions has always been characteristic of the bohemian, who sees in marriage only an institution for hampering one's freedom and self-expression and cramping one's personality. This is especially true of the woman in bohemia, who objects to giving up her individuality, independence, and name. It is not uncommon to see two names—John Jones; Mary Smith—on "village" mail boxes, indicating a man and woman living together unmarried. Such a union is usually extremely casual, taken up because you like the back of someone's head, or agree that John Masefield is an old maid, or that the proletariat is being crushed under capital's heel; and terminated when it gets in the way of your ambition, or interests diverge, or you meet someone who suits you better, or the other person begins to bore you by talk about getting married. It's all in the open, an accepted pattern of behavior in the "village." All these attachments are sincere while they last. Occasionally one lasts for years, or passes over into marriage.

The anonymity and unconventionality of "village" streets attracts to them many who merely want to be "let alone." I was talking one night, near "Bughouse Square," about life in the "village." Afterward a girl came up to me and said: "Why can't social agencies let us alone? There's at least a year in everybody's life when he wants to do just as he damn pleases. The 'village' is the only place where he can do it without sneaking off in a hole by himself."

Plenty of individuals do use the anonymity of "village" life, however, to sneak off into holes by themselves. Business and professional men use its studio apartments to keep their mistresses. B—— and her mother live in a beautiful apartment, with Japanese servants and every luxury. B—— is supported by a wealthy business man, married, with a wife and family, who spends occasional week-ends with her. Intervening nights she entertains an army officer, a penniless adventurer, to whom she even gives money. G—— is a well-to-do lawyer and bachelor and keeps his mistress in the village. There are many such cases, especially of young men, "philistines" through and through, who nevertheless like the laissez faire of bohemia. R—— is a wealthy dilettante in the arts whose elaborate studio parties are celebrated for the fact that all the women present are his mistresses—past, present, and prospective.

Distorted forms of sex behavior also find a harbor in the "village." Many homosexuals are among the frequenters of "village" tearooms and studios. B—— L—— keeps a vermilion kitchenette apartment, with a four-poster bed hung with blue curtains and an electric moon over it. When he has his loves he gets violently domestic, tailors, mends, and cooks. S—— was married, but indifferent to her husband, and lived in a "village" studio, posing as a homosexual and having a succession of violent affairs; when she finally "fell" for the blond lion of the "village" she went around and bade her former "flames" dramatic farewells featured by long, passionate kisses and embraces. A number of times I have followed a cab through the "village," the lights of my car revealing its occupants, two men or two girls, fondling each other. A nurse told me of being called on night duty in an apartment in the "village" and of being entertained every night by the girls in the apartment across the well, some of whom would put on men's evening clothes, make love to the others, and eventually carry them off in their arms into the bedrooms. A friend of mine was asked by an acquaintance to accompany him to the studio of a well-known "villager" to Sunday afternoon tea. There was a large group there. The men were smoking and talking in one end of the room, the women in the other. There was a good deal of taking one another's arms, sitting on the arms of one another's chairs, and of throwing an arm about one another's shoulders. But he thought it was merely that the group were old friends. He was asked to tea again a few weeks later. This time he remained in the evening. Soon the men were fondling one another, as were the women. A man he had met that afternoon threw an arm about him. He got up, went over to the acquaintance who had brought him, and said, "I'm leaving." When they got out on the street he asked, "What sort of a place was that, anyhow?" "Why, I thought you knew," his companion replied, "the best-known fairies and lesbians in Chicago were there." There used to be a group of male homosexuals who frequented the "village" known, after their leader, as the "blue birds." Warm summer evenings they would distribute themselves along the benches on the esplanade. The leader would start walking by, down toward the Drake. From bench to bench would go the whisper, "Here comes the blue bird!" They would flirt with him as he passed by until he selected a partner for the night. Then the rest of them would pair off and seek their "village" haunts.[1]

GARRETS AND STABLES

The intimate and artistic life of the "village" is passed unnoticed by the rest of the city, to which Towertown stands only for these bizarre garret and stable studios, long hair, eccentric dress, and free love. This is due largely to the fact that certain shrewd individuals were not slow to see possibilities in the commercialization of bohemia. Some of these individuals were of bohemia themselves. A group of young women writers in Towertown organized "Seeing Bohemia" trips, at seventy-five cents a head, and conducted curious persons from the outside world through tearooms and studios bizarrely decorated for the occasion. Tradition has it that the Dill Pickle Club had itself raided two or three times, secured an injunction to make it safe, gazetted itself, and began to charge admission. The Coal Scuttle and the Gold Coast House of Correction were other efforts of Towertown's business men to commercialize bohemia. They were dingy, out-of-the-way places, marked by an ostentatious bohemian poverty—catch-penny devices to lure the slummers who nightly crowd the district. Few real bohemians crossed their thresholds.

In Towertown, as in the Latin Quarter and Greenwich Village, the night club has seen the possibility of exploiting the reputation of bohemia. Bert Kelley's Stables, the Tent, the Paradise Club, the Little Club, and Chez Pierre are among the better-known night clubs of Towertown. Unlike the "Rialto" cabarets that draw a local patronage from

[1] Document 22.

"the street" and "Little Hell," unlike the bohemian tea-rooms with their little groups endlessly discussing obscure poets and schools of art, Towertown's night clubs, with their "Paris revues," singing waiters, and jazz, trade upon the fast-spending, semifashionable after-theater crowds out to "make a night of it," or upon the respectable citizens of outlying communities seeking stimulation and adventure. In the anonymity of this mobile area "anything goes," and persons seeking unconventional experiences escape from the regulations of better organized communities into the promiscuity of its supposedly bohemian night life.

THE "VILLAGE" PASSES

The days of Towertown would seem to be numbered—even of the "village" of the would-be artists, the bohemian experimenters with life, the persons who seek license under the cloak of artistic freedom. The passing of Towertown, as of the bohemias of Paris and New York, is incident to the march of the city. The old *Montmartrais* looks sorrowfully at the seven-story buildings cutting into the sky, annihilating with their immense façades the small one-story houses around with their stuffy *gargotes* and cafés, all adorned with windmills like a Flemish landscape, in which painters and sculptors worked and lived their reckless lives, and sighs "Montmartre is dead!" The "Quarter" gives way before the modern Paris of commerce. The Greenwich Villager somberly watches the old dwellings that harbored cheap studios leveled to the ground as great apartments as splendid as those on Park Avenue rear their ten, twenty, or thirty stories from Fourteenth Street down to Eighth Street; laments the building of a new subway and the approach to a new vehicular tunnel which cut block-wide swathes through the

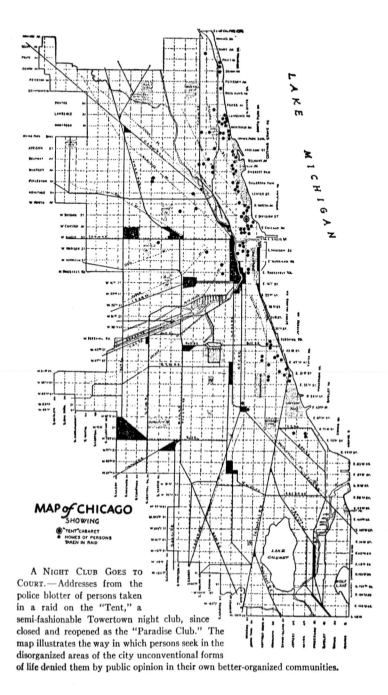

MAP of CHICAGO
SHOWING

◉ "TENT" CABARET
● HOMES OF PERSONS
TAKEN IN RAID

A NIGHT CLUB GOES TO
COURT. — Addresses from the
police blotter of persons taken
in a raid on the "Tent," a
semi-fashionable Towertown night club, since
closed and reopened as the "Paradise Club." The
map illustrates the way in which persons seek in the
disorganized areas of the city unconventional forms
of life denied them by public opinion in their own better-organized communities.

heart of the Village; observes apprehensively the northward press of business and the renovation of picturesque old houses into a real estate agent's paradise; waxes indignant at the enforcement of a tenement law that forbids gas plates and sterno stoves; bemoans the passing of the pleasant Italian and French table d'hôtes with the convivial bottle of wine, the spaghetti "meccas," the "chip-in" sketch classes, and the open-house studios that only a short time ago made the locality famous.

And so, in the tearooms of Towertown, one hears talk of the "good old days" when Sandburg and Kreymborg walked its streets, and of the "fine old radicalism" of before the war. Meantime the Loop, crossing the river, pushes northward. Great office buildings and towering apartment hotels cast their shadows over the old stone fronts that harbor studios. Rising land values and rents make Towertown too expensive a place for young artists and students, for bohemians and itinerant radicals, to live. Studios and tearooms are replaced by offices and shops. The tides of the city rush along the streets. The life of the "village" begins to disintegrate. There is talk of demolishing the old water tower to speed the flow of traffic down Michigan Avenue. A decade more, and Towertown may be little more than a memory.

The passing of Towertown has a deeper significance than to serve as an illustration of the succession of the city. It is indicative of pervasive changes in the nature of the city's life. As the city expands, the slum moves on. Towertown, the Village, bohemia, however, passes out of existence— passes out of existence because it no longer has a rôle to play in the life of the city. As the outlying areas of the city become increasingly mobile, as contacts become increasingly secondary and anonymous in the great areas of apartment-house life, group sanctions disintegrate, unconventional behavior is tolerated or ignored, and the "radical" no longer faces the necessity of seeking refuge from community opinion. The bohemian way of life becomes increasingly characteristic of the city at large.

CHAPTER VI

THE RIALTO OF THE HALF-WORLD[1]

In the heart of the Near North Side, in the center of the rooming-house district and on the frontier of the slum, lies North Clark Street. By day it is a street of queer contrast between the shabbiness of the slum and the march of the city. Occasional new office buildings, real estate offices, and banks mark the struggle of business in its conquest of the slum. But its atmosphere is more that of busy dilapidation than of hurrying commerce. Most of North Clark Street's buildings are run down, many of them ramshackle old dwellings unconvincingly converted into store fronts. And the stores are largely such as cater to the migrant population of the rooming-house, or the submerged population of the slum—pawnshops, cheap theaters, second-hand stores and resale shops, white tile restaurants, cigar stores, news and taxi stands. The people who walk its streets are cheaply and carelessly dressed, and stand hesitatingly before store windows before they enter. The few short blocks from the smart shops of North Michigan Avenue to North Clark Street seemingly take one into a commonplace and workaday world.

But at night North Clark Street shakes off somewhat its shabbiness and its dinginess. Its electric signs and brightly lighted windows, lighted late into the night, have earned for it the name "little white way," for at night it is a street of lurid cabarets, of all-night "chop sueys" and "chili parlors," of innumerable small dance halls where jazz is king.

[1] The identity of all persons referred to in documents in this chapter and throughout the book, has been disguised. Where names occur, they are fictitious.

By day or by night, it is a street of queer and exiled types, a street whose people are in the city but not of it—the hobo, the radical, the squawker and the stick-up man, the panhandler and the prostitute, the dopey, the jazz hound, the gold digger, and the charity girl. To all these denizens of the half-world North Clark is Main Street.

THE HOBO

North Clark Street is the north side "stem" of Chicago's hobo population, one of the streets of hobohemia—and Chicago is the hobo capital. All the roads that the hobo travels, or tramps, lead to Chicago. From 300,000 to 500,-000 of these migratory men pass through the city every year. Chicago's lodging-houses and cheap hotels harbor from 30,000 to 50,000 of these homeless men, depending upon whether times are good or times are hard.[1] Perhaps half of this population are stationary casual laborers—men who once were wanderers, but who now, because of age or physical handicap, find the "road" too hard. They are the dregs of hobohemia, to whom the hobo and the tramp contemptuously refer as the "home guard." Of all these, North Clark Street has its share.

North Clark Street has, to be sure, no "slave market" like West Madison Street, no hobohemian playground like South State Street; but it is near to both of these, and it boasts in Washington Square the congregating place of the hobo intellectual. Above all, its cheap hotels and lodging-houses afford "flops" to the migrant or the down and out. In the few blocks between the river and Chicago Avenue there are fifty men's hotels and men's lodging- and rooming-houses. And on Lower La Salle, Dearborn, State, and Rush streets, and on the cross streets below Chicago Avenue,

[1] See Nels Anderson, *The Hobo*, chap. i.

there are scores of other cheap hotels and rooming-houses which open their doors to the homeless man. Here one can get a room, or a bed, for from 25 to 75 cents a night, according to his purse. Rooms may be had by the week for as little as a dollar.

Along Clark Street have located all sorts of stores that cater to the trade of the homeless man and to the poverty-stricken family back in the slum. There are clothing exchanges, resale shops, and second-hand stores along North Clark Street and in the vicinity of Clark Street on Chicago Avenue. They deal in used articles of clothing which perhaps the Gold Coast has discarded, in sample suits and shoes, in imperfect garments. Prices are not high; complete suits may be had, if one looks around, for as little as three dollars, and shoes for much less. And the homeless man may eat along North Clark Street as cheaply as he may clothe himself. There are forty-four lunchrooms and restaurants on the street between the river and Chicago Avenue, and seventy-six between the river and North Avenue. Many of these are of the cheapest sort, and frequented only by men; others are of a higher grade, and appeal to the men and women of the rooming-houses on Dearborn and La Salle.

Nearly every block has its barber shop; many blocks have two and three. The barber shop is a sort of local news bureau, passing along bits of gossip on the "stem." The "lady" barber is also becoming popular along North Clark Street—for the homeless man has few associations with any other woman than the prostitute. Perhaps the mission owes much of its popularity to the same cause; or perhaps, again, to its warmth on chill nights, to its free doughnuts and coffee, to its theatrical evangelism, and to its ability to stir old associations. At all events, the "church on the stem," be it a mission meeting or a street meeting, is assured of an interested if curious audience. And the mission and street meeting are also characteristic of the vicinity of North Clark Street.

There are book stores, too, on "the street," the stalls of which are filled with books and pamphlets calculated to attract the hobo and the financially unsuccessful. One of the most interesting, not to say picturesque, of these is the Gold Coast Book Store.

The Gold Coast Book Store is in the basement of an old residence, built back from the street, and now sandwiched between two business blocks. The space in front is filled with stalls, and striking placards and posters.

These posters advertise such books as will arrest the attention of the down and out. One reads: "All of the world reads Nietzsche. Why not you? He is the greatest, boldest, the most original thinker Europe has produced in 200 years." While another reads: "Men in thousands pass this spot daily, but the majority of them are not financially successful. They are never more than two jumps ahead of the rent man. Instead of that, they should be more bold and daring, 'Getting Ahead of the Game,' before old age withers them and casts them on the junk heap of human wrecks. If you want to escape this evil fate—the fate of the vast majority of men—come in and get a copy of *The Law of Financial Success*. It will put some new ideas in your head, and put you on the highroad to success. 35c."

There are always men loitering before its stalls. But they seldom buy. Success comes high, even at thirty-five cents, to the hobo.[1]

It is difficult to estimate the numbers of the "hobo" on the Near North Side, but there are perhaps five thousand of these homeless men to whom North Clark Street is the "main drag."[2] They are mostly the misfits of society. They can't or won't fit in. And however much they may boast

[1] Document 23.

[2] Nels Anderson, *The Hobo*, p. 4: "Every city has its district into which these homeless types gravitate. In the parlance of the 'road,' such a section is known as the 'stem' or the 'main drag.'"

of their freedom, they are always on the defensive against the condemnation of a larger society, sensitive to the opinion of a larger world.

The younger men compensate with a boastfulness—they are eager to talk about their experiences, and to impress upon their listeners that they are having the times of their lives. Especially are they boastful of their sexual experiences—for status has little more than a physical basis in a situation of anonymity and isolation. One claims to "have had intercourse with more women than any other man" of his age; another "can sure kid the girls and get them to fall" for him; a third boasts of his virility which enables him to earn a living as a male prostitute; many insist they have sexual relations only with "women of the higher classes."

But the older men have a sense of defeat. They are suspicious and reticent, and talk only to justify themselves: "If I only had done so and so when I was young"; "life has stacked the cards against me"; "hell can beat this world all hollow." They try to give the impression that they have never been immoral, either with women or with their own sex.

There are those, though, who are queer beyond feeling any lack of adjustment. Paul claims to be an inventor. He has invented a new kind of lens which will enable a person to see things 1,000,000,000 times as large as they actually are. He has ground the lens himself, with emery cloth. He says he has been offered $1,000 for his invention, but is holding out for $5,000. When he was asked how he knew the lens was so strong, he explained his experiment upon a bedbug: "You know, when I put one of those live bedbugs under this glass, I can see every muscle in its body. I can see its joints and how it works them. I can see its face, and I notice it has no expression in its eyes. You couldn't do that with an ordinary lens."[1]

This population of homeless men of the casual laborer or hobo type brings with it a high degree of personal and social disorganization. All that has been found true of the population of the better-class rooming-houses is true of the "homeless man" in an exaggerated fashion. In meeting his

[1] Document 24: "A Study of Hobo Life," an unpublished manuscript on the hobo in Washington Square, by Alfred E. Nord (adapted).

sex problem he spreads disease—for he can afford only the broken-down prostitute. He is the victim of the bootlegger, the dope peddler, and the "jack roller." Gamblers and pickpockets thrive in his precincts. His economic insufficiency and his mobility are constant problems to the mission, the police, and the welfare agency. He is not a part of the larger community; often he is at war with it.

THE SQUAWKER

"Everybody on Clark Street has his squawk." There are hundreds of men, and women too, on the Near North Side who are "getting by" with petty grafts of one kind and another. In the parlance of the street, these "grafts" or "games" are known as "squawks." And Clark Street is a favorite working place of the "squawker."

Peddlers are constantly on the street, standing on corners, or going from store to store, with shoestrings, safety pins, pencils, postal cards, anything on which a few cents' profit can be made. But peddling is work, and many prefer to beg. The majority of these beggars are mere "panhandlers," able-bodied men who try to work upon people's sympathies with a "hard luck" tale and to pick up a nickel, a dime, or a quarter here and there. But there are the physically handicapped, too, who exploit their loss of an arm or a leg, of sight or hearing.[1] Then there are the élite of the

---

[1] Clark Street might well be called "the street of forgotten men." There are several old hotels and rooming-houses in its vicinity which are populated largely by the physically handicapped beggar—especially the blind beggar—and by those who through simulation and "make-up" are able to ply the same trade. The old Revere House, for one, has a considerable coterie of blind "professionals."

K——, for example, is a well-known Clark Street character. She is a graduate pianist from a conservatory in a midwestern city. Her sight having been greatly impaired, she passes as blind, though she still has some vision. She has taken up the violin for street use and, as occasion necessitates, plays

profession, such as the "throw out" and the "black hood," who simulate paralysis or throw fits for a street audience, and reap a harvest of coins from the sidewalk. The "squawker" is a professional man and a student of human nature. The "panhandler," for example, picks his victims carefully. Often he will let half a dozen people pass before tackling one with his hard luck story; and he is nearly always successful in reaping some small return for his yarn. The "flopper," too, studies his public, and soon learns what corner is most profitable for his particular game. And the game is profitable. For while peddling rarely enables a man to live much above the "coffee and" level, a clever squawker will make as much as fifty dollars on an exceptional day, and it is a poor day indeed when he cannot make ten dollars for five hours' work.[1]

---

to street and restaurant crowds. The night before she goes to "work" she puts her hair on curlers and sits propped up with pillows all night in order not to muss her hair. She also writes poems and music, which she sells. She usually "works" the after-the-theater crowds, and then sells to patrons of restaurants and poolrooms, often till three o'clock in the morning. She occasionally has programs printed of concerts to be given by herself—selections from Bach, Chopin, and others. Armed with these she goes about restaurants selling tickets. Needless to say, the concerts never materialize. One day on the street she came upon a blind man playing a violin. She stopped and took up a collection from the passing crowds as he played. Then she calmly walked off with the proceeds. What could illustrate more astonishingly the mobility of the city street? (incident related by L. Guy Brown, who is soon to publish a study entitled "Physical Defects and Problems of Personality").

[1] Document 25: The "Squawker"; and Nels Anderson, *The Hobo*, chap. iv, " 'Getting By' in Hobohemia." The professional beggar knows his associates by odd terms. The flopper, for example, is a man or woman who has lost both legs, and sits or "flops" along the sidewalk, begging for alms. The "black hood" is a woman who sits along the street with a baby in her arms and a cup by her side. The "throw out" can throw out his joints at will, thus simulating various deformities. A "high-heeler" is a female beggar who works with a "squawker."

Street faking is another popular game along Clark Street. Any pleasant summer afternoon or evening one may see these fakers on the corners. A man shows you the sun through a long telescope, for ten cents. A street astrologer asks the month when you were born, tells you some commonplaces which might be true of anyone, but which are always flattering, and tries to sell you, for a half-dollar, a little red book with your horoscope. A conjuror pastes a stamp on a wooden paddle, turns it to a dollar, then back into a stamp—and sells the paddle for a quarter. A gypsy woman, colorfully garbed, does a trick with a magic egg, and tells your fortune. "Hawkers" are selling cheap books on sex, or patent cuff-links, or "snake oil" that is guaranteed to cure all human ills.[1]

Occasionally some "genius," with an imagination that might have taken him far in a more reputable profession, conceives of a scheme that at once marks him as an aristocrat on the street and yields him a steady and handsome income. Such a scheme was the "Christ Brotherhood."

The "Christ Brotherhood" yesterday found itself beset by devils in the form of court action, recalcitrant members, and a general disagreement as to whether the cult's hand points to heaven or to perdition.

[1] Sex is an ever interesting theme on the street. Several "doctors," well-known characters of the Near North Side, make a living selling mimeographed works on "Secrets of a Vital Sex Life" or "How To Escape Disease." Remedies for restoring virility are constantly and profitably peddled to drifting men who frequent the street. Medicines for rejuvenation are frequently feature displays in drug store windows. Until recently the Near North Side boasted a flourishing if questionable "Institute of Glandular Therapy." The promise of restored sexual potency will separate the older frequenters of "the street" from their last dimes. It is difficult for the average person to appreciate how intimately the status in life of the denizens of the half-world depends upon sex exploits.

The brotherhood was formed by David Thompson, who had as his temple the second floor of a rooming-house at 601 North Clark Street.

David set out to become mankind's savior, on a platform of no sex, no money, and no meat. He gathered half a dozen women and half a dozen men at his shrine, and proceeded to send them out every day to work at odd jobs and to bring the money back to him.

There were charges yesterday, however, that David was not perfectly in accord with his profession of the rules of conduct. Miss Helen Miller appeared before Judge Barasa.

"He got me in a month ago," she said. "He made me work and give him the money. Then he—well, he came into my bedroom and made improper advances, though his religion said there must be no relations between men and women."

"She's a devil," quoth David to the judge. "God tried to save her by sending her to me, but she won't be saved. She's—well, the devils have her."

And then, at the cult's shrine, came another diagreement, but that has not reached any court. A woman and a boy, firm believers in David, and a man who says it's all flim-flam, did the talking.

"David is Christ," quoth the boy. "He knows all."

"The boy's feebleminded," whispered the man. "Moral oddities, that's what caused it—and that's what David causes here."

"We are one for all, and all for one," remarked the woman. "No one owns anything."

"No one but David," whispered the man. "He makes us all work and give him the money. He's bought real estate in Florida with it, though he's not supposed to own anything. All we get is raw carrots three times a day. That's the only thing he lives up to—no meat."

"There is no sex," continued the woman.

"But I saw David rubbing a girl's back as she lay in bed," interposed the man.

"Anointing," explained the woman. "We anoint each other with olive oil—just like the early Christians, you know."

"David is the chief anointer," answered the man. "Only women anoint him. And I saw him kissing and fondling a girl one night."

"He kisses the girls goodbye when he goes away," was the explanation offered. "It is the sexless kiss of a savior."

"There is no death," explained the woman.

"That's what he tells 'em," answered the man. "Live on raw carrots and raw spinach, and you'll live forever. Most of the dupes here make about $5 a day and David gets all except a nickel's worth of carrots."[1]

Getting by on the "Rialto" is a game with its lure, and its scope for the play of genius, as well as its professional compensations—as much so as is watching the ticker on La Salle Street.

BUG HOUSE SQUARE

Chicago is the "wobbly" capital of America. It is the headquarters of the I.W.W. The Workers' Party, official mouthpiece of the Russian Third Internationale, is moving its offices to Chicago. The *Novy Mir*, a Russian-language paper, the only open champion of Sovietism in America, is also moving to Chicago. The *Liberator*, formerly the *Masses*, has already moved to Chicago, and now publishes from 1009 North State Street.[2]

Because Chicago is America's "wobbly" capital there is an unusually large element of intellectuals and agitators, of I.W.W. sympathizers and "reds," and of professional malcontents in its population of drifting men. And it is in the vicinity of North Clark Street that these types have made their gathering place. Their favorite place for setting up their soap boxes is in Washington Square, between Clark

[1] Newspaper item. It may be suggested that "David" was a subject for a psychopathic clinic rather than for a judge on the bench. Quite possibly this is true. Indeed, "the street" would provide an excellent interneship for a young psychiatrist. But genius is, after all, relative to the social situation. And many of the most colorful and, within limits, "successful" personalities of "the street" would be psychopathic in the alienist's consulting room. The social adjustments of the "half-world" are not so exacting as those of the world of industry. That is one of the causes of the "half-world's" existence.

[2] *Chicago Tribune*, August 5, 1923.

and Dearborn streets, in front of the Newberry Library. By day its benches are filled with men reading newspapers, talking, or just sitting in the sun. But at night, crowded along its curbstones, are gathered groups of men, often as many as a hundred in a group, listening to the impassioned pleas of the soap-box orator, the propagandist, and the agitator. All their arguments come down to one or the other of two propositions: the economic system is all wrong, or there is no God. Occasionally a dreamer dares raise his voice, or a street-speaker for a rescue mission takes issue with a proselyting atheist. After getting down from the soap box the speaker often will pass the hat, making his living by reading up on some subject or other in the library during the day, and speaking at night. Sometimes he will have a partner, who acts as heckler, thus adding a dramatic element which holds the crowd. Because of the constant and violent agitation from its soap boxes, night after night, Washington Square has come to be known as "Bughouse Square," and there are many who know it by no other name.[1]

THE "LITTLE WHITE WAY"

At night North Clark Street is a street of bright lights, of dancing, cabareting, drinking, gambling, and vice. There is a colorful night life in which bohemia and the underworld may meet with the curiosity seeker and slumming parties from the world of fashion. The bohemian and the fashionable world, however, tend to frequent the tearooms and cabarets east of State Street, leaving the haunts of North Clark Street to the denizens of the underworld.

We have seen that before the abolition of legalized vice, North Clark Street was honeycombed with houses of prosti-

[1] See Nels Anderson, *The Hobo*, pp. 9, 10.

tution and disreputable hotels, was a "red light" district only less widely advertised than the notorious segregated district on the South Side, old Customs House Place. And before prohibition every corner along North Clark Street had its saloons. In 1918 there were along North Clark Street, between North Avenue and the river, fifty-seven saloons and twenty cabarets. It was not uncommon in those days to hear the district spoken of as the "Wilds of North Clark Street."

The efforts of committees for the suppression of vice, and of federal prohibition agents, have altered the nature of vice rather than abolished it. There is still soliciting along North Clark Street, but it is carried on less openly. There is still gambling and drinking, but it is done behind closed doors and drawn blinds. The chief result of campaigns against vice has been to drive it from the lights of the street into back rooms, on into the anonymity of the rooming-house. The street is not the show place to the curious man from the small town that it once was. But it remains the center of the worst police district in Chicago, and the haunt of a large element from the underworld.

The night life of this underworld element centers about the cabaret. There are now seven cabarets along North Clark Street between Grand Avenue and Chestnut Street: the Poodle Dog, the Derby, the Royal Café, the Erie Café, Spark Plug Inn, the Palace Garden, and the "606"; while the Red Lantern, Camel Gardens, and the Tile Bar have only recently passed out of existence.[1] These cabarets are continually at war with the police and prohibition agents, many of them operating under injunctions secured in the Thompson régime. The Juvenile Protective Association and

[1] This was in 1923.

THE RIALTO OF THE HALF-WORLD 117

the Committee of Fifteen are constantly taking them into court.[1] They are frequently "padlocked" and as frequently reopened.

Shrill laughter, masculine as well as feminine, shrill talk, shrill singing: "A'm nobuddies' weakness it seems, for no deah boy haunts mah dreams, and—so—ah want some lovin' papa, ah want. . . . ." Cigarette smoke denser than a London fog . . . . smell of bad alcohol, cheap cosmetics, rich cigars, ginger ale, cold cream, sweat, disinfectant. . . . . Swirling, twirling figures. . . . . The hoarse plea of the saxophone . . . . a crash as a drunken patron knocks a glass from the waiter's hand . . . . young boys with young girls . . . . old men with young girls . . . . young men with thirty-five-year-old women . . . . couples kissing. . . . . "Let's go somewhere else." . . . . "Gimme a drink."

And yet the Erie Café, one of the élite of the Near North Side cabarets and saloons, looked at less hysterically is not a bad place. It is, for the most part, a much better place than the other cabarets in the neighborhood. The owners are more circumspect about selling liquor; the patrons are more orderly; there is less "rough" dancing on the floor; there is better ventilation; the women are not so easy to "pick up"; and the entertainers are better behaved.

This does not mean that the entertainers do not accept the hospitality of the patrons. Any girl is glad to drink with any customer. She will even dance with the customers who look as if they had money. And it does not mean that there is no drinking. Unless otherwise specified, the waiter only half fills a glass of ginger ale. It is understood that no one drinks just ginger ale.

But still, the Erie is a class above the Derby, the cabaret at the other end of the same block. The Derby is newer, cheaper, and wilder. . . . . The ventilation is far worse than at the Erie. The dining room, originally intended for a mere back room of the bar, is overfilled with shouting, screaming patrons. The chorus of entertainers at the Derby is younger and prettier than at the other cabarets. They are also very much more friendly with the patrons. A wink, properly directed, will bring a girl to your table. Another wink, equally properly directed,

[1] See Cases 2746–47, 2854–59, and others in the records of the Juvenile Protective Association.

will bring the waiter, willing to serve you as much and whatever kind of liquor you may desire.

There are more habitués at the Derby than at the Erie. The Erie seems to be less friendly and strives more for the fast-spending traveling man in town on a holiday than for the "cabaret hound," the roué and his lady, and the other types which night after night find their way to the little tables of the Derby and its like.

A block farther south and a step farther down in the social scale is the Six-O-Six. It has not even a door leading directly into the dining room. Egress is only obtained after a journey down a dark passageway or a walk through the barroom. The place is frankly dirty; dirtier table cloths, dirtier waiters, dirtier walls, dirtier floor, dirtier glasses and dishes than any other cabaret on the street boasts. On one door, in plain view, hangs an obscene sign.

The entertainers—there are only three—are low and coarse. Prices are low at this place. Beer—it is served in a stein, a concession to good taste which the other cabarets of the neighborhood refuse to make—is only twenty-five cents. Whiskey and gin are obtainable, but the head waiter is very cautious. "We little fellows got to watch out for the pro'bition agents. It's us little guys they go after." But nevertheless he was not afraid to saunter from table to table, soliciting for the three women who sat at the table back of the three-piece orchestra, and for the neighboring hotel.

The Spark Plug, a smaller place across the street, is tenanted almost entirely by habitués of the street, and actors from the loop, and offers but very cold welcome to new patrons.

A few blocks farther north is the Poodle Dog, a new and more up-to-date place than the others, but otherwise exactly the same.[1]

The North Clark Street cabaret makes little pretense at respectability. It draws, of course, a few of the curious, who come to get a vicarious thrill. But the most of those who sit at its tables are men looking for drink and women; prostitutes soliciting business; gold diggers looking for generous daddies; vamps, whose profession is blackmail, looking for victims; crooks—rouged dandies of the underworld, Robin

[1] Document 26.

Hoods of the boulevard, rather than the hard guy of the old detective story—with their "broads,"[1] making a night of it, or meeting "fences." Most of the cabarets have their habitués, their cliques. The cabareting party receives a cold shoulder unless it spends freely. Unlike the big cabaret of the Loop, or the cabarets to the east, the North Clark Street cabaret has a local patronage from the slum. It belongs to the underworld.

Closely associated with the cabaret is commercialized vice. North Clark Street is still—with West Madison Street and the "avenues" of the "black belt"—a district of commercialized vice. The Committee of Fifteen and the Juvenile Protective Association are constantly reporting and closing disorderly houses along or near North Clark Street. Most of the places closed are small hotels; others are rooming-houses.[2] Since the police have made soliciting in the street unsafe, it is only the lone girl with a room somewhere

[1] A daddy is a man of past middle age, wealthy and a free spender, usually married, who supports a girl and keeps her in an apartment in return for her favor on one or two nights a week. The rest of the time she is free to do as she pleases. Daddies are much in demand along the "little white way."

A "broad" is a crook's woman—his common-law wife or his mistress.

[2] Norman S. Hayner, in *The Hotel*, writing of the relationship of vice to the old hotel in the disintegrated community, says: "There are many 'cheap hotels' of this kind on North Clark Street. The old Revere House is an example of this kind of deterioration. At one time it was a respectable hotel; it is now frequently in the courts because of the disorderly conduct which it houses. An investigator recently got a bellboy there to "get him a wife" by tipping him fifty cents, and this woman in turn went out and brought in another prostitute for his friend, giving clear evidence of the nature of the place. The Normandy is another North Clark Street hotel with a history of deterioration (adapted from pp. 44–46).

The *Chicago Tribune* (February 9, 1923) proclaims "City To Fight Rain of Writs in Vice Vigil," and lists a number of small hotels picketed by the police because of complaints that they were "resorts." Seventeen places were

who ventures it. The "houses" get their business through the waiters and doormen of the cabaret, or through the taxi driver who takes patrons to and from the cabaret.[1]

Quite different from the rôle of the cabaret in the night life of the "little white way" is that of the dance hall. The dance hall does not draw to its waxed floors the man with money to spend, the gold digger, or the underworld. It draws rather men and girls from the world of furnished rooms and the slum, with only occasional pickpockets, professional prostitutes, and charity girls. Many of the lonely and heart-hungry men and women from the rooming-houses here form the "intimacies" which lead to a few weeks in a light-housekeeping room on La Salle Street. The transient prostitutes of the rooming-house district—girls who can no longer get into "houses" since the attempted suppression of vice, and get furnished rooms near the Loop and bright light areas to which they take men—use the larger dance halls for picking up customers. And the rougher element

under guard in the Chicago Avenue district. Besides thirteen places on North Clark Street and others on Wells, State, Huron, and Ohio streets, Captain Collins picketed the New Albany Hotel, at 413 Rush Street, the Revere House, Clark Street and Austin Avenue, and the Astor, 176 North Clark Street (adapted).

[1] An increase of cabarets followed upon the breaking up of the segregated districts. They largely took over the functions of the saloon and the house of prostitution, prohibition accelerating the change. The abolition of the segregated district has also broken up the prostitute "caste." In the days of the levee and the red-light district the "painted lady" was an outcast. Now women can get into and out of prostitution easily. The cabaret facilitates this. The prostitute of today, instead of being a woman of professional nature, grown old in the game, is typically a young girl, neither a professional nor an outcast. This indicates a tremendous change in the mores, and is coincident with the gradual letting down of all sexual conventions, as, for example, the prevalence of the intimacy, in which the cabaret also plays a part.

from the slum, the gangs and "athletic clubs" with their "shebas," are regular patrons. Practically all the patrons are workingmen and shopgirls. Such are the larger dance halls.[1]

Another type of dance hall, the "closed" dance hall, is also found along North Clark Street. These closed halls admit only men, and are peculiar to areas of homeless men, particularly homeless men of foreign birth. Dancing is on the "park plan": men buy tickets and pay a ticket a dance, usually ten cents. The girl "instructors" are required to dance with any man who asks them, and get half the value of the ticket for each dance. This "closed" dance hall is the type of dance hall that flourished on the old "Barbary Coast" of San Francisco, and is intimately associated with vice. Its appeal is frankly sexual.[2] The girl's returns depend upon her ability to attract men to dance with her. And the men who go to these halls are those who are not welcomed elsewhere because of their dress, or of their nationality, or color. One of these North Clark Street "closed" halls is frequented altogether by Greeks, and another chiefly by Filipinos and Chinese.

In addition to the cabaret and the dance hall, there are a vast number of bars, soft-drink parlors, chop sueys and chili parlors, all-night restaurants, and pool and billiard halls along North Clark Street, which are nightly gathering places for the people who live in the rooming-houses and slums of

[1] Document 27, and records of the Juvenile Protective Association.

[2] "The writer was accosted one night on Clark Street by an unkempt and ungrammatical young fellow wanting to borrow a quarter. The writer fell into conversation with him. It seemed that a quarter, with the nickel which he already had, would buy three tickets to the Atheneum, one of the closed dance halls on Clark Street. 'You see,' he said, 'it's hard for a fellow who doesn't know any girls. You can go with prostitutes, but you're likely to get a disease' " (document 28).

the Near North Side. Indeed, as we have said, North Clark Street is Main Street to much of the world of furnished rooms, the half-world, and the slum.

THE THREE GILDED BALLS

No one, perhaps, knows more of this Main Street, of its comings and goings, its gaiety and its tragedy, than does the pawnbroker, over whose counters many of its stories are told. The following document vividly pictures North Clark Street as seen through a pawnbroker's eyes:

Clark Street is known among the "half-world" all over the globe. A certain element, transient and traveling about—crooks, actors, prostitutes, dope fiends, hoboes—pass its fame around. When habitués of the underworld come to Chicago they immediately go to Clark Street, because they know that they can find friends there, and everything that they want or need.

Clark Street is at once the melting-pot and the hangout of the "hectic crowd." It is a "dumping ground" for all classes. Transients, professionals, actors, etc., of all sorts live at its cheap hotels and rooming-houses. Twenty per cent of its population is drifting. There is a certain lure to the street. I went out of the business a few years ago, and had to leave Clark Street. But I didn't like it; I wasn't satisfied; the old associations drew me; and "I had to get back to the street."

Why are all the pawnshops located here within a few blocks of one another, and not back toward the river, where the slums are? Well, the answer is twofold. In the first place, not one person in ten who pawns an article needs the money for a legitimate reason—for bread and butter or for rent. Nine times out of ten it's for gambling, for booze, for dope, or for women. So the business of the slums wouldn't keep us going. The reason why we are all here is largely because North Clark Street, before the "lid" was clamped on, was an area of open vice, of gambling houses, of houses of prostitution, of saloons. And it was from the people who frequented these places that we got our business. A fellow wanted booze or "coke," and he'd pawn a ring; or he went broke in the game, and wanted to stay in because his luck was due to change, he'd pawn his watch; or he'd spent his money on booze and wanted a woman, he'd pawn something. So it went. The pawnshops naturally located where you could pawn, and that brought business to the street. It's just as it is with the piano business. You have all your big music stores along Wabash Avenue. When a man wants a piano, he naturally goes down to Wabash Avenue to look for one. The avenue gets a reputation as a piano street, and that brings that sort of trade to it. So it is with North Clark Street and the pawn-shops. The street is known as a pawn street, and business comes from all over the city, and even from out of town, to sell money there. Now, a pawnshop couldn't move to Wells or State without going out of business. And there is no need to move, for even though the "lid" is on, the same sort of people frequent Clark Street; its cabarets are the center of Chicago's night life; and it is a good business street.

In a pawnshop "you get everything from soup to nuts." Men speculating on the Board of Trade, dignified fellows with gold-headed canes, pawn jewelry or stock; people—hundreds of them—and es-pecially "kept women," come from the Wilson Avenue district, where they are living from hand to mouth and life consists in "putting on dog." I saw a couple like that in a restaurant one day—men, dressed in English walking suits. One ordered mashed potatoes, and the other ordered coffee, and they were counting up the pennies they had between them to see if they could pay. Then there are the "cokes," "snow-birds," they call them, who will pawn everything they have for a shot. One came in one day and said, "I just closed a deal this week on this building, and I'm going to raise your rent three hundred dollars a month." But before he left he was willing to pawn an old wedding ring for a few dollars to get a little heroin. Then there is the "dreamer" type, the socialist, and the fellow who wants to revolutionize the world. He tries to get something out of the pawnbroker by working on his emotions and getting a "touch." I remember one fellow came in here; he had me sitting on a cloud playing a harp before he left with twenty-five dollars I'll never see again.

Then, of course, there are the "slummers." They want to see some wild life, want a little jazz and a little booze. A fashionable society woman came in here one night, drunk as a lord, with her hair all down over her face; said she'd lost heavily gambling, and wanted some money. She pawned one of her diamond earrings. I saw her on the street later that night, singing, and minus the other earring; anybody could have picked her up then if he had tried; she was out for a hell of a time.

Then there are professional people, vaudeville troupes and actors and musicians with some cheap show that goes broke, who want to make another town. About all they have to pawn is their musical instruments; that's why we have so many in our shops.

Women from the Gold Coast, and from out around Wilson Avenue, drive up in limousines to pawn things for money to settle bridge debts. People do some inconsistent things. One fellow came up in a cab and paid a fare of a dollar and a half to pawn an old suit that he got only four dollars for.

Every article in this shop has a story behind it, if you can only get at it. There was a 'bo on Clark who got his leg cut off one year and couldn't ride the rods any more. He got a wooden leg, and hung around, getting by with just enough work to keep him going. But he boozed, and was always going broke. The only thing he had to pawn was his wooden leg, and he would pawn that, and use a crutch until he could redeem it. He did that half a dozen times, and then he pawned it once too often, and has never been able to redeem it.

Numbers of people have pawned plates of false teeth. We have an Irish lace nightgown that a "sporting" woman left one day. Then, a year or two ago, a Russian woman brought in a diamond bracelet and pawned it. We found later that she had pawned, all told, a hundred thousand dollars' worth of jewels in the shops on the street. She was a princess before the revolution, and her family, all but herself, were executed. She escaped with some of the family jewels and came to America. Then, of course, there are the stolen articles that crooks try to pawn here. One day a pretty girl came in crying because she had to pawn her engagement ring. It was a beautiful stone, and I offered her two hundred if she would sell it, but she said she would never sell her engagement ring, so I gave her the eighty dollars. A few hours later the police came around looking for the ring. It turned out that the girl was a member of a criminal gang, that she had entered service as a maid on the Gold Coast and had stolen the ring along with a lot of other jewelry.

The pawnbroker has a bad name for squeezing and beating his clients, the sort of notion you get in reading Dickens. But that is not really so. The pawnbroker has a heart and helps out many a fellow who would go down and out otherwise. Herman Cohen, down the street, could buy a row of buildings with the money he has given away. He has a card index of twenty-five thousand dollars that he has loaned without security, to down-and-outs, in the forty years he has been on the street. Just for example now: one day a little girl came in here with tears in her eyes, and wanted to pawn her wedding ring. I couldn't have given her more than a couple of dollars on it; it was cheap. So what the hell, I just gave her the two dollars, and got it out of the next customer. No, its not a Shylocking business; we help the deserving fellow, often by allowing him more on his article than we need to, and more than it is worth. The poor men who *do* come to the pawnshop couldn't get money in any other way. They have no security, and can't get a loan from a bank; their friends don't have money, and it's either the pawnbroker or charity. A man can pawn and still keep his self-respect, but he can't keep it if he asks for charity.

When we take an article we have to hold it thirteen months before we can realize on it. That means that capital turns over slowly. About six men to every four women pawn articles, and not over 30 per cent of the articles pawned are ever redeemed. No, we don't work in chains or have any central clearing house to dispose of all this stuff that is left. Most of it we sell right here on the street. And then there are firms who keep their eye on all pawnshops, hoping to buy certain articles. One dealer comes around looking for antiques, another for odd and old jewelry, another for watches, still another for old gold, silver, and platinum, etc. The people from the Gold Coast come a good deal looking for antiques. Senator Ham Lewis comes around regularly on Clark Street and picks up antiques and odd jewelry; he's an eccentric in his dress anyhow, you know.

It all sounds as though it's a pretty tough neighborhood, doesn't it? But environment isn't everything. Some good men have come off Clark Street. There's Justin McCarthy, who was prosecuting attorney; he was a kid right around here; and Dorsey Crow, the alderman, was raised here too.[1]

Such is the Rialto of the half-world. It is a bizarre street when contrasted with the Mayfair of the Gold Coast, three

[1] Document 29: "The Pawn Shop," an interview with the proprietor of the Pal Re-Sale Shop on North Clark Street.

blocks to the east. Its people, its ways of thinking and doing, like those of the world of furnished rooms, are incomprehensible to the people of the conventional world. Yet those who frequent the "Rialto" are typical of an increasingly large population in the modern city, who, living in the city, are not of it; who, in the ever increasing anonymity, mobility, and segregation of city life are coming to constitute a half-world, a world apart.

CHAPTER VII

THE SLUM

West from Wells Street, and south from Chicago Avenue until Rush Street is reached, then south from Grand Avenue, ultimately merging with the wholesaling and manufacturing district along the river, stretches the slum.

We have already seen that this western and southern area of the Near North Side has had a long history as a slum. The land has always been low in the river district. This low-land early marked the division between the fashionable residence district and the slum, the sandflats at the river's mouth and the lowland to the west being populated by a poorer element. The fire limit established after the fire of 1871, allowing cheap wooden structures to be erected in this west district, while requiring more substantial ones to the east, perpetuated this division. Finally, the streets in the west district were elevated four to eight feet, leaving the buildings with dark, damp basements, a situation favorable to tenement conditions.

One alien group after another has claimed this slum area. The Irish, the Germans, the Swedish, the Sicilians have occupied it in turn. Now it is being invaded by a migration of the Negro from the south. It has been known successively as Kilgubbin, Little Hell, and, as industry has come in, as Smoky Hollow. The remnants of these various successions have left a sediment that at once characterizes and confuses the life of this district. Originally close to the river, the slum has pushed eastward as the city has grown until it now bids fair to sweep across La Salle Street and submerges much of the area of furnished rooms.

The slum is a distinctive area of disintegration and disorganization. It is an area in which encroaching business lends a speculative value to the land. But rents are low; for while little business has actually come into the area, it is no longer desirable for residential purposes. It is an area of dilapidated dwellings, many of which the owners, waiting to sell the land for commercial purposes, allow to deteriorate, asking just enough in rent to carry the taxes. Except for the sporadic building of factories and business blocks, no building goes on in the slum, and most of its structures have stood for a generation and more.[1]

The slum is an area of freedom and individualism. Over large stretches of the slum men neither know nor trust their neighbors. Aside from a few marooned families, a large part of the native population is transient: prostitutes, criminals, outlaws, hobos. Foreigners who come to make a fortune, as we used to go west, and expect to return to the Old Country as soon as they make their "stake," who are not really a part of American life, and who wish to live in the city as cheaply as possible, live in the lodging-houses of the slum. Here, too, are the areas of immigrant first settlement, the foreign colonies. And here are congregated the "undesirable" alien groups, such as the Chinese and the Negro.

The slum gradually acquires a character distinctly different from that of other areas of the city through a cumulative

---

[1] No residences have been built on the entire Near North Side in the past ten years. Building has been confined to the erecting of large hotels and apartments, or to the remodeling of old houses in the Gold Coast district; while along the river and in the slum only office buildings, factories, stores, garages, and the like have been built. See K. Young, *A Sociological Study of a Disintegrated Neighborhood.*

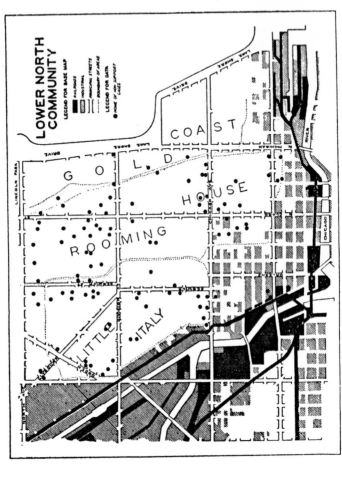

NON-SUPPORT CASES, COURT OF DOMESTIC RELATIONS.—It is often said that desertion is the poor man's divorce. This is substantially true. This map of non-support cases indicates that in the "world of furnished rooms" and the slum area the family is both unstable and economically maladjusted. Consequently the family in these areas does not meet situations for its members as does the family in better organized communities (data after Mowrer, *Family Disorganization*).

process of natural selection that is continually going on as
the more ambitious and energetic keep moving out and the
unadjusted, the dregs, and the outlaws accumulate. This is
particularly noticeable in the more static European cities.
In America, where competition is uncontrolled, change is
rapid. But even in American cities this selective process
lends the slum a submerged aspect. The city, as it grows,
creates about its central business district a belt of bleak,
barren, soot-begrimed, physically deteriorated neighborhoods. And in these neighborhoods the undesirable, and
those of low economic status, are segregated by the un-
remitting competition of the economic process in which land
values, rentals, and wages are fixed.

HUMAN DERELICTS

The slum comes to be characterized, then, not only by
mean streets and ramshackle buildings, but by well-defined
types of submerged humanity. The Near North Side slum
falls into two parts: an area of cheap lodging-houses along
Clark and Wells streets and the streets south of Chicago
Avenue, and an area of tenements from Wells Street west.
The tenement area is the world of foreign tongues and
cultures; the area of cheap lodging-houses is a jungle of
human wreckage.

The cheap lodging-house is filled with economic failures:
the broken family, the rooming-house family, the "marooned" family. A desolating poverty is one of its most
striking characteristics.[1] It is filled with derelicts, all man-

---

[1] The poverty of the slum moves men to strange deeds. An actress died
in a North Side rooming house. While the United Charities were discussing
means for her burial, her estranged husband, having read in the paper of her
death, slipped in to where her body lay and pried loose a diamond and gold
filling from one of her front teeth.

ner of the queer and unadjusted. Its bare rooms house the non-family laborer, the factory worker, the waitress, the migrant, the hobo. The criminal and the bohemian find refuge from the conventional world in its haunts.

All the characters that are cast in the sordid episodes of slum life are to be found in the case records of charity organizations. Indeed, the case records of such an organization as the United Charities, supplemented by the police blotter, constitute a sort of dramatis personae of the slum. The following stories from the United Charity case records dramatize somewhat the life of the economic failure and the derelict of the North Side streets that lie in the slum.

The stories of lodging-house families bring out most strikingly, perhaps, the relationship of economic inadequacy to the slum. These lodging-house families live chiefly in the cheap rooming- and lodging-houses that lie south of Chicago Avenue.

R—— (LOWER NORTH DISTRICT, UNITED CHARITIES)

The Agency has been in touch with this family for eight years. Scarcely a month has passed but what the family has required assistance. In the eight years the family has lived in more than a dozen rooming-houses. Sixteen agencies, at one time and another, have been interested in the case. The problem, as stated by the agency, consists in epilepsy, intemperance, tuberculosis, maternity, imprisonment, unemployment, and bad housing. The story, as adapted from the case record, follows:

The father, mother, the father's mother, and five children live in one room and an alcove. The blankets are worn; there is no stove; and the floors are bare. Cooking is done on an inadequate gas plate. The children are dirty and undernourished. The father is out of work. The mother is pregnant, expecting confinement shortly.

The family is continually in debt, always behind in the rent, has several times been evicted. The father, an electrician by trade, drinks heavily, once having been arrested for having a still in his room, and works irregularly. The record shows eight years of continuous effort to keep the man placed; he has had a hundred jobs in that time. The mother works occasionally.

The father, when drunk, is maudlin and irritable. He demands money from the mother for whiskey. When she refuses, he throws the teapot full of hot tea at her, scalding her and the baby. There is a family brawl; the police are called; he gets thirty days in the Bridewell. The woman, in constant fear of pregnancy, tries to keep from sleeping with him, and they quarrel. A woman taken in to room brings a man to live with her; a brawl results.

The Agency is constantly trying to get the man to "brace up," to supply the morale normally supplied by some group. He is always promising and failing. An interesting group of attitudes cluster about the case. The family formerly had a fairly comfortable home out on Artesian Avenue, but they were burned out in 1914. Since then the man has believed luck was against him; has lost his grip, drifted, drunk. Both he and his wife blame it all on "luck" and "this furnished-room life." They show shame, occasionally, at their condition and the way of living, at having to accept relief. But these moments are rare and passing. Usually they take it as a matter of course, and show no glimmer of self-respect or hope.

Their relatives have long since turned against them—"like pouring money into an empty well." At a family conference, called by the Agency, the brother refused to take the case into court because "the newspaper publicity would be too humiliating." The uncle, fairly well to do, said he was "through with them." The one time that the Agency succeeded in getting the family out of the slum, the man soon wanted to move back, saying he did not want to work in the neighborhood, "because everybody knows me." The whole group of conditions and attitudes serves to isolate the family and to keep it in the slum.

Another case, an immigrant family of the second generation, after having moved out of the slum, is forced back into it again by the protracted illness of one of the children, and the heavy hospital bills which ate up all the family had saved. A visiting nurse told of a case where the family was gradually forced into the slum because the priest kept insisting that they have children until they had more than the father could support.

All the records of these families tell more or less the same story: economic misfortune or failure, physical inadequacy, drink, dope or gambling, a loss of grip, *and finally a set of attitudes* that at last accommodates the family to the slum, and isolates it.

Into the slum there drift, for similar reasons, a large number of men and women derelicts, users of opium, drunkards, the "queer," criminals and outcasts, men and women of unstable or problematical character who want to get away from their own communities to a place where they will not be known, or who are forced out and down into the slum by failure or unwillingness to adjust themselves elsewhere.[1]

An elderly woman applied through letters to several wealthy women for aid. She told a pitiful story of her past, and gave the usual appeals for assistance. She was referred to the United Charities, much to her chagrin. She did not want to fall back upon public charity for her living, she said. Circumstances made it necessary for her to accept help, but it cut her pride, and she made every effort to conceal her identity. It was discovered later that she had formerly had social position and wealth, and had been a member of several prominent clubs in the city where she had lived. Through her husband's and her own drinking the family had been reduced to desperate circumstances. In the slum of Chicago's Near North Side she had endeavored to cover up her life-story.

A young couple applied to the United Charities for assistance, saying they had come from Omaha, where they had had clerical positions, to Chicago, in the hope of bettering their condition. They said they were but temporarily stranded. A great many of these people tell stories of their past successes and their sure prospects. They often

---

[1] The following stories are taken from the case records of the Lowei North District of the United Charities.

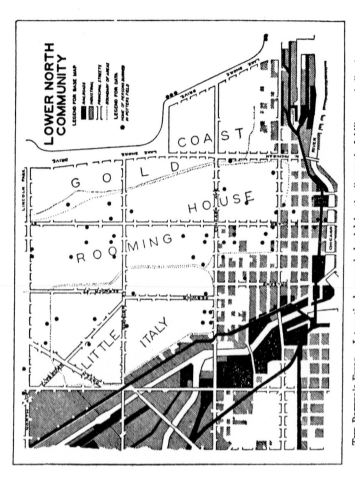

THE POTTER'S FIELD.—Interestingly enough, burial in the "potter's field" seems indicative not so much of the poverty of the slum as of the isolation and lack of group contacts of the rooming-house areas. The above map shows the addresses of persons buried from the morgue when their bodies were left unidentified and unclaimed.

insist that they are quite embarrassed at having to appeal for help. This latter attitude is quite in contrast to that of the professional beggar, the man or woman who makes a living by going from one charity agency to another. It turned out that neither of the young people had lived in Omaha, as they claimed, but that they had run away together, against the advice of their parents, from a small town down state.

Mrs. L. V. was quite a character along Clark Street. She claimed to be of a noble German family; that she had been deserted by her husband; and that she was trying to give her son a musical education. She applied to the Lower North Community Council, and was referred to the United Charities. She turned out to be a dementia praecox case, with a history of petty graft, prostitution, and blackmail. Her address and culture (her early history was never uncovered) enabled her to get by. The son had real musical talent, but had developed an exceedingly erratic "shut in" personality, due to conflict over his inability to study.

G. is an actor, of a long and checkered career. After a year at Harvard, where he roomed with Frank Bacon, he went on the stage. Early in life he displayed considerable talent and was with several successful shows. He married a professional woman of great beauty. But two years after their marriage she died, and he immediately began to drink heavily. He sank rapidly to stock, small road shows, unimportant parts, nothing at all. Now he goes about the Near North Side, living in cheap rooms, from which he is often evicted, sleeping in ten-cent "flops" or in parks. He rarely has over twenty cents in his pocket. A regular visitor at the agency, he is continually promising to look for work, but never doing it. Periodically he goes on a spree, turning up again with his clothes ragged and tattered, and his face haggard. He has had a score of odd jobs, distributing quack pamphlets (for which he was put into the Bridewell), peddling patent medicines, but never sticking to anything for very long, feeling that these jobs were beneath his professional dignity. His whole life is now organized about dreams of the glory of his past, and his purely imaginary dignity as a member of "the profession." He peddles early mornings and at night after dark for fear some of his old associates might see him. When offered three dollars a day to be a super for a movie company in a mob scene, he said, "When I take part in a mob scene, it will be in a coal yard or a graveyard, but never in the profession." Many of his old friends have tried to help him, but his pride keeps him from seeing them. G. is always dreaming of getting back on the stage. "If I could only get a wardrobe!" But every time he gets a wardrobe he pawns it and gets drunk.

B. came into the office. She said that her husband had deserted her. They were formerly vaudeville people. For nine years he was a good husband. Then he was converted and became an evangelist for a city mission. Since then he has never supported her, and for a year she has had no word of him.

At ———— Larrabee Street lives a broken-down hag of a woman in a store piled with junk and filth: old china, broken furniture, old papers, etc. She sits by the hour in a rocker in the midst of it all, seldom going out. The Sicilian children in the neighborhood call her "teacher." She was graduated from the University of Chicago in the early nineties, a Phi Beta Kappa student. She never married, but was a teacher of English in a large city high school. She began to take dope. Then she disappeared. Several years later she was found at the present address in the slum. She refused all help from social agencies, whose workers she considers her inferiors. She has a letter from a wealthy woman in Hyde Park, an old college friend: "I would be glad to help you. But of course, if you won't have anything to do with your old friends. . . . ."

Stories like the foregoing could be indefinitely multiplied from the case records of charitable agencies. For the slum is full of unadjusted, often psychopathic personalities who are isolated from their old associates. And the barrier is never one of disease, or failure, or vice alone. It is always accompanied by a set of attitudes that serve to shut the person off from the rest of the world.[1]

[1] It is this complex of attitudes, through which the person has become accommodated to the slum, that often makes the behavior of the slum dweller so incalculable to the budget-minded social agency. It is often remarked how difficult it is to get a family to consent to move out of the slum

It will have been remarked, in the foregoing cases, how frequently drink and drug addiction play a part in the descent to the slum. Indeed, a few years ago there was a block below Chicago Avenue known as "dopey block" be-

---

no matter how advantageous the move may seem from the material point of view, and how much more difficult it is to keep them from moving back into the slum. The story of the old woman who insisted upon being moved from a pleasant country home back to the slum, giving as a reason "People is more company than stumps, nohow," is a classic of social work. The person's behavior becomes conditional upon stimuli of slum life. Without these familiar stimuli the person becomes restless, lonely, uncontrollable. The story of Jenny well illustrates this hold of the slum upon its dwellers.

Jenny was the daughter of "Ella the High," a notorious madam who lives near Wells and Superior streets. They lived in the worst of basement rooms, in which water was always standing on the floors after spring rains. Jenny was accustomed to scenes of drunken carousal and viciousness when her mother entertained men. The mother had cancer, and at fourteen Jenny accepted the responsibility for the family and went to work in a factory. Her mother kept encouraging her to form an alliance with some traveling man who could help support the family. But at seventeen she met a young man who worked at the bottling works whom she was crazy to marry. Since he made but twenty-two dollars a week, her mother would have none of it, insisting that she live with a man who made fifty and would turn it all over to her—the fact that this man had a wife in Minnesota being immaterial. Then one night Jenny was kidnaped on the street and raped. She had a frightful experience and was in the hospital for weeks. Such was the slum to Jenny.

The young fellow from the bottling works still wanted to marry her. A group of women on the Gold Coast learned of the case through a social worker and said that if the man wanted her that badly they would make it possible. So they gave her a wedding at River Forest—so "swell" that her mother was reconciled. Then they put the couple in a little wooden house on Oak Street just off the Gold Coast. They fitted it up with bright chintzes and things, and were terribly pleased with what they had done. But one morning not long afterward the social worker found the house empty. The couple had moved in the night. A few weeks later they were found in a single basement room back again on Wells Street—dark, damp, and dirty, but on Wells! Jenny's explanation was that over on Oak Street life was too quiet; there was no excitement; "the wagon never backed up to anybody's door!"

cause of the number of drug addicts who lived in it. It has since been cleaned up. But "dope" is still liberally peddled in the slum. The following excerpt from the "Diary of a Dope Fiend" is from the story of a formerly influential business man of Chicago, who in a few years of drug addiction, became a derelict in the slum:

January 1. Slept all day. Up at 7 P.M. Had the blues. Nowhere to go. No money; no friends. Would have had plenty if I had been a different man. Oh, how one feels to have no one to be with. Took my first nip of morphine—just a nip. Wonderful dreams. Lifted me out of my misery.

January 4. Pawned my razor. Went to doctor. [The doctor who let him have the opiate.]

January 22. Up at 9 A.M. Looked for work. No money. Tired, sick, all in.

January 28. Went to doctor. Feel bad. When a fellow's broke, he's no good to himself or anyone else. Hell on earth. I owe everyone. What is a fellow to do?

January 29. Went to bed with my thoughts. God! It's awful.

January 31. Took three and one-half grains.

February 1. No money. Am hungry. No place I can go. Don't know what to do. Took five grains. [He got a few jobs during the month, but could not keep them.]

February 11. Must try to get away from this thing. It's growing on me. Cut down my dose today to three and one-half grains.

February 18. Had to have seven grains today.

February 21. What's the use of trying to quit? Took ten and one-half grains today.

February 25. Had dream last night about Dora.

March 1. Sold coat. Borrowed $15. To pay back $9 each pay day.

March 7. Took twelve grains today.

March 24. Used lots of ——— today. Don't know why. Wish I did not have it.

March 25. Use more and more. Can't let it alone. Don't know what to do. Tired and sick. Damn fool. A fool there was and that am I.

March 26. Seven grains. Nothing left. Am glad. Will now let it alone. Never again. What a fool one is when he has this stuff. Those who know nothing about it are fortunate. [In the month of March twenty-two visits to the doctor to get the drug are recorded.]

April 3. Slept all day. And without a dime. I know I am a fool, but I went to the doctor.

April 4. Got $1.50 on my bathrobe. Sorry to pawn it, but I had to.

April 5. Got 15 cents to live on. It's a lot. Ha, ha! To hell with everything.

April 6. Another damn day. Wish things would go up in smoke. This is a hell of a place—this world. Some have everything; others nothing. Hope the war raises hell with all things and people with money.

April 7. I wish something would happen. This is awful. I'm thinking of someone tonight. I wish she were here.

April 11. Put gray suit in pawn. Paid doctor one dollar. Ate good meal once more. But the three dollars for my suit, it won't last long.

April 12. What a boob I am without a dime! Gee, I wish I were like I used to be. How would it feel, I wonder?

April 21. Tried to pawn my overcoat. One dollar is all I could get. When is this going to end? Wish I was like I used to be. Oh! what I have lost because of a girl.

April 29. I wish I was dead. What in hell am I living for, anyway? Saw Mrs. Williams today. She told me B. was going to get free. Best girl in the world. Hope she gets a good man. None like me.

May 2. I must get work today. Only coffee and rolls in two days now. I've only five cents. I think I'm going crazy.

[On May 6 he pawned his fountain pen to get morphine. The next entry is written in pencil. May 21 he vowed again to quit the drug, declaring he would cut off a grain a day. The dose that day was nine grains. The next day it was eight, the next seven, and so on down to four. He made his final entry on May 28, after taking nine grains. "No use trying," the entry read, "I can't quit!"][1]

It is in the lodging-house of the slum that the rank and file of the underworld "hang out." Many of these North Side

[1] Document 29.

lodging-houses are criminal haunts. A "flower girl" writes of such a house on La Salle Street:

Effie's avarice had prompted her to keep the house full of lodgers. Some of them were morphine addicts; some smoked "hop"; others were "cokeys." All belonged to that stratum of society referred to as the "underworld." There was Paddy Gallagher the "wire," a pickpocket who lived with his "mob" in comparative harmony; "Dago" Charlie, who talked of social inequalities as rapidly as any parlor bolshevik, and played his violin to soothe himself between smokes; "Boston" Nell, a large, matronly looking, gray-haired woman, whose respectable appearance belied her professional activities as a nationally known "lifter." "Dad" Miller, an old thief who looked like a great general, and Ada, his young wife. "Dad" didn't drink, and he rarely "smoked," but he had a record of twenty-seven years done in various prisons. Ada was both a shoplifter and a pickpocket—an unusual combination of talent, for your criminal is usually a specialist if he is wise. She made a pretty picture on occasional afternoons, wheeling the baby along State Street, and here and there "lifting a poke" from some unsuspecting admirer of the child. But she was overly addicted to morphine and thin as a rail, boney, like a woman after a fever. But "Dad" loved her. He even forgave her frequent lapses from faithfulness to him, which is not usually the way with crooks, who mostly require their women to be "straight." But "Dad" was a philosopher, of a sort. There was "Frenchy," a dark, sharp-nosed little man, who from long imprisonment and brooding was what "Paddy" called "stir nuts," and was always muttering and praying. There were others too numerous and transient to mention: beggars, "dingers," "D.D.'s," and "T.B.'s," and so on. That is, they twisted an arm or a leg, or they played mute, or coughed as though they had tuberculosis, each of his own line. There were quarrels and brawls when some drug-crazed man would go "blind" and break up things until he tired himself out, or was overpowered by some of his friends who feared police interference.

Police there were, occasionally, but they came in search of one man or one "mob," and made no more to do about it. It is convenient for the police to let criminals hang out together, for then they know where to look when one is "wanted."[1]

[1] Document 30: "Durfie—The Autobiography of a 'Flower girl.'"

In another lodging-house on La Salle Street lived Katherine Malm, the "tiger woman" of a recent and sensational episode of automobile banditry and murder.[1]

[1] In testifying, Katherine said that Malm was introduced to her as "the biggest crook on the North Side." Another girl who roomed on La Salle Street spent her nights at North Side cabarets, luring victims for stick-up men.

The lodging-house area of the slum is an area in which women must live at men's terms, as is brought out in the following excerpt (*Chicago Tribune*, February 4, 1923) from the sensational "Hate Diary" that was to have been the primary evidence of the State's Attorney's office in prosecuting L—— K—— for the murder of her husband, but which at the trial the State's Attorney failed to produce. L—— K——, keeper of a slum lodging-house on the Near North Side, shot the husband who deserted her. The following lines are from a diary reported to have been found in her room:

"Alone, alone, always alone. Washing from babyhood up—corn bread and bacon to eat. Clothes to wear to school that other children would make fun of. No school but that I walked miles to get to.

"Then six months a year snatched between wash days. No mother, no father, no real friends. . . . .

"A few months of happiness in Chicago with Frank until I found that also false. A few months with Harry, my husband, until that awful day when I found that letter, and then my heart broke. My husband was false to me in every way, and I was sick, tired, and disgusted. . . . .

"My faith has had cuts and jags all my life. When I found that letter I died. Five long years of hell! The only diversion I had from that old dull hurt has been work, work, work, some dissipation, and—I must not lose or die!

"Men, how I hate them. I hope the day will come soon so that—damn them—I won't need them. . . . .

"I will play the damned man; he is my only hope. . . . .

"I saw last night the damned man. I was as nice as I could be to him. He forced his attentions on me. How can women swallow the hot air that men try to hand them. . . . . O, I would like to say, 'Shut up, you fool; you are after what you can get; I am after the money. You want me and I need you.'

"Well this is a man's world, say what you will. At last I will have to admit it is a man's world. It took me thirty years to find that out."

GHETTOS—OLD AND NEW

The ghetto was the name given to an area in European cities in which for centuries the Jews were confined. This confinement was the creation of the racial religion of the Jew himself, however, and not a product of Christian coercion. The ghetto formed a more or less independent community, with its own customs and laws, and was always in controversy with the larger community.

Most of the foreign colonies in American cities are after the pattern of the medieval ghetto—especially the Negro quarters or black belts, the Chinatowns, and the Little Italys. They have their own traditions and customs, their own regulations and laws, to which the Mafia and Tong wars bear evidence.[1] The Chinese Tongs, for instance, enforce

---

[1] The following item from the *Chicago Tribune* of July 11, 1922, part of which was quoted in chap. i, well illustrates the way in which the foreign colony tends to set up law within law, and to settle its own disputes in its own way without appeal to the American courts:

SYRIANS AND ASSYRIANS IN DEADLINE FEUD

"Three men were stabbed, several badly beaten, and ten arrested during a pitched battle between rival factions of Persians in a coffee shop at 706 North Clark Street early yesterday evening. Police in answering a call of a riot were forced to fight their way through more than 200 men engaged in the fight.

"Patrolman G. V. Magnuson and Police Surgeon William Smale of the Chicago Avenue station were the heroes. Together they dashed into the coffee shop and dragged out the wounded men and placed them in an ambulance. Then they drew revolvers and held the fighters at bay until reinforcements arrived.

"For several years there has been an unwritten law that no Syrian Persian was allowed north of Huron Street on Clark Street. Five members of the race wandered into the coffee shop of Titian & Sayad and sat down at a table to play cards.

"In a short time six Assyrian Persians entered the place and saw them. They walked to the table, it is said, and remarked that the Syrians had better get off the street. At that the five Syrians started to fight.

"In a moment other men in the place drew knives and advanced on the battlers. Chairs were overturned and windows broken. The fight led out to the street. Finally more than 200 had taken up the fight. Some one sent in a call to the police."

their own laws and impose their own fines; the American
courts and law are only resorted to when help is needed to
enforce the Tong law against a rebellious member. There is
always a "boss" or a "king" in the colony—several, perhaps,
if it is a large colony. The boss or king knows more English,
has been in America longer, knows the city and the police,
has influence both with his countrymen and with the in-
scrutable American law. The police seek to deal with the
colonists through him and his ability to enforce the unwritten regulations of the colony. The colony is little understood, either by the law or by the rest of the city, and comes
to constitute a little world by itself.

These foreign colonies, both in the cities of Europe and
America, are located in the slums. It is in the slum, in every
city, that one finds Little Italy, Little Poland, Chinatown,
and the black belt. As we have already remarked, this does
not mean that the immigrant necessarily seeks the slum, or
that he makes a slum of the area in which he lives. But in
the slum he finds quarters that he can afford, and relatively
little opposition to his coming. Moreover, as the colony
grows, the immigrant finds in it a social world.[1] In the
colony he meets with sympathy, understanding, and encouragement. There he finds his fellow-countrymen who
understand his habits and standards and share his life-
experience and viewpoint. In the colony he has status, plays
a rôle in a group. In the life of the colony's streets and
cafés, in its church and benevolent societies, he finds response and security. In the colony he finds that he can live,
be somebody, satisfy his wishes—all of which is impossible
in the strange world outside.

The slum district of the Near North Side harbors a half-

[1] See John Daniels, *America via the Neighborhood*, pp. 96–97; and Robert
E. Park and H. A. Miller, *Old World Traits Transplanted*.

dozen fairly well defined foreign colonies. The largest of these, Little Sicily, will be described in another chapter. But besides Little Sicily there is a Persian colony, a small settlement of Greeks, a little black belt, and the poorer elements of Chicago's German and Swedish populations. Each of these has given an area within the slum its characteristic stamp, and is living a life more or less to itself.

PERSIA IN AMERICA

The largest colony of Persians in the United States is located on the Near North Side of Chicago. It is difficult to estimate its numbers, as the United States census groups the Persian with the natives of Hedjoz, India, China, and Japan, as from "Other Asia." Prominent men of the colony claim for it a population of from three to six thousand. Three thousand would seem to be a fairly accurate estimate.[1] The greater part of the colony lies between Dearborn and Wells streets, south of Chicago Avenue. But there is a scattering of Persians east of Dearborn, and north along Clark and Wells. Indeed, during the past two or three years there has been quite a noticeable movement north along Wells Street.

The majority of this colony came from the province of Urmia, though there are others from Hindustan and the Transcaucasus. In their native country, which is rugged and mountainous, they worked vineyards and orchards, and were distinctly provincial and rural people. Practically the whole colony call themselves Assyrians (Christian Persians); there are not a dozen Mohammedan Persians in Chicago. And their emigration from Persia was due to the religious intolerance and persecution which flared up in the Mohammedan

[1] Documents 31 and 32.

countries of Asia Minor during the war. There were but two or three hundred Persians in Chicago before the war, the remainder of the colony having arrived since 1918.

By far the larger part of the colony consists of single men between twenty and forty years of age. There are few women and children. Consequently most of the Persians live in lodging-houses, or in buildings which the few families take over and convert into rooming-houses for friends and relatives. The colony is pretty well scattered among the other groups in the slum. There are no blocks that are solidly Persian. There are, however, many houses which have only Persians living in them; and groups from the same town settle in the same block. Thus the Persian colony, like every foreign colony, tends to be a mosaic of miniature Old World villages.

Most of the Persians, because of their rural origin, have no trade or profession. There are a few skilled laborers in the colony, a number of small shopkeepers, and a score, perhaps, of professional men. But the most frequent occupation is that of cook or waiter in a restaurant or hotel; many others are janitors, or work in factories.[1] The standard of living is much higher among the Persians than among similar immigrant groups, however. The Persian does not save and send money to the Old Country, as does the Italian, for example, but spends his wages for his immediate needs.[2]

[1] Among eighty-five Persians studied through the records of the immigrant Protective League, the following occupational distribution was found:

Workers in hotels or restaurants..	29	Painters....................	4
Janitors......................	17	Tailors....................	3
Factory laborers...............	8	Bakers....................	2
Shopkeepers..................	6	Other occupations..........	11
Garagemen....................	5		

[2] Florence Nesbitt, director of the Lower North District of the United Charities.

The Persian brings with him, of course, a heritage of Old World custom and tradition. But in a colony of single men, where families are few, custom does not play the part in social life and control that it does in a more normal community. A great part of the life of the colony centers about the coffee house. The men gather in the coffee houses in the evenings, eat Assyrian dishes, talk, smoke, and play cards. The gossip of the coffee house plays a large part in the forming of opinions. There used to be a Persian paper in Chicago, and among the Persians the editor of the newspaper is always influential. But there were too few subscribers to support the paper. Control in the colony is now largely vested in the steamship agent and in the church. There are no politicians, as we use the term, among the Persians. But the steamship agent, knowing every Persian in Chicago, and many in Persia, is politically influential and takes the place of the "boss" of Little Italy or Little Poland. The real power in the colony, however, is the church. For the Chicago colony is a religious sect, driven to America by religious persecution. It is Assyrian first, and Persian afterward.

The future of the colony is difficult to predict. Just before the passage of the immigration law of 1921 many of the men were bringing over families, wives, or sweethearts. But the law limits the number who can be admitted to the United States from all of "Other Asia" to seventy-eight a year. So the growth of the colony has closed, and it will be impossible to bring more Persian women into the colony. At the same time there is at present considerable sentiment against intermarriage. On the other hand, the religious situation in Asia Minor precludes the return to Persia of any great number. If our immigration policy remains as it now is, the Persians will probably intermarry with other nationalities and gradually lose their identity.

ATHENS ON THE "L"

East of the "elevated" on Chicago Avenue, and south of Chicago Avenue on Clark Street, one sees curious Greek lettering on the windows of stores, coffee houses, and cafés. Here, in the lodging-houses of the slum, mingling with the Persian colony, is a population of nearly one thousand Greeks. In the vicinity of Chicago Avenue and North Clark Street is a suburb of the large Greek colony about Halsted and Harrison streets which is the second-largest Greek colony in America. Like the Persians, most of the Greeks come from rural districts, though some come from the cities of Tripolis and Sparta, and small coastal towns. But, unlike the Persian, the Greek comes solely from an economic motive, the desire to get away from the extreme poverty of his native country and to make a small fortune in America.

The North Side colony is made up largely of the lower class, or "tramp" type of Greek, who migrates from city to city. His migratory tendency is evident in every phase of his life: his constant changing of lodging-houses, of occupations, and of habits. The majority of these Greeks work in restaurants, factories, or stores. Those who work in factories usually have mechanical knowledge, gained while "tramping" about on boats.

Like the Persians, again, they are largely an adult male population. But they do not live together in houses as the Persians do. They usually live in pairs, in lodging-houses which often contain as many as five nationalities. Nevertheless the Greeks are very clannish. The majority of Greeks are employed by Greeks; there are five restaurants to the block in the vicinity, and half of them are owned by Greeks who employ only Greeks. All trading and dealing, so far as possible, is carried on through fellow-countrymen. In many cases a Greek will try to "beat" an American to help one of his countrymen. Consequently he has the reputation of being "tricky" in business. Few poverty cases come to the charities from among the Greeks, the well-to-do helping out their unfortunate countrymen.

Yet with all this clannishness the Greek population is relatively unorganized. It has no lodges and orders. The only Greek organization in America is the Orthodox church, and scarcely a fourth of the Greeks in Chicago belong to the local churches. The Greek laborers do not join labor unions. There are no Greek political organizations of any importance.

The men spend their evenings in coffee houses, moving picture theaters, pool-rooms, and dance halls along Clark Street and Chicago Avenue. A great deal of card-playing and gambling goes on. Turkish coffee is served, and everyone sips it. There is much talk upon a variety of subjects. Socialism is a frequent topic. Many believe they are being abused; yet out of fifteen who were questioned as to whether they would like to return to Greece, not one answered in the affirmative. Politics is sometimes discussed; old-world affairs get their share of attention. There is usually a dominant conversationalist at each table, and his ideas prevail. The talk is largely in Greek. In the pool-rooms the talking is loud and rough. At times it is necessary to warn of the possibility of police raids if the place does not quiet down.[1]

Chicago's Greek newspaper, the *Greek Daily*, is little read by this North Side population. Little interest is taken in local questions or politics. The Greek proceeds about his business of making money, with little regard for the com-

[1] Document 33.

munity about him. Indeed, these North Side Greeks scarcely form a colony of their own. They are merely a part of the lodging-house population of the slum, a shifting population held in temporary equilibrium by common language and economic interest.

A LITTLE BLACK BELT

Into the heart of Little Hell has come, since the war, a fourth invasion which has gradually darkened its streets: the Negro from the rural South. "Shore-croppers" and cotton pickers from rural Georgia, Mississippi, and Arkansas, ignorant and poverty stricken, they have succumbed to the lure of high wages that have prevailed in northern industrial cities since the shutting off of the stream of immigrants from southwestern Europe. Settling first in small numbers along Wells and Franklin streets, as the immigration grew they pushed westward into the tenements of Little Sicily until today on many of the streets of Little Sicily one hears the soft voice and sees the black face of the Negro as frequently as he hears the staccato speech and sees the brown skin of the southern Italian.

The story of this Negro invasion is the old story of the competition of standards of living. Willing to live in dwellings that even the Sicilian had abandoned, willing to pay higher rents than the Sicilian had paid, meeting these rents by overcrowding, the Negro has slowly but steadily pushed his way in among the Sicilians, who, in turn, have begun to move northward toward North Avenue, into the German slum. With the district steadily deteriorating before the encroachment of industry, the ultimate replacement of the Sicilian by the Negro would seem only to depend upon the continuance of the immigration from the South.

A recent survey of five hundred Negro families in the area bounded by Chicago Avenue, Larrabee, Division, and Franklin streets, made by the Chicago Urban League, gives an interesting picture of this Negro population. Eighty-nine per cent of it is native to the rural South; 55 per cent of it has come from the South to the Near North Side since 1918; 63 per cent of it has come to the Near North Side since 1922. It is a population evenly divided as to sex, composed largely of young wage-earners. The modal family size is two persons. The Near North Side Negro lives in rundown dwellings, with stove heat, falling plaster, outside toilets. Sixty per cent of the Negro families live in rear flats or basements, for which they pay a modal rent of less than four dollars per room. A third of the families take lodgers. Negro families move about frequently within the area, 63 per cent having lived at their present addresses less than one year. The men have irregular employment as unskilled laborers, 85 per cent of the men earning less than 32 dollars per week. The modal wage for men is $20–$24, and for women $12 or less. Poverty is extreme and mortality is high.[1]

The Sicilian has not retired before the Negro without a show of resistance. On the school and public playgrounds are re-enacted the scenes of a generation ago when the Sicilian was forcing out the Swede. The Negro child is often mistreated and ostracized. There are gang fights on playground and street. The police patrol clangs along the streets of Little Hell in answer to not infrequent riot calls. Sicilian fathers protest to the schools against admitting Negro children. Sicilian landowners band together to keep the Negro from acquiring property. But the resistance is in-

[1] Document 34, "The Negro on the Lower North Side," a survey made by H. N. Robinson, of the Chicago Urban League, in 1925.

effective and sporadic, and the invasion is on the whole a peaceful one. A Negro population of several thousand has already penetrated Little Sicily, bringing with it its barber shops and pool halls, its markets, and its "store-front" churches.

There remain on the Near North Side many remnants of the German and Swedish populations that formerly lived there. Not far below North Avenue, on North La Salle Street, is the Svenska Klubben, a club of well-to-do Swedish business men. And at the corner of Germania Place and Clark Street are the Lincoln Club (formerly the Germania Club), a fashionable German club, and the Red Star Inn, a famous old German restaurant. Farther south on Clark Street, just above Chicago Avenue, is the old Turner Hall, still the home of several German and Swiss *Turnvereine*. The very names of the streets are reminiscent of the German population: Germania Place, Goethe Street, Wieland Street, Beethoven Place, and Schiller Street.

North Avenue is still a northern European thorough-fare, the street of the poorer elements of the German, Hungarian, Swedish, and Swiss populations of the North Side. Its many German cafés—Wein Stube (with a bunch of huge gilded grapes over the door), Pilsner, Wurz'n Sepp Family Resort, Komiker Sepp—give it a distinctive color as contrasted with the Greek and Persian coffee houses on Lower Clark Street, or the Sicilian shops and soft-drink parlors along Division Street. Drug stores have no soda fountains. The windows of the many delicatessen shops plainly proclaim Swiss, German, or Hungarian; and they have little tables about which men eat lunches of rye bread, sauerkraut, sausage and pickles, perhaps with *alpenkräuter*, and talk in German. At the corner of Larrabee and North Avenue is the Immigrant State Bank (with name in German, Hungarian, and Italian, as well as in English), the Chicago Hungarian Athletic Association, a Hungarian daily, and a Hungarian barber shop. To the east are a building and loan associations and several steamship agencies. On Halsted, near North Avenue, are two German labor newspapers, and St. Michael's Bavarian Church. North Avenue has a few chain grocery stores, but most of its groceries are neighborhood stores; it has several five-and-ten-cent stores; and it has a "loan bank" where, the pawnbroker says, articles are pawned, not for drink, dope, or women, as along Clark Street, but to buy food and pay the rent. The names along the street are nearly all northern European: Carl Bocker, Cigars and Tobacco; Stroup & Happel, Architects; A. Schlesinger, Schiffskarten.

The large part of this German and Hungarian population now lies between Clybourne Avenue and Center Street, with the Swedish population north of it. The more well-to-do and influential elements of both the German and the Swedish populations long since crossed North Avenue and moved northward before the pressure of the Sicilian immigration. That many German, Hungarian, and Swedish clubs and newspapers are located on the Near North Side is significant only historically; the center of influence, economically, culturally, and politically, now lies farther north. The Teutonic population, chiefly German, which remains below North Avenue, consists of the poorer element which has lagged behind in the general exodus, clinging to the old wooden tenements on the narrow, often crooked, streets of this district. Its chief contribution to the life of the Lower

North Side is a poverty problem. But since there is practically no German, Swedish, and Hungarian immigration, and the Sicilians are pushing steadily northward, it would seem to be a matter of but a few years until the last remnant of this early population moves out of the Near North Side.

SLUM PATTERNS

It is apparent that the slum is more than an economic phenomenon. The slum is a sociological phenomenon as well. Based upon a segregation within the economic process, it nevertheless displays characteristic attitudes, characteristic social patterns which differentiate it from adjoining areas. And it is this aspect of slum life that is especially significant from the standpoint of community organization. The slum sets its mark upon those who dwell in it, gives them attitudes and behavior problems peculiar to itself.

The slum is a thoroughly cosmopolitan area. Foreign colonies, urban, rural, and alien cultures, diverse tongues and creeds exist side by side, mingle, and interpenetrate. Moreover, in the foreign colonies, especially in the black belts, Chinatowns, and Little Italies, where a whole people is segregated by virtue of color or culture, one finds more grades of people living together than in any other area within the city. This Near North Side slum, with its history of cultural succession and its twenty-eight nationalities, is one of the most cosmopolitan areas in a distinctively cosmopolitan city.

The cosmopolitanism of the slum means more than a polyglot culture. It involves a breaking down of prejudices, until in an area like "Bughouse Square" social distances are reduced to a minimum. There is tolerance of "foreign" customs and ideas not to be found without the slum. Groups in accommodating themselves to one another assimilate one another's folkways and mores. Cultures lose much of their identity. The mores tend to lose their sanctions. And in this cosmopolitan world, by virtue of this tolerance of the "foreign" and interpenetration of customs, traditional social definitions lose their meaning, and traditional controls break down. Groups tend to lose their identity, and the social patterns of these groups tend to merge into a hybrid something that is neither Sicilian nor Persian nor Polish, but of the slum. This is particularly true of the smaller groups, like the North Side Jew, Pole, and Greek, who do not live in colonies but are scattered throughout the slum.

The life of the slum is lived almost entirely without the conventional world. Practically its only contacts with the conventional world are through the social agency and the law. The social agency is looked upon as a sort of legitimate graft whereby small incomes may be considerably supplemented;[1] and the law, symbolized by the "copper," the

[1] It is not exceptional to find families who make their entire living by exploiting charity organizations (see Document 35). One such character, "Honest to God Sam," had fourteen charities helping him at one time, each ignorant of the aid he was receiving from at least ten of the other thirteen. The "basket rush" at Thanksgiving and Christmas becomes a sort of game. Families pride themselves on their ability to get more baskets than their neighbors; and the champion basket-getter thereby secures status. Often the baskets are not wanted for any other reason. A visiting nurse tells of visiting a family three days after Christmas and finding the children playing with turkeys dressed up in sweaters, as dolls. A Polish woman was furious because Nick and Alec had been drunk Christmas Day, and as a result the family had got but seven baskets from the Salvation Army, when they might have got nine. One block organized to get baskets and then held a street market and sold the baskets at five dollars a piece.

Yet basket-giving is spectacular. It gets status for the giver as well as the receiver. The newspaper photographs the lines waiting for baskets. A

"bull," the "flivver," and the "wagon," is to the dweller in the slum a source of interference and oppression, a cause of interrupted incomes, a natural enemy. The Lake Shore Drive is as "foreign" to many a resident of Little Hell as though it were separated from him by the Atlantic Ocean.

The slum is a confused social world to those who grow up in it. This is due on the one hand to what we have referred to as the cosmopolitan nature of the slum, its lack of common social definitions, and its many conflicting definitions that arise out of its various cultures. But it is more directly due to the functioning of the slum family and the slum community.

The "normal" community tends to meet crisis situations for its members. The "normal" family does the same thing. But the slum community and the slum family fail in this respect. Over a large area of the slum, the area of cheap lodging-houses, there is nothing of the nature of a community. And the persons and families who live in these lodging-houses are segregated there because they have failed, for one reason or another, to adjust elsewhere. Many of these families are broken families; others are disorganized; still others are merely ineffective. Moreover, the very physical conditions of lodging-house life, particularly its

---

fashionable Near North Side church recently discontinued a constructive social experiment in favor of basket-giving and financing of "poor" families (see Document 36). Indeed, the contact of the conventional world with the slum has, until recently, largely consisted in these spectacular gestures. The city mission, with its bread line and its ragtime gospel, is not the least interesting in these gestures. Missions are found only in the slums, and only in the slums of English and American cities. This fact is likely enough the result of the Anglo-Saxon's individualistic philosophy. "You must not interfere with a man's private life and affairs until he is down and out and gone to the devil. Then, however, you are permitted to step in and see what you can do for him."

mobility, make impossible that constellation of attitudes about a home, with its significant ritual, which affords the basis for that emotional interdependence which is the sociologically significant fact of family life. As a result, the person who dwells in the lodging-house of the slum has to meet his problems alone. This is peculiarly significant in the behavior patterns of the child.

Much the same situation meets the second generation in the foreign colony. The immigrant generation, feeling little other pressure than the necessity of learning the minimum of the English language required to get along economically, shuts itself off in a Little Sicily or a ghetto and lives to itself. The American-born generation, however, is not able to live to itself. The law requires it to attend American schools; and in many other ways it is precipitated into American cultural life. It finds itself living in two social worlds, social worlds which define the same situation in very different ways. At once cultural conflicts arise; perhaps merely vague bewilderment and unrest, but often definite problems of personal behavior. In the normal native community, we have said, the family and the community meet these problems for the child. But the foreign family and community are not able to do this completely or successfully. Their attempts as likely as not but serve to mark the child as a delinquent in the eyes of the *American law*. The child, consciously if vaguely, feels this inadequacy of the family and community in helping him to make his adjustments; nor can he find in the Old World life of the colony satisfaction for his wishes as defined by his contact with American life.

Herein lies the significance of the fact that there is an ecology of the "gang." The boys' gang is an adjustment that results from the failure of the family and community to meet the boy's problems. This failure is especially characteristic of the foreign family and community, which economic necessity has segregated in the slum. Hence it is that the slum, particularly the foreign slum, is gangland. For gangland is but the result of the boy's creation of a social world in which he can live and find satisfaction for his wishes.

The characteristic habitat of Chicago's numerous gangs is that broad twilight zone of railroads and factories, of deteriorating neighborhoods and shifting populations, which borders the city's central district on the north, on the west, and on the south. They constitute a sort of medieval empire in a modern city. This empire is divided into three great domains: the North Side Jungles, which lie north and east of the north branch of the Chicago River; the West Side Wilderness, which lies west of the Loop and the river; and the South Side Badlands, which extend south of the Loop and east of the South Branch of the river. The realm of the gang also extends into the better residential areas along railroads and business streets which reach into these communities like tentacles of the slum. In addition to these chief regions of gangland, there are certain appended areas attached to industrial and other suburbs and satellites which include slum-like districts and foreign communities of the poorer type. The haunts of the gang, however, are chiefly to be found in the so-called "poverty belt" about the loop.

The beginnings of the gang can best be discerned in one of those crowded sections of the city that comprise its characteristic habitat. On a warm summer evening, for example, the formation of gangs may be easily observed in the twilight life of the slum. Groups of children at play are everywhere. They readily meet in their social environment, hostile forces which knit them together and give them solidarity. The embryo gangs often have their beginnings in the fighting that takes place between rival streets. While many of them are ephemeral, others develop considerable social self-consciousness. They often get a name from their own street or of their own choosing. In this way the embryo gang becomes solidified and permanent and acquires considerable stability. Boys may hang together in this manner throughout the whole period of adolescence, and when they arrive at manhood they represent a well-integrated group. After the gang has developed for a period, it is likely to become conventionalized, taking on some traditional form like a club, or following some social pattern in the community. The dominant social pattern for the gang in Chicago is the athletic club, a type of organization which is the dream of every street gang. In the conventional stage, however, the formal acquirements are largely external and the group still retains many of its old gang characteristics. Out of these gangs of boys and young men the criminal gangs develop, and often these dangerous associations masquerade under the name of clubs. The crime commission of Chicago estimates that there are 10,000 professional criminals in the city. It is more than likely that their training was in such gangs, which, usually unsupervised, are veritable cradles of crime.

Besides creating juvenile delinquency and training criminals, the gang acts always as a source of disorder in the community. It is a problem for school, for park, for playground, and for settlement. It thrives on conflict. When there are riots, the gang takes a leading part in them; and it easily becomes a nucleus for the mob. In its more mature forms, in unscrupulous hands, it becomes the instrument for evil. It may be used in labor slugging, in strike breaking, or in violent competition. In Chicago, as in other cities, it has become a favorite tool of political bosses, who subsidize it and protect it in its delinquency in return for strong-arm work and votes.

Yet it would be erroneous to suppose that the gang is inherently evil. It is simply a spontaneous expression of human nature without social direction. It is a product of neglect and repression. It flourishes like weeds in the formal garden of society. If properly directed and encouraged, the energies of the gang can be turned into highly desirable channels. Supervised, the gang may become an instrument for the personal development instead of the demoralization of its members. Socialized, it may become a constructive agency in the community.[1]

The gang originates as a conflict group, a group in conflict with the social definitions of one or all of the family, the

[1] Document 37, prepared by Frederic M. Thrasher, whose significant study, *The Gang*, has recently been published.

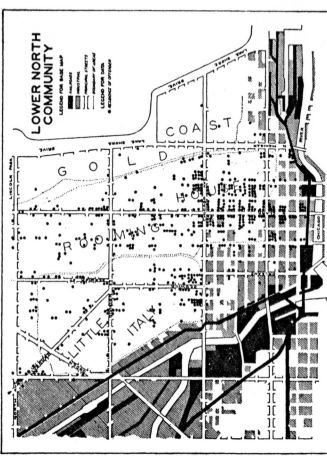

CRIME.—The Near North Side, including "Little Hell," "Death Corner," and the "Rialto," is notorious as the worst police district in Chicago. Crime concentrates in the southern end of Little Sicily and in the slum lodging area about the Rialto. This map gives the distribution of adult arrests from the East Chicago Avenue and the Hudson Avenue stations from August 15 to September 15, 1924, totaling 674.

community, and the conventional world. The "gang" often becomes the most sensitive and intimate zone in the boy's social world, the focus of his loyalties and his emotional life. But membership and status in the gang is the reward for behavior that is defined by the larger community as "delinquent."[1] In the conflict situation these delinquent patterns are fixed in the boy's personality. The "vice lords" of the passing generation were the products of the "gang" life of the Irish slums, many of them of the old "Market Street Gang" of Little Hell; and the underworld kings of today are the products of the gang life of the Jewish and Italian slums.[2]

Taking into consideration the segregated nature of the population of the cheap lodging-house, with its mobility and anonymity and its lack of group life, common social definitions, and public opinion, and taking into consideration the social patterns that grow out of the cultural conflicts of the life of the foreign colony, it is not surprising that the slum is a world of unconventional behavior, delinquency, and crime.[3]

And this Near North Side slum, with its frontier and rialto along North Clark Street, is the worst police district

[1] An extreme but interesting illustration is the following, given by Shaw in *The Boy's Own Story*. Membership in a gang of boys "back o' the yards" was contingent upon the promise that all money that came into a member's hands, no matter in what way, should be turned over to the gang. One day a boy was given five dollars by his mother to pay a grocer's bill. He paid the bill and was given a receipt. Later in the day, at the gang's shack, when he was taking some things from his pocket, the receipt fell out and was seized upon by another member of the gang. When it was discovered the boy had violated the code of the gang, he was beaten to death by the other members.

[2] The late Dean O'Bannion, for one, was a product of the Market Street Gang. The Miller boys grew up in the "valley."

[3] All that has been said in chap. iv on the effect of mobility on the life of the rooming-house district applies to the life of the cheap lodging-house as well.

in the city of Chicago.[1] The police court of Chicago Avenue, like all other police courts in the slum, is the stage upon which the drama of slum life is enacted. In the police court all the troubles and conflicts of the slum are brought to light. In the police court the slum's strangely divergent patterns come into uncompromising conflict with the patterns of the conventional world.[2]

[1] The map facing p. 157 shows the distribution of residence of 674 persons arrested August 15–September 15, 1924, in the district bounded by the river, the lake, and North Avenue. It clearly shows the correlation between crime and the life of the slum. It is interesting to note that the world of furnished rooms, unconventional though it is, comes into relatively little conflict with the law, as compared with the slum. The population of the world of furnished rooms, largely from small towns and suburban communities, does not bring to the rooming-house conflict patterns. Its unconventionality lies rather in the realm of the private life, centering about the rise of a new code of sex relationships.

[2] Document 38: a police court journal.

CHAPTER VIII

LITTLE HELL

West of the rumble and roar of the elevated, bounded on the south by "Smoky Hollow" and on the west by the river, notorious Goose Island, and a brick and steel barrier of railroad and industry, looking toward the German slums to the north, lies that tract known variously to the police, the newspapers, and the world at large as Tenement Town, Little Sicily, and Little Hell. Standing on sinister "Death Corner,"[1] in the heart of Little Hell, one can see, beyond the elevated structure and less than a mile to the east, the fashionable Drake Hotel and the tall apartments of Streeterville; while less than a mile to the south loom the Wrigley Tower and the broken skyline of the Loop. Yet Little Hell, or Little Sicily, is a world to itself. Dirty and narrow streets, alleys piled with refuse and alive with dogs and rats, goats hitched to carts, bleak tenements, the smoke of industry hanging in a haze, the market along the curb, foreign names on shops, and foreign faces on the streets, the dissonant cry of the huckster and peddler, the clanging and rattling of railroads and the elevated, the pealing of the bells of the great Catholic churches, the music of marching bands and the crackling of fireworks on feast days, the occasional dull boom of a bomb or the bark of a revolver, the shouts of children at play in the street, a strange staccato speech, the taste of soot, and the smell of gas from the huge "gas house"

[1] The corner of Oak and Cambridge streets, at the very steps of the church of St. Philip Benizi.

by the river, whose belching flames make the skies lurid at night and long ago earned for the district the name Little Hell—on every hand one is met by sights and sounds and smells that are peculiar to this area, that are "foreign" and of the slum.

Two generations ago this district was an Irish shanty-town called Kilgubbin. A generation ago it was almost equally Irish and Swedish. Then the "dark people" began to come. At first they came slowly, meeting no little resistance.

I interview Pastor _____, of Chicago's largest Swedish church, at the corner of Elm and Sedgewick, to learn why he opposes the intention of the Lincoln Park Commission to put a playground there. "This is *our* neighborhood, a *Swedish* neighborhood," he explains. "The dark people have come in farther south in the ward. If a playground is put in our neighborhood we fear these people will come with their children to live in our neighborhood. . . . ."

The Sicilian girls, timid and shy, come to Seward Park. They run to an empty swing. Two Swedish girls jump in, pushing them away. "Get out! Dagoes! Dagoes! You can't play here!" It is the same at the sandpiles and the "shoots." It is the same on the beaches. After the playground has been opened several months I pass one day and see a colored girl at the gate. She is talking earnestly to the Sicilians. "Sure you can go in. You got as much right to dem swings as anybody. I'm gwine in right now and show you—you come along." They follow Mattie, the colored girl, who seizes the first empty swing in spite of protesting pushes from Swedish girls. The Sicilians look scared and defiant, but they get into a swing. Their Americanization has begun. . . . .

The boys fight over the playground, too, but mostly outside. These fights are only partly for Seward Park; they are chiefly nationality gang-fights. The Swedish and Irish always win against the Sicilians. Even an onslaught led by a Sicilian boy on a horse ended in a rout for the Sicilians. . . . .[1]

[1] Document 36: "The Dark People Come."[1]

But the Sicilians pushed slowly into the district. Industry was demanding cheap labor. Sicilians came in great numbers, especially in 1903-4, the tremendous Italian immigration year. In this river district of the Near North Side they found cheap living quarters. It was the old story of a competition of standards of living, colored somewhat by national antagonisms. The Irish and Swedish, more prosperous, moved out of the district and northward. And by 1910 Kilgubbin and Swede Town had become Little Sicily.[1]

Little Sicily this district has remained. It now has a population of about 15,000 Italians of the first and second generations. Save for a few Genoese in the south of the district, this population is almost solidly Sicilian.[2] The heart of the colony lies in the area from Sedgwick Street west to the river, and from Chicago Avenue north to Division, though there is a considerable movement of the more well-to-do north among the Germans along Cleveland, Clybourn, and Blackhawk streets, and even north of North Avenue.

[1] Documents 37, 38, 39, and 40. In 1910, according to the United States census, there was in the Twenty-second Ward a population of 65,231 persons. Of these, 18,639 were Italian, and 14,709 German. The Germans formed a distinct colony between Division and Center streets: and the district in question, from Division Street south, had become almost solidly Sicilian. There were in 1910 but 1,716 Irish and 4,313 Swedish persons left in the entire ward. The Sicilian population has declined since 1910, with the general decline in population of the district as industry has moved in and as the Negroes have come in.

[2] How solidly Sicilian the population is, is revealed by a study of six blocks in the heart of the district. The schedules yield the following figures:

United States	43	Jewish	10
U.S. Colored	100	Polish	95
German	54	Swedish	90
Greek	5	Swiss	4
Irish	40	Russian (Jew)	5
Italian (Sicilian)	2,300		

Little Hell is an area of first settlement, an area into which immigrants have come directly from Europe, bringing with them their Old World tongue, and dress, and customs—persistent and divergent social patterns that condition the Sicilian's participation in American life.

"We are *contadini*." This phrase from the lips of the immigrant Sicilian is most revealing as to his social attitudes. The Chicago Sicilians have come largely from the villages and open country of Sicily, where they were poor, illiterate peasants, held down by the *gabelloti* or landlords in a state little better than serfdom. Generations of this condition have led them to look upon this status as fixed, and as the horizon of their ambitions. Why should *contadini* send their children to schools to bother their heads with letters? And besides, in Sicily the boys go to work in the fields at fourteen. Why should they not go to work here? The peasant attitudes and devices that sufficed for the primitive agriculture of Sicily, moreover, are utterly inadequate to adjust the Sicilian to the laboring conditions of the industrial city.

The spirit of *campanilismo*, of loyalty to *paesani*, is another trait of the Sicilian significant for his attempts to adjust to city life. The Sicilian peasants' interests are literally limited by the skyline. His only interests are the local interests of his village. The man from even the adjoining town is a foreigner. The government is a vague something that collects taxes. The spirit of *campanilismo*, of dwelling under one's own church tower, of jealous loyalty to *Paesani*, to his fellow villagers, circumscribes the Sicilian's social, religious, and business life. Social control in the village is largely in terms of gossip; one must not be *sparlata*—spoken badly of. The old men, too, occupy a respected and influential position in the life of the family and the village.

But the family is the center of the Sicilian's life and interests. The Sicilian's virtues are domestic virtues. The events of his life center about the birth, christening, marriage, and death of members of his family. The man is head of the house, and exacts obedience from his wife and children. He even has a say in the affairs of his grown-up sons and grandchildren; it is a custom with force of law that the first child be named for the paternal grandfather or grandmother. The family becomes almost a clan. Even the godfather and godmother are looked upon as blood relations. The interests of the family take precedence over those of the village. Its honor is jealously guarded, and upheld by feuds that endure for generations. Within the family the status of each member is fixed. The women and daughters are carefully protected and much secluded. The young girl is kept in the home until her marriage. The marriage and dowry are arranged by the parents. Grief over a death in the family is genuine and violent. But the funeral must have the proper degree of pomp to maintain the family's status in the community.

The attitude of the peasant toward the church is interesting. He is nominally Roman Catholic. A vein of superstition holds him to the church, but not to the point where it clashes with his own interests. His attitude toward the saints is proprietous and patronizing rather than reverent. His support of the church is part of his spirit of *campanilismo*. For generations he has been part of a community which centered about the parish church. He knows the advantages that may come from standing in with the church and the priest, who in Sicily is often a peasant like himself. While he harbors a skepticism as to the power of his local madonna, and has no illusions as to her, he would violently resent her being held up as a fraud by any other village. He goes little to church, yet there lurks in his mind the ghost of a fear that things might turn out, after all, to be as the priest pretends. The peasant woman, however, is very close to the church. It has been for generations the church of her family. Its colors, lights, miracles, and relics are an escape from her everyday life. It serves as a social meeting place for herself and her friends. The priest often acquires considerable power over the women, and every devout mother hopes to see one of her sons enter the priesthood. And yet the priest or friar is often enough jeered at. As in the time of Boccaccio, he is still the subject of jokes with double meaning.

Truth-telling is not counted among the virtues in Sicily. It has been remarked that there are liars, expert liars, and Sicilians. The Sicilian's attitude is well expressed in the proverb *La verità si dici a lu confissuri* (one tells the truth to his confessor). The truth is a distressing curb to the vivid Sicilian imagination. Moreover, hospitality is counted among the greatest virtues; the host never distresses a guest or friend; and the truth is so frequently unpleasant.

Gambling is the great national Sicilian pastime. Lotto banks are as frequent as wine and tobacco shops. Government lotteries are patronized even by the very poor, who thus squander most of their small earnings. Gambling contributes to the devastating poverty so characteristic of Sicilian life. If you ask a Sicilian in New York or Chicago, Why did you come to America? the answer is always the same, "We came for bread." Begging is a well-nigh universal practice seemingly attended by no disgrace. One is accosted every hour in the day, "*Eccelenza, morto di fame*" (Kind sir, I am dying of hunger).

The *Mafia* is another significant Sicilian tradition. It has its roots in the long history of political oppressions and is purely political in nature. But its pattern of swift, violent, and secret vengeance has become a part of Sicilian life. The characteristic Sicilian attitudes of reserve and suspicion are bound up with it.

The net result of these Sicilian patterns is the "individualism" which is the Sicilian's outstanding characteristic from the point of view of the American community.[1]

THE COLONY

From the various towns of western Sicily they have come, settling down again with their kin and townspeople here, until the colony is a mosaic of Sicilian towns. Larrabee Street is a little Altavilla; the people along Cambridge have come from Alimena and Chiusa Sclafani; the people on Townsend from Bagheria; and the people on Milton from Sambuca-Zabut.[2] The entire colony has been settled in like fashion.

The colony centers about the church of St. Philip Benizi, and Jenner School, which is jealously spoken of as "our school."[3] It has appropriated a "movie," which it has

[1] Document 41: "Sicilian Traits," by Helen A. Day, head resident of Eli Bates House, a social settlement in Little Sicily, who lived for a number of years in Sicily. (See Monroe, *The Spell of Sicily;* Rose, *The Italians in America;* and Park and Miller, *Old World Traits Transplanted*, for similar descriptions of Sicilian traits.)

[2] Document 41.

[3] By an almost imperceptible pressure the Italians are forcing the Negro children out of Jenner school. See Document 41.

rechristened the "Garlic Opera House." West Division Street, the colony's principal street, is lined with Italian businesses and shops: numerous grocery stores and markets, florist shops, the Sicilian pharmacy, undertaking establishments, cobblers' shops, macaroni factories, cheap restaurants, pool rooms and soft drink parlors which are the lounging places of the second generation, and the barber shops which have replaced the saloon as the center of gossip for the older people. On the corner of Elm and Larrabee is a curb market. Along Oak Street are numerous stalls where fruit, vegetables, coal and wood, and oysters on the half-shell are sold. The shingles of the doctor and midwife are frequently seen. The vicinity of Oak and Townsend is the center of the colony's population. Many of the influential Sicilians live along Sedgewick however, the colony's eastern boundary and more prosperous and fashionable street.

Because of its isolated situation, due to poor transportation and the barrier of river and industry, Little Hell remained until the war relatively untouched by American custom, a transplantation of Sicilian village life into the heart of a hurrying American city.

Until 1914 the Sicilian colony in Chicago was an absolutely foreign community. The immigrants were mostly from villages near Palermo, though nearly all the Sicilian provinces are represented. The most important of the village groups are those from Alta Villa, Milicia, Bagheria Vicari, Cimmina, Termini-Imarezi, Monreali, and the city of Palermo. These groups retained their identity, living together as far as possible, intermarrying, and celebrating the traditional feasts. Immigrants who settled in Louisiana came up to join their village colony. Those who had been leaders in Sicily retained their power here and, having greater force and intelligence, made contracts with local politicians, police officials, labor agents, and real estate dealers, and became the go-betweens for their colony and the outside-world labor agents.

Women continued to live as they had in Sicily, never leaving their homes except to make ceremonial visits or to attend mass. The presence of several garment factories in the district made it possible for them to earn by doing finishing at home. In later years hundreds of women went into the garment factories to work, some taking the street cars out of the district; but they went to and from work in groups, their shawls carefully wrapped about them.

In the entire district there was no food for sale that was not distinctly foreign; it was impossible to buy butter, American cheese, sweet potatoes, pumpkins, green corn, etc., but in season artichokes, cactus fruit (*fichi d'India*), pomegranates, cocozella, and various herbs and greens never sold in other parts of town were plentiful. There were no bookstores. Italian newspapers had a limited circulation, and the Chicago daily papers were sold at only two transfer points on the edge of the district. There were no evidences of taste in dress or house decoration. This group seemed to have had no folk music, but took great pleasure in band concerts when spirited marches and melodies from Verdi's operas were played. There was no educational standard; the older people were almost all illiterate; they accepted this as natural, and explained it by saying, "We are *contadini*, and our heads are too thick to learn letters." Some of the younger ones had had a little elementary training, but with very few exceptions no one in the colony had gone beyond the *quarto elementario*. Few had seen military service or learned trades, except, of course, the tailors, barbers, and shoemakers. One heard of an occasional cabinet maker, harness maker, solderer, carpenter, or mason, but none followed his trade here, as the training did not fit him to American methods. Many who had worked in the orchards in Sicily found their way to South Water Street and worked as truckers and fruit packers, and, becoming familiar with the way produce was handled, started their friends out as fruit and vegetable peddlers, thus establishing a wholesale business for themselves. Most of the men, however, were sent by their leaders to the railroads and building contractors as laborers. . . . .

Individually, Sicilians seem to vary as much in their manner and ideals as Americans, but as a group they have certain very marked characteristics: reserve, suspicion, susceptibility to gossip, timidity, and the desire to *fa figura*. Intense family pride, however, is the outstanding characteristic, and as the family unit not only includes those related by blood, but those related by ritual bonds as well (the *commare* and *compare*), and as intermarriage in the village groups is a common practice, this family pride becomes really a clan pride.

The extent to which family loyalty goes is almost beyond belief; no matter how disgraced or how disgraceful a member may be, he is never cast off; the unsuccessful are assisted; the selfish are indulged; the erratic patiently borne with. Old age is respected, and babies are objects of adoration. The self-respect of a man can be gauged by the number of his children, and the women seem to accept the yearly bearing of a child as a privilege. Both children and adults seem satisfied with the social opportunities offered within the family itself. The births, baptisms, christenings, betrothals, marriages, and deaths furnish the occasion for ceremonial visits and festivities. Traditional religious forms and superstitions are observed on these occasions, but the church and the priest seem adjuncts rather than the center of the various rites.

The leaders of the village groups organize brotherhoods for the purpose of perpetuating the feast of the patron saint and to arrange the elaborate funerals with which they honor the dead. The societies meet each month, collect dues, have endless and excited discussions over the petty business that is transacted, with, however, most serious regard for rules of order. Some of the *fratellanza* have women's auxiliaries, but they are directed entirely by the men, and the women seem to have no voice in the conduct of affairs; they pay dues and march in the processions. The annual feast is the great event of the year, exceeded in importance by Easter only. The group responsible for a feast put up posters announcing the day and the program, and through committees arrange for all the details of the celebration; electric-light festoons are strung across the streets, concessions for street booths are sold, bands are hired, band stands are erected, and the church is paid for a special mass and for the services of the priest who leads the procession. The whole community participates to some extent, but those from the village whose patron is being honored make the most elaborate preparation in their homes. . . . . Those who have been ill or suffered physical injury during the year buy wax figures of the part that was affected—legs, hands, breast, etc.—to carry in procession; others carry long candles with ribbon streamers to which money is affixed by a member of the brotherhood who rides on the shrine and exhorts the crowds to make their offering. The shrine is lowered to the street every hundred feet or so, and little children are undressed, their clothes left as an offering, and they are lifted to kiss the lips of the saint. Sometimes a blind or lame child is carried about on the shrine in the hope of a miraculous cure. The climax is the flight of the angels. The shrine is set in the middle of the street in front of the church, and two children are lowered by strong ropes so that they are suspended just over the figure of the saint, where they sway while chanting a long prayer.

The offerings made during the most important of these feasts amount to from four to six thousand dollars. This money goes into the treasury of the *fratellanza* and is used for the expense incurred by the *festa* and for the death benefit. There are those who say that tribute is paid to certain individuals as well.

These feasts are not approved by the priest, and people say that trouble is started by the jealousy aroused when one village tries to outdo the other. It certainly is true that at these *festas* there is often a shooting.

The position of women in the Sicilian homes in this district is hard to define. The general impression is that women are slaves to their husbands, but this is far from true except in the cases of very ignorant and primitive types. The head of the family takes the responsibility of protecting the women and girls very seriously, and for this reason women have little life outside their homes. It is a mark of good breeding for a man to show *la gelosia* regarding his wife and daughters, and it would be a sign of disrespect to them if he did not guard them carefully. Within the home, however, the wife directs the household, and it is not unusual for her to take the lead in family affairs, such as the expenditure of money, plans for the children, or the choice of friends.

When a girl reaches the age of twelve her freedom comes to an end; she is considered old enough to put away childish things. Until she is married she is not supposed to have any interest outside her home, except school or work, and with these two exceptions she is not supposed to be out of her mother's sight. A family that fails to observe this rule is subject to criticism.

A marriage is arranged by the parents as soon as a suitable young man of their village presents himself. The girl is not consulted and often does not even know whom she is to marry until the matter is all settled. After the girl is promised her fiancé must be consulted before she can go out, and she never appears in public without her mother or father in attendance. It has become the custom to have a civil ceremony performed shortly after betrothal. This does not constitute a marriage, and often it is several months or even a year or two before the actual marriage takes place. Meanwhile the engaged couple meet only in the presence of their parents or attend various family ceremonies together, always suitably chaperoned.

Sometimes a girl is coveted by a man considered undesirable by her parents, or by one who did not know her before she was engaged. In such a case the man may try to force his attentions on her in the hope of attracting her in spite of her parents or her promise. If she does not respond and will not elope voluntarily, it is not unusual for him to try to take her by force, either carrying her off himself or getting his friends to kidnap her and bring her to some secret place. When a girl becomes engaged her family is on the lookout for just such occurrences, and if they have any suspicion that she is being pursued she is kept a prisoner until she is safely married. If the man is known he is dealt with in no uncertain way—told to stop or take the consequences.

If a girl permits herself to be kidnaped the affair is usually ended with the blessings of all concerned, though the jilted one sometimes makes it necessary for the couple to move to another part of town, at least until he consoles himself with another wife. If a girl is carried away entirely against her will there may be bloodshed as a result.

Not all kidnapings occur in this way; often impatient men, tiring of the long and ceremonious period of betrothal and failing to persuade the fiancée to elope, try to carry her away. A well-bred girl will put up a good fight to escape, and if she succeeds, the engagement is broken; but if she is forced to submit, the family accept the situation and all is forgiven. There are, of course, many voluntary elopements by young people who are attracted by one another and who, because of family differences, could never get the consent of their parents.

Seduction is an almost unheard-of thing among this foreign people, and in the few instances where a girl has been wronged it has meant certain death to her betrayer. Not long ago a man seduced a girl and left town when he discovered she was pregnant. Her family moved from the district, and after a few months the man, Piazza, returned. The girl's brothers met him and seemed friendly, so he agreed to visit their new home. Shots were heard by neighbors, and when the police arrived they found Piazza and the girl's oldest brother dead. The bodies were seated on opposite sides of the table, and it is supposed that both drew and fired their revolvers simultaneously.

During the last four years there has been a great change; the colony is slowly disintegrating; old customs are giving way. Contacts with the outside world, through work and school, have given boys and girls a vision of freedom and new opportunity. They are going to night school and making their friends outside the old circle. They are out of patience with the petty interests and quarrels of the older group, and refuse to have their lives ordered by their parents, whom they know to be ignorant and inexperienced. Families are not being broken up; the deep affections still persist; and though the old folks have misgivings, in their indulgent way they are letting the new generation take the lead and are proud of their progressive sons and daughters. Young married couples are making their homes north of the old district, within easy reach of their parents, but away from the old associations. Evidences of refinement are seen in their homes and in their manner, and their children are dressed and fed according to most modern standards.[1]

"DEATH CORNER" AND THE BLACK HAND

Before the war, contacts with the outside world were few, and principally those made by the men on the job. But even on the job they worked chiefly in gangs of their countrymen. Such accommodations as had to be made with the larger city were made through the steamship agent, the *padrone*, and the banker, who were powers in the colony in its early days.

Certain of their Sicilian traditions, however, inevitably brought them into conflict with American custom and law. The corner of Oak and Cambridge streets long ago became

[1] Document 42: Report on the Sicilian colony in Chicago (manuscript) by Marie Leavitt, quoted by Park and Miller, *Old World Traits Translated*, pp. 153–58.

known throughout the city as Death Corner, because of the frequent feuds that were settled there by shootings or stabbings. Little Hell has been long notorious for its unsolved murders.[1] The American courts and police are powerless to deal with the situation. This is due in part to the nature of the American legal machinery. In Sicily the police worked secretly; an informant's name is never known. But in America an informant must appear in court. And to inform is to invite swift reprisals. Consequently the already reserved and suspicious Sicilian shrugs his shoulders—"And if I knew? Would I tell?"

Taking advantage of this situation has grown up the Black Hand. Weekly bombings are almost a tradition in Little Sicily. The Black Hand is not an organization.[2] Its outrages are the work of lawless individuals or of criminal gangs. But it trades upon the reputation of the *Mafia*, the fear of which is deeply ingrained in the Sicilian heart.[3]

[1] Every year for the past eighteen years there have been from twelve to twenty murders in the square half-mile of Little Sicily (Marie Levitt, *loc. cit.*).

[2] Document 43 and Park and Miller, *Old World Traits Transplanted*, pp. 238-60.

[3] Document 44: "Antonio Moreno versus Tradition." Antonio Moreno lived on Cambridge between Chicago Avenue and Oak. He was a day laborer, but had gotten a little money. He received Black Hand letters stating that his boy would be kidnaped unless he gave a certain sum of money. After much worry he decided to break the Sicilian custom and to tell the police and ask for their help and protection. The boy was kidnaped and no trace could be found of him for several weeks. With advice from the police Moreno answered the next Black Hand letter with marked money. The boy was returned at the place and hour promised. Moreno had told what persons he suspected, and there were arrests and convictions. Two brothers, prominent in politics, were sentenced to the state's prison for a term of years. It was learned, of course, that Moreno had talked to the police. He was furnished protection, one detective with him by day as he worked on the city streets and one by night guarding his home. This protection continued for a

This type of crime has been carried on to such an extent that, though the majority of those in the colony are honest and industrious laborers, nearly everyone seems to feel that he is in constant danger of either becoming the victim of a plot or of being forced to involve himself with the gang.

Continental Italians and those of other nationalities who live in the district may own well-stocked stores or acquire a reputation for wealth, but are never molested or threatened, but a Sicilian who shows any sign of prosperity almost invariably begins to receive threatening letters, and, though a love of display is a national characteristic, few have the courage to raise their standard of living as long as they continue to live in the district. The streets lying in the heart of the colony are thought to be centers of danger, so there has been a tendency to move toward the boundaries, or a few blocks beyond, and though they still live within easy walking distance and return daily to visit friends, attend church, patronize the shops, etc.

In the district itself it is considered very bad form to discuss these affairs. No one alludes to them voluntarily, or in plain terms speaks of a murder. A murdered man is spoken of as the "poor disgraced one," and the murders or persecutions as "trouble." Certain men are called *mafiosi*, but this generally means only that they are domineering, swaggering, and fearless, and no one would think of making a direct accusation. There are men who are said to be "unwilling to work for their bread," and certain names are never mentioned without a significant raising of eyebrows. The term Black Hand is never used except jokingly, nor does one hear the words *vendetta, omertà,* or *feudo,* though everyone is imbued with the sentiments for which they stand. In the whole colony there is no one so despised as an informer, nor is it thought desirable to show an interest in another's private affairs.

---

year or more. Moreno's wife died—it was said, because of her terror over the whole affair. The house in which he lived was practically deserted because people feared it would be dynamited.

After a short period the two brothers were pardoned, having served practically none of the sentence. When they returned to the city they were met by a brass band. An automobile awaited them, and in this they were driven slowly through Cambridge Avenue to their home, escorted by the band and a good procession of men and boys. This procession was perhaps chiefly political adherents. Moreno lived in constant terror of Black Hand vengeance.

There is a general belief that men who are murdered usually deserve their fate. Murdered men are not buried from the church unless a large sum is paid for a special mass.

The American press and police attribute all these "Italian killings" to the Black Hand, and consider them inevitable. Every so often the newspapers print an interview with a police official in which a certain number of murders are prophesied to occur in this district, and the public is given to understand that the situation is hopeless. When a murder is committed it is either reported as a minor occurrence, in a single paragraph, or absurdly elaborated in highly romantic style. A few years ago the chief of police, on being urged to have a careful study made of the situation, dismissed the matter by saying, "Oh, we've always had trouble up there; they never bother anyone but each other."[1]

This attitude of the police, based upon their inability to deal with the situation, dealing harshly with the occasional Sicilian criminal apprehended and ignoring the rest, is reflected in the Sicilian's attitude toward the American law.

There is no respect for law in Little Sicily. The law collects the taxes. It takes your children away when they are old enough to work, and puts them in school. It batters down your door and breaks open your kegs of wine. The Sicilian fails to comprehend all this. C____ came in the other morning. . . . . "No free country, no free country! I pay four policeman $16 each a month. Then they bring in police from other district and raid me! No free country!"

You can't convince a Sicilian that the police, the courts, or the law are on the square. A gang of Sicilians was arrested recently for stealing butter. One of them skipped. "Police no good. It blow over. New election, I all right. If me know big man, he talk to judge. Judge no want to lose job. He say 'you go home.' " Everyone is supposed to have his price. The "fixer" is one of the colony's most influential men.

But the wife of this man wrung her hands, and tears ran down her cheeks: "Oh, he will go to Joliet, he will go to Joliet, even if he did not do!" There is no faith in justice. They see the innocent "sent up" while the guilty walk the streets of Little Sicily.

[1] Document 42: Report on the Sicilian colony in Chicago, Marie Leavitt.

To a large element in the colony the law is a natural enemy. Even to the younger boys, baiting the "cop" is a game, and a ride in the "wagon" is a joy ride. Those who successfully defy the police are among the colony's heroes. Young men openly boast of their "hauls" and of their gun-play. When the bands march up Sedgwick during the festas, they always stop in front of the house of T____, the moonshine king, to serenade him. A year ago the whole colony turned out, with white horses, and thousands of dollars' worth of flowers, and blaring bands, to march in Rini's funeral. And who was Rini? Formerly the proprietor of a tough dive on Clark Street, and convicted of murder and hung in New Orleans. The hero of the colony.[1]

This attitude of the Sicilian toward the law, and of the police toward the Sicilian, has made of Little Hell a stamping ground for criminal gangs. Their operations center about the "bootlegging" and "hi-jacking" business. Politics plays its part in the situation; and there have been in the not distant past "understandings" between the "kings" of Little Hell and officialdom.[2]

The economic status of the Sicilian has involved him in another train of maladjustments. The greatest concentration of poverty in Chicago, as revealed by the giving of relief, is in Little Sicily. The Sicilian, of peasant origin, is inevitably an unskilled laborer. His acceptance of his status as *contadini* makes him difficult to unionize effectively. Seventeen per cent of the incomes of Sicilian families in this district fall short of the dependency budget worked out by the United Charities of Chicago; and 35 per cent fall short of the minimum independence budget. Considering these facts in the light of the prevalence of begging in Sicily, it is

[1] Documents 41 and 64.

[2] Not long ago Aiello, leader of a North Side beer gang undertook to dispute "Scarface" Al Capone's sovereignty on the South Side. Aiello's bakery shop on Division Street was riddled by machine gun fire from a passing automobile, and Little Hell was precipitated into another gang war.

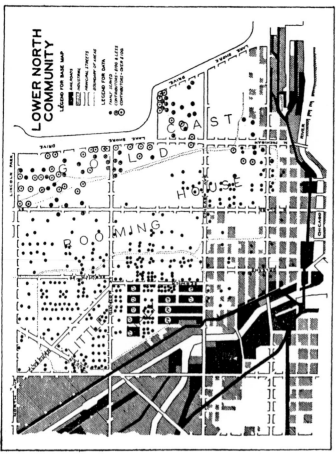

POVERTY AND PHILANTHROPY.—A map of the relief cases of the United Charities might well serve as a map of the slum. Economic inadequacy is an outstanding characteristic of the slum. The map, with its marked concentration of poverty in Little Sicily, indicates the difficulty faced by the immigrant family in making the economic adjustment to American life. The concentration of contributors along the Gold Coast, and of those receiving aid in Little Hell, brings out clearly the amazing distances which separate the adjacent but highly segregated areas of the inner city.

not surprising to find much pauperism and many professional charity cases.[1]

The immigrant is utterly unable to comprehend or to participate in the political life of the American city. The spirit of *campanilismo*, limiting the Sicilian's interests to his village group, paralyzes his political competence. The Sicilian vote, with the immigrant vote at large, is a commodity upon the market. It is controlled by the bosses and kings of the colony, marshaled, if need be, with the aid of gangs and automatics, and traded to the higher-ups for petty political favors. There is no "Italian vote" in Little Hell.[2]

In spite of these maladjustments which have grown out of the Sicilian's Old World background, there is not the disorganization to be found in Little Hell that is to be found in many other immigrant areas—across the river in Little Poland, for example. This is due to the persistent emotional attitudes that center around the Sicilian family tradition.[3] Family control in Little Hell has remained remarkably effective. The map showing divorce and desertion on the Near North Side reveals that Little Sicily is an area practically without divorce, and with relatively little desertion.[4] And

[1] Document 47: "A Short Study in Poverty in Chicago's Little Sicily," by E. L. Rauber; Document 48, a summary of family schedules on file at the Lower North Community Council; and family schedules of the Lower North District of the United Charities and of Eli Bates House. Less recent studies are "The Concentration of Misery in Chicago," the *First Semiannual Report of the Department of Public Welfare to the Mayor and Aldermen of the City of Chicago* (March, 1915); and "The Italian in Chicago," *Bulletin of the Department of Public Welfare of the City of Chicago*, Vol. II, No. 3.

[2] Documents 49 and 50.

[3] Document 51: A group of several hundred papers, written by school children of the Near North Side about their communities and activities, interestingly bring out the persistence of this family organization into the second generation of the Sicilian.

[4] See p. 129.

this family control has persisted despite economic and cultural tensions within the family, and the family's slum environment.

But even the Sicilian family is slowly disintegrating with the increased contacts of the second generation with American life. These contacts are made on every hand. The school holds up customs and ideals unlike those of the family and the community. The movie, for which Sicilian children have a passion, presents situations wholly outside the definitions of the community. The increasing mobility of the second generation, of the boy driving his truck or taxi, of the girl working in the Loop, takes it out of the old community into situations beyond its controls, into contacts with divergent standards and behavior. And there is an increasing amount of personal disorganization among the American-born. The second generation finds itself trying to live in two social worlds. The same situations are defined in contradictory terms by the school, for example, on the one hand, and by the family on the other. If the child conforms to the American definition he is a delinquent in the eyes of the family; if he conforms to the family definition he is a delinquent in the eyes of the American law.

The child cannot live and conform in both social worlds at the same time. The family and colony are defined for him in his American contacts by such epithets as "dago," "wop," "foreign," and the like. He feels the loss of status attached to his connection with the colony. In his effort to achieve status in the American city he loses his *rapport* with family and community. Conflicts arise between the child and his family. Yet by virtue of his race, his manner of speech, the necessity of living in the colony, and these same definitive epithets, he is excluded from status and inti-

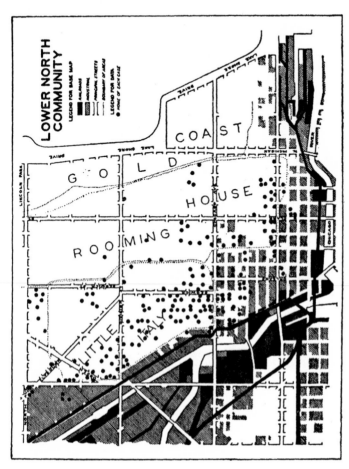

JUVENILE DELINQUENCY.—Juvenile delinquency is characteristic not of nationality, race, nor intelligence, but of the slum. It is particularly characteristic of the foreign slum, where the second generation is trying to live and adjust in two worlds with conflicting definitions of situations (data after Shaw).

mate participation in American life. Out of this situation, as we have already seen, arises the gang, affording the boy a social world in which he finds his only status and recognition. But it is by conforming to delinquent patterns that he achieves status in the gang. And every boy in Little Hell is a member of a gang. This is substantially the process of disorganization of the Sicilian boy of the second generation. Out of it grows all manner of social disorganization. There is, however, relatively little disorganization among Sicilian girls. The old family controls still seem effectively to define their behavior.

SOCIAL FORCES IN LITTLE HELL

Control in the colony is largely in terms of personal relationships. There are no organizations, nor individuals, that have an effective influence throughout the colony. Rather, control goes back to the spirit of *paesani* and the village neighborhoods. Every village group has its lodge. Each lodge is organized about the most influential man of the village. And it is these men, with their lodges, who are the social forces, the foci of attitudes and collective action, in Little Sicily.[1]

The church retains little effective control in the colony. This is not remarkable in the light of the peasant's attitude toward the church in Sicily itself. Moreover, as in nearly every Sicilian colony, the priest is a northern Italian, which makes *rapport* between church and community difficult if not impossible. All things considered, the priest at the church of St. Philip Benizi has remarkable prestige and influence. The immigrant generation still desires to dwell in the shadow of the church's tower. Even the second genera-

[1] Document 52.

tion would not think of letting a christening, a marriage, or a death pass without the traditional sanction of the church. But the church is none the less rapidly losing its control over the second generation. And it has no great influence upon community action.[1]

Little Hell, like every immigrant colony, has its settlement. And the settlement aids those whom it reaches in innumerable accommodations. However, the activities of Eli Bates House, following the settlement tradition, are institutional in nature. It does not participate in the currents of community life, and, like the church, has little or no effective influence upon the direction of community action.[2]

Far more influential in the currents of community life than any social agency is the local politician, the ward boss, and the precinct captain.

These political leaders are not theorists; they are workers who set for themselves an objective, definite and alluring, and then go about organizing all the forces around them to work together for that goal. Their methods may seem crude and unscientific, but they are human; a United States congressman who hails from a ward of foreign-born citizens in a Middle West city seems to have a private key to the mint, so full are his pockets always of half-dollars available for friends in need. A Polish washerwoman in this man's district said to her employer, "I cannot come next Tuesday."

[1] Document 53.

[2] Out of the settlement grew the Italian Progressive Club. It numbers among its members bankers and attorneys once boys in the colony and the settlement. It is a fraternal organization with educational aims, and takes no part in politics, as an organization. It attempts to draw into its membership the more promising of the younger generation. But its influence in the community is limited. Its members, like the progressive members of the second generation of any immigrant group, tend to move out of the colony. It is a fact not without significance, however, that not one in five of the second generation leaves the colony. And the population of Little Sicily is now more of the American-born second generation than of the Sicilian-born immigrant generation. See Document 41.

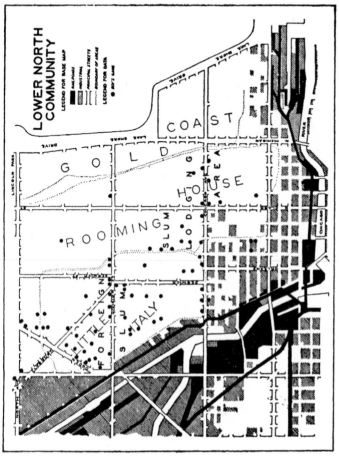

THE GANG.—The boys' gang, like juvenile delinquency, is characteristic of the life of the slum, particularly of the immigrant slum. It is a juvenile pattern of life that grows up in the interstices between old world cultures and the cultures of the American community, and in those areas of the city where family and community control are disintegrating (data after Thrasher).

"Why not, Maggie?"

"It's election day and I must stand on the corner."

"What do you stand on the corner for?"

"For five dollars."

"But what do you do on the corner?"

"I do nothing—Stanley K. pins a paper on me."

Tangible proof that Stanley is a more generous friend than the employer is found by Maggie in the two dollars' difference in the daily wage, and as adviser in matters of general interest he must be wiser than less generous friends. No hour is too late or too early for this honorable member of Congress to get out of bed to go to the police station to bail out an unfortunate neighbor who has imbibed too much and become too noisy, or by other ways that are dark has found himself in the clutches of the law. Not only Mr. K.'s unfailing willingness to go, but his demonstrated influence with the powers that be when he arrives, makes him a worthy leader in the eyes of his followers. At local weddings and neighborhood funerals he is the outstanding social ornament; his well-cut suit, white spats, top hat, and stick lend dignity and grace to the occasions, and it may be that he has started the subscription paper that has made so grand a ceremony possible. His objective—a seat in the municipal council, or in Congress, or a judgeship, or even a place on the precinct or ward committee—may not seem to us worthy of the coherent, enthusiastic following he is able to acquire, but he has it, and unless we have something better to offer, or take our place at the wire with him, he and his fellows will leave us far behind in the race for neighborhood organization and achievement. . . . .

We often wonder at his stock of detailed knowledge; and envy. But it isn't strange; he has visited again and again in every home in the precinct, and each time he goes he has a definite errand: an invitation to a precinct meeting, a visit, and some new family situation is revealed. If in any settlement we had such an aggregation of knowledge of the homes and lives of the neighbors in one precinct as the "boss" of that precinct has, we would be rich indeed. We could acquire it if we would. They are not trained social workers, these precinct leaders; they are just neighborhood people, and perhaps that is one of the secrets of their success.

They are not only in, but of, the neighborhood. Most of our charity organization society visitors, our school teachers, our visiting teachers, our park and playground staff workers, and certainly most of our boards of directors live miles from the neighborhoods where people they serve live. No matter how kind and friendly and helpful they are, "there are some things about us they cannot understand because they do not live here." Even our settlements, who like to feel that we are a stable and stabilizing element, have an astonishing "labor turnover," and are always having to introduce new workers to our neighbors. The precinct boss has lived, does live, and will live there, and although he may now and then switch from party to party, "for the good of the service," or some other reason, he still is he, and the neighbors know him.[1]

The village lodges, the precinct captains, and the kings who have utilized their local followings to secure understandings with the police, the ward leaders, and the politicians higher up, constitute the hierarchy of control in Little Sicily. There is no consciousness in the colony of itself as such, no common sentiment, no common interest. Only twice in the history of the colony has there been anything approaching community feeling: once a dozen or more years ago, when the proselyting activities of Protestant missions resulted in several nights of street fighting; and more recently, in the growing sentiment against the invasion by the Negro. In the last analysis Little Sicily is still a mosaic of Sicilian villages.[2]

West of the elevated, blackened by the smoke of industry, crowded against the gas house, known to the city at large as Tenement Town and Little Hell, Little Sicily is a different world from the world which parades the Esplanade, a different world from the world which cooks over sterno

[1] Harriet E. Vittum, "Politics from the Social Point of View," *Proceedings of the National Conference of Social Work* (1924), pp. 423–25.

[2] Document 54.

stoves in rooming-houses, a different world from the world that gathers in stables and garrets to argue heatedly and endlessly over obscure schools of art. There are those who, knowing it only through headlines in the newspapers or appeals of social agencies, knowing only its poverty, its squalor, and its crime, think of it merely as a world of tragedy. But to those who have participated in its life it has its pathos and humor as well.

We like living here. The Italians are good neighbors, and we like them. They do funny things, of course. Garbage cans disappear from alleys, to reappear on stoves as washboilers. Spring finds the winter's ashes in the bathtub—if there is one. An Italian making six dollars a day at the least takes food from the charities, the proceeds of the *Tribune's* "Give till It Hurts" campaign, and anything else that he can get. A father went to a public school to protest against paying for his children's books. "Free country, everything free!" he exclaimed from his seal-lined overcoat. The Italians save—but when they die they spend all the insurance on a funeral, bound that no one shall have a grander.

Yes, they are funny. But after all I wonder if there is as much happiness on the Gold Coast as over in these basement rooms. When the father comes home at night, six or seven children run to meet him, and a warm supper is always ready; and summer nights—the streets—you would go a long way to hear the concertinas.[1]

[1] Document 55.

CHAPTER IX

COMMUNITY INSTITUTIONS AND
THE SOCIAL AGENCY

The most striking thing about the local life of the Near North Side, as we have seen it in the light and shadow of the foregoing pages, is the fact that, from the lake on the east to the river on the west, there is scarcely an area that may be called a community. From the mansions of the Gold Coast to the tenements of Little Hell there is startlingly little of local feeling, consciousness, or action. The local areas of the Near North Side represent communities in process of disintegration, or areas, like the "world of furnished rooms," from which all traces of community life have vanished. The comparative status of local institutions and social agencies on the Near North Side significantly reflects this aspect of life in its local areas, and the possibility of anything approximating community action in these areas.

In the village community the church, the school, and the "town meeting" or political organization exist as community institutions and function under community sanctions. But on the Near North Side the church has ceased to bear any vital relationship to local life; the school, while still in the "community," is part of a great system of schools, centrally directed, and little interested in local problems; and the "town meeting" has become a ward club, where "the boys" and political jobholders gather to take orders from the ward boss, and perhaps to "sit in" on a few hands of poker.

THE CHURCH, THE FAMILY, AND THE SCHOOL IN THE CHANGING COMMUNITY

In the town or village the status of the church was defined in the mores of the community. Sects might compete with one another; but the church played a definite rôle in community life. Significant family events—christenings, marriages, burials—centered about the church. The church took a leading part in community celebrations, and was looked to in time of crisis. The church was intimately identified with the life of the locality, and was the visible symbol about which centered a great part of the community's ritual and tradition. The church plays a very different rôle in the life of the local areas of the Near North Side, the rôle varying with the degree of "community" remaining to those areas. Throughout the Near North Side the church finds the necessity of adjusting to a changing community. It is attempting this adjustment in various and interesting ways.

There are a few churches that are intimately related to local groups, express group life, and are mediums of group action. These churches are found among the Persian and Negro populations. The Persian, calling himself Assyrian, a sectarian name, and coming to America because of religious persecution, lives a great part of his life in the church. The Negro recently from the rural South, where the church played a large part in his life, continues, on the Near North Side, to organize much of his life about the church. What collective action takes place among the Persian and Negro populations takes place through the church. But the Negro and Persian populations are scattered among other groups, and have little influence upon the trend of "community" events.

The churches of the Gold Coast and of Little Sicily are

nominally community institutions. As we discovered in looking about the Gold Coast, however, most people in the neighborhood of the Lake Shore Drive "simply don't go." As the old contributors—whose relationship to the church is defined in terms of the day when the church was a community institution—leave the church, or die, it becomes increasingly difficult to finance these great churches.[1] An analysis of their membership reveals the fact that their members are scattered all over the city, and that a large number of them live far outside the "community," while of the members who live in the neighborhood of the church a large proportion belong to a totally different social world from that of the Gold Coast.[2]

These churches, realizing that the "community" is changing, and that they are losing touch with local life, are making various efforts to accommodate themselves. Their efforts but re-emphasize how far away from the community the church has grown. One of these churches split its con-

[1] The Fourth Presbyterian Church, for example, is feeling the necessity of endowing itself. The ultimate result of endowment is to give the church the same status in the community as has the social settlement.

[2] Of the membership of the Fourth Presbyterian Church, for example, a large proportion live without the boundaries of the Near North Side, and of those members living within the Near North Side, many are of the drifting rooming-house population, and are members only in name.

This church is a "community" institution only in its own eyes. The "community" feels keenly the barrier between itself and the world of fashion of which the church is a part; and the church is commonly referred to about the "community" as the "Millionaires' Club." The Gold Coast attends the morning service; the "world of furnished rooms," the evening service; the two rarely mingle. The "Life Story of a Charity Girl" (p. 80) and Document 56 show how little a part of the church these people from the world of furnished rooms feel themselves. They contribute little to the support of the church, and their memberships are brief in duration, and relatively inactive.

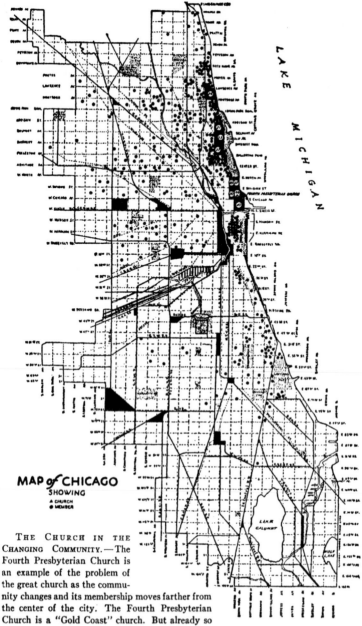

MAP of CHICAGO
SHOWING
▲ CHURCH
● MEMBER

THE CHURCH IN THE
CHANGING COMMUNITY. — The
Fourth Presbyterian Church is
an example of the problem of
the great church as the commu-
nity changes and its membership moves farther from
the center of the city. The Fourth Presbyterian
Church is a "Gold Coast" church. But already so
large a proportion of its membership has moved to outlying communities or to suburbs
not shown on this map, that it is in no sense a community church identified with the life
of the Near North Side. The concentration of spots back of the church represents the
transient contact of its institutional activities with the lodging house area.

gregation over the question of giving dances for the girls working in nearby shops and offices; and recently the "radical" element, after establishing its own church and building a beautiful parish house, voted to discontinue "community center" work in the rooming-house district (on the border of which it is located) in favor of giving Christmas baskets and putting a few "old ladies" in homes.[1] The churches of the Gold Coast have little identity with local life.

The church of Little Sicily is perhaps more intimately identified with local life. The membership of the Catholic church is limited to the local parish. The traditional relationship of Sicilian village life to the church still persists. Family celebrations and village festivals have at least a nominal relationship to the church. But we have seen that the church is losing its hold on the second generation. It is the church, rather, of the diminishing immigrant generation, and is participating less and less in the life of the colony.

Even less intimate in its relationship to local life than the church on the Gold Coast or the church in Little Sicily is the church in the world of furnished rooms. The rooming-house district is a district of many church spires, relics of the day when this was a fashionable residence community. But it is a district of dying and abandoned churches. Without exception, these churches are supported by members who now live far outside the community, but cling to the old church out of sentiment for the days that were. A few of these churches have withdrawn into themselves, content to let the life of the city rumble faintly by without their doors. But others are attempting to reach down into the life of the area.

One of the most interesting of these is the New England

[1] Document 57.

Congregational Church. It is one of the oldest churches in Chicago. Its traditions reach back through Plymouth to the England of the Restoration. Visible relics bind it to the past. Inlaid in the wall on the sides of its outer portals are two small original slabs, one from Scrooby Manor, dated 1606, and the other from Delft Haven, dated 1670. Within the church may be found a large fragment of the Plymouth Rock. The baptismal font was used three hundred years ago, in the Pilgrim colony in Massachusetts, by Elder Brewster, in the baptism of the sons of Governor Bradford. A generation ago the New England Church was a fashionable church, numbering among its members those whose blood was the bluest of the blue, and was famed for its orthodoxy. As the years have passed its membership has dwindled until today it is but two hundred, 70 per cent of which lives without the Near North Side. But it still numbers among its members some of the oldest, wealthiest, and most conservative families of Chicago.

The fashionable residence district that once surrounded the New England Church has been displaced by an area of cheap rooming-houses. And in Washington Square, directly opposite its door, where nursemaids once wheeled the children of the rich, the hobo now lounges while the agitator harangues from his soap box. The late pastor, a former army chaplain, with modern ideas on all subjects from the immaculate conception to the meaning of the brotherhood of man, attempted to compete with "Bughouse Square" by opening Sunday forums on such subjects as "War," "Narcotics and Drug Addicts," or "If I Were the Devil." Finally a Sunday school class for the hobo was organized, and Dr. Ben Reitman, that colorful adviser and friend of the migratory man, was invited in to lead it. This, however, proved too much for the conservative element of the old congregation. Shades of Plymouth were conjured up; purse strings were drawn; the minister was asked to resign; and the pulpit gave up its competition with the soap box.

Another church in this district has inaugurated a "bread and coffee line" for drifting men. Others have become little more than missions, striving to awaken old memories by familiar hymns and an "old time religion." Many have given up the struggle altogether, have been abandoned to livery stables and auto-repair shops, or have been torn down, to be replaced by office buildings, industrial plants, and play parks for the children of the slum. The people on the streets hurry by their doors. They belong to another world. The church bell has been replaced by the newspaper advertisement.[1]

Little need be said of the relationship of the school to the local life of the Near North Side; there is none. The schools, centrally directed and standardized, are interested in turning out "Americans" at so many per year, not in

[1] The situation cannot be laid wholly to the futility of the church, of course. The church meets in the rooming-house area with a total lack of response, if not with positive opposition. The social worker of one of these churches remarked, "We are desperate to know what to do. There is no response, no matter what we try. We have a large old plant, but our members nearly all now live far outside the community. Many of them have no automobiles, and they don't come. If we could make a congregation of our membership the church would be crowded. But we can't. We are going to try the experiment of sending out auto busses Sunday mornings to bring our members to the church. We cannot reach the neighborhood. We tried children's clubs, only to discover there are no children. We went around from rooming-house to rooming-house, inviting the people who lived in them to a social club. Without exception, the keepers of the houses refused to let us see the roomers. We were allowed to leave programs on hall tables. But there was no response. Not a person from these houses ever came" (see Documents 58).

making adaptations to the problems and needs of a Little Sicily, a gang world, or a life in furnished rooms. The attitude of the Board of Education practically killed the school community center movement.[1] As we have seen in the case of Little Sicily, the school rather creates local problems than adjusts or controls them. Outside the Gold Coast, with its private schools, there is not a parent-teachers association within the entire Near North Side. The school is in this area no longer a community institution.[2]

Like the church and the school, the family, considered as an institution, functions far differently in an area like the Near North Side than in the town or village community. The maps showing the distribution of desertion and divorce over the Near North Side and the distribution of juvenile delinquency are indicative of the extent of family disorganization. Over large areas, like the rooming-house district, the family as an institution does not exist.[3] In practically every immigrant group, as in Little Sicily, the family is going to pieces in the conflict with an alien culture. The fact that there is no occupational continuity and tradition within the family, that the child tends to follow a different trade from that of his father, and is taken into a world of different values, materially contributes to this conflict and dis-

[1] Document 59. The attitude of the Board of Education to the problems of the local community is illustrated by the reply of an assistant superintendent of schools to a Near North Side social worker who asked his help in studying a disorganizing gang situation: "My dear woman, why worry about such things? You have more important work to do in giving baskets and helping the poor."

[2] The private schools of the Gold Coast, of course, are exceptions. They arise out of a felt need of the Gold Coast, and are a conscious attempt on the local community to control the second generation in terms of its folkways and mores.

[3] The family, that is, as a nucleus of ritual, tradition, and emotional definitions and attachments.

integration.[1] The map of United Charities cases indicates that the family is failing, also, in those areas of the Near North Side to function as an economic unit. The fact that it is only on the Gold Coast that the family functions as an institution, functions more or less as the family in the village community, would seem to indicate that the family institution is conditioned by the community, and that where the community sanctions disintegrate the family ceases effectively to function as an agency of social control. The community may persist without the family, as in the womanless colonies of the Persian and the Greek. But the family disintegrates without the community.

THE MERCHANTS' ASSOCIATION

The economic life of the Near North Side presents an equally significant contrast to the economic life of the town, even to the economic life of the outlying areas of the city. From the Gold Coast to Little Sicily the person's occupational activities take place outside the area in which he lives. There is no local organization of physicians, lawyers, or artisans. The guild of the medieval city has been replaced by the "local" of the trade union. There are locals on the Near North Side. But these locals are parts of city-wide organizations without local interests.[2]

[1] Document 60, five hundred themes written by eighth-grade children in the schools of the Near North Side, throws interesting sidelights on this process. Children who state "My father does a kind of work called labor" are universally looking to stenographic and clerical "jobs" because "they are easy," "they pay good money," and "you can dress swell."

[2] The guild was a community organization. The members of the guild lived together in a local area of the city, and the guild organization bore an intimate relationship to the life of this area. But even a casual reading of the history of the American Labor Movement (Commons, Hoxie, and Williams), its attitudes, and its structure discloses how remarkably little relationship unionism bears to local life in the city.

As we have already noted, with the exception of the professions of the Gold Coast there is little continuity of occupation from generation to generation. Not only do occupational attitudes not become a part of family and community tradition, but the occupation of each generation takes it into a world of values that often conflict with those of its community. A tendency toward community disintegration is the inevitable result.

Outside the foreign colonies, the trade of this area tends increasingly to be drawn into the Loop or to go to stores that are managed by persons living outside the community. The only "neighborhood" stores are in Little Sicily or along North Avenue. The entire economic service of the Gold Coast is furnished from without, and much of that of the the world of furnished rooms. The majority of the stores of the Near North Side, with the exception of the smart shops on North Michigan Avenue or the corner stores of the foreign slum, depend largely upon a transient trade. The relationship of business to local life is reflected in the brief careers of two local newspapers, the *North Side Shoppers' News* ("From Goose Island to the Gold Coast") and the *Clark Street Booster*. Both of these papers, after existing a few months and with free distribution, passed out of existence because it did not pay to advertise in them. The majority of the owners of these stores live beyond the boundaries of the Near North Side.

Consequently the merchants' associations that exist in the Near North Side bear a very different relationship to local life than do those in outlying communities. There are four merchants' associations having members within the area. Of these, the largest and most influential, the North Central Association, is a Loop organization interested in

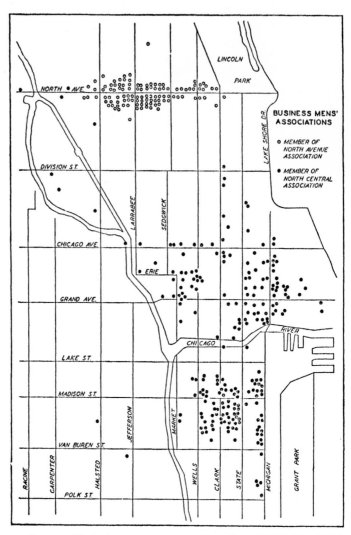

BUSINESS MEN'S ASSOCIATIONS IN THE NEAR NORTH SIDE.—Near North Side Merchants Associations are little identified with the social life of the area. The North Central Association is interested merely in pushing the Loop development in the North Michigan Avenue district. The North Avenue Merchants Association is identified with the local interests of the German and Hungarian colony about North Avenue.

pushing the North Michigan Avenue development, and taking no interest in the local life in that vicinity. The three others are associated with local business streets: Clark Street, Division Street, and North Avenue. Of these, only the North Avenue Merchants' Association has any stability, and it is identified with the German community to the north. The Division Street association is a by-play of a politician in Little Sicily, and is periodically having to be resuscitated. The North Central Clark Street association has but just come into existence, after years of futile attempts to organize the street. The association is a reaction to the Michigan Avenue development. Its president, asked to present its program at a meeting of Near North Side agencies, declined, on the ground that all they had in mind was a better street lighting system. The relationship of the Merchants' Association to the area is much like that of the social agency or the Bureau of Streets. Its function is one of physical reclamation.

LOCAL LIFE AND THE NEWS

As with the church, the school, and the Merchants' Association, so with the news. The newspaper, which in the town, and even in outlying communities of the city, is an institution of control and intimately identified with local life and local issues, has, on the Near North Side, little to do with the formulation of local issues and local opinion.

Beyond the stories of murders on "death corner" or tales of girls gone wrong in rooming-houses, the larger part of the life of this Near North Side rarely is reflected in the news. The modern metropolitan newspaper, with its emphasis on the romantic episodes of life that have a universal appeal, many of which come over the wires, bears little relationship to the life of local areas of the city. Outlying communities, such as Englewood and South Chicago, have successful community newspapers. But within the non-family and slum areas of the inner city, where advertising does not pay, "news" and local life belong to different universes.

The Gold Coast, however, in this as in every other aspect of its life, presents a contrast to the rest of the Near North Side. The comings and goings of the world of fashion are "news" everywhere; they have a glamor and a romantic interest, and pages are devoted to them. The society pages of the daily papers are really local newspapers of the Gold Coast, resembling, in their get-up and in the intimate nature of the news which they print, the newspaper of the small town. Affording, as they do, a tally of tricks in the social game, these columns are a prominent factor in social control.

THE CLUB AND THE GANG

The church, the school, and the occupational group, then, as well as the newspaper, play no intimate rôle in the local life of the Near North Side. But the life of this area is far from unorganized. The Gold Coast has its clubs; intimate groups gather in "village" studios; the foreign areas have numerous lodges and mutual benefit societies; the slum has its "gangs." Even in the rooming-house area, where group life is at a minimum, occasional cults and sects spring up, and every pool hall and cigar store has about it a nebulous group. And these groups may play an enormously important rôle in the lives of their members.

But these groups, with the exception of the clubs of the Gold Coast, are interstitial groups, not only from the point of view of the larger society, but also from the standpoint of the local community. They represent communities in process of disorganization. They are segmental rather than communal expressions of the life of the local area. The horizon of interest of the clubs of the Gold Coast, on the other hand, is city-wide and local issues rouse but faint echoes in the ballroom of the Casino or the lounges of the Racquet Club.

LOCAL POLITICS

The extent to which community life has broken down on the Near North Side, the extent to which local institutions and groups fail to function as agencies of social control, is reflected in the host of problems which the area presents from the point of view of organized society. With the physical inadequacy, poverty, ganging, delinquency, and crime of its slums, the clandestine vice of its rooming-house district, and the commercialized vice of its "little white way," with an almost total indifference to community issues and interests and an extreme individuation of personal behavior, with prejudice of group against group, with political corruption and graft, the Near North Side is not only an area of physical change and deterioration, but an area of extreme personal and social disorganization.

Yet these "problems" lie almost completely outside the realm of political action. In the slum area, from Wells Street west to the river, politics is a game, a mere struggle for office with its concessions and booty. These local "problems" are not election issues. The vote is organized from "higher up" outside the community. Elections are decided on party lines. Party lines are emphasized, if need be, by gangs of "strong-arm" men backed up by automatics.[1] The

[1] At the presidential election of November, 1924, the late Dean O'Bannion patroled the polling places with his "lieutenants." During the recent aldermanic election (February 24, 1925), gangs of gunmen stole ballot

vote of the northern part of the slum is a part of the larger "German" vote. The vote of the Negro, recently from the South, is traditionally Republican. The vote of Little Sicily is peddled by local bosses to ward politicians. The vote of the "flop" is a downright commodity. The local politician switches his loyalties to keep on the bandwagon.[1] An occasional alley is paved, as a sop to the popular vote. "Understandings" and "concessions" are granted to keep the more powerful kings of Little Hell in line. The Gold Coast, when at home, takes a dilettante interest in better-government campaigns and political reforms. But while it helps to elect a judge to the municipal bench, Little Hell elects the ward alderman. The large population living in furnished rooms to all intents and purposes does not vote at all. To the Gold Coast politics appear as an avenue of "uplift"; to Clark Street, as a means of "protection"; to the foreigner, as a source of income. Politics on the Near North Side is nothing more than a game, a game played without well-defined rules, a game played only incidentally in the local community and bearing little or no relationship to the problems—they can scarcely be called issues—of local life.[2]

---

boxes, intimidated voters and candidates, kidnaped election judges. A North Side aldermanic candidate mounted a machine gun on his home after receiving threatening letters demanding his withdrawal. See *Chicago Tribune, Chicago Daily News,* and the *Herald* and *Examiner,* February, 1925.

[1] Document 61.

[2] Hyde Park becomes aroused over the delinquency which it discovers in the tenements along Fifty-fifth Street, and after numerous community meetings, at which precinct captains and aldermen are much in evidence, a community program for meeting the situation is adopted (Document 62); Woodlawn, with its *Woodlawn Gazette,* Woodlawn Business Men's Associa-

GOVERNMENT BY THE POLICE AND THE
SOCIAL AGENCY

As a result of the breakdown of community life and community institutions, the indifference of the local population to local "problems," and the failure of local "problems" to find their way into politics, the greater part of the Near North Side is incapable of political action and self-government. There is no common culture or common body of interest out of which political action can arise. And as a matter of fact, the greater part of this area does not govern itself, but is governed by the police and the social agency.

The relationship of the law to this area is largely one of repression. Municipal legislation, passed for the city as a whole, and embodying the values of the more homogeneous and stable outlying communities, attempts to fix certain limits to individuation of behavior and to compel compliance with certain standards. But the values of these outlying communities are not the values of the population of the greater part of the Near North Side. They have to be forced upon this population by the police. And the police are suc-

---

tion, Kiwanis Club of Woodlawn, etc., with great community spirit and enthusiasm, takes a high ranking in the Better City Campaign (*Chicago Daily News*, July 28, 1923); Rogers Park holds mass meetings and organizes a Citizens' Vigilante Committee for the suppression of "polite vice" (Document 63 and *Chicago American*, October 12, 1923). Delinquency, healthy children and clean streets, and vice are community issues in these outlying areas, and not only result in extra-political community action but get into politics. But on the Near North Side a criminal situation that completely overshadows that in Hyde Park, filthy streets and a high rate of infant mortality, and vice that is far from "polite" have existed for decades without arousing any great degree of local feeling, without giving rise to local action, without becoming issues in local politics.

cessful only in enforcing compliance with the negative values, the prohibitions, of the law.[1]

The social agencies, for their part, are interested in setting standards in situations undefined by the law, or in situations where the law is not enforced. There are more than fifty social agencies on the Near North Side, ranging from gospel missions and settlements to children's clinics and charity organization societies, endeavoring to set standards of private life and public conduct; to persuade, cajole, or force the population of the district to conform to the values and mores of the larger society—values and mores derived from generations of village life, and often unadapted to the life of the city.

Much of this effort is directed at mere physical reclamation. A visitor from a community council endeavors to force the slum to keep its streets and alleys clean, its floors scrubbed, and its windows washed. A "Charities" family case worker tries to hold families together and to enforce a higher standard of living. The visiting nurse requires that the mother bring up her baby in what are to the mother

[1] As is inevitable in an area without a public opinion, there is a long history of graft in connection with law enforcement on the Near North Side. The police, the courts, and the city hall are parts of a larger political organization. Politics is constantly complicating the problems of law enforcement. Cabarets and "soft drink parlors" operate under court injunctions. Politicians "frame" police squads who raid places which these politicians have pledged to protect. The police themselves have not been guiltless. The report of the Senate Vice Committee in 1917 disclosed a network of police protection of disorderly houses. Police captains in this district have, in the past, been accused of understandings with its "kings." Under the present reform administration, the morale of the police department has been heightened, and the captains of the police precincts in the Near North Side seem to have made genuine efforts to curb graft. But individual policemen still "protect" moonshine parlors, gambling dens, and questionable resorts. See K. Young, *A Sociological Study of a Disintegrated Neighborhood*, and Document 64.

strange and inconvenient ways. Clinics and societies exist for the reclamation of the maimed, the blind, the deaf, the tubercular, or the socially diseased. Other social agencies are more interested in redefining the population's wishes and values. Of this kind are the settlement and the mission. But beyond the sphere of physical reclamation the social agency is hardly more successful than the police.[1]

The police and the social agency alike meet with little co-operation or response on the part of the population. Those who see an opportunity for profit give a nominal or calculating co-operation. Others are indifferent, suspicious, resentful, or in open opposition. For the police there is no respect, but rather a complete indifference. Those who run rooming-houses or soft-drink parlors make it a point to stand in with them. There is a universal belief that no policeman is "on the square." The sanitary squad is taken as a matter of course; promises are made that are never fulfilled. Investigators and detectives are everywhere, and consequently the attitude toward the stranger is one of active suspicion. The population takes no interest in the social uplifter. When parks, playgrounds, social centers, and public baths are established, there is merely resignation to what is believed to be an inevitable increase in taxation. The crusading reformer meets everywhere with opposition. In the rooming-house district the church visitor is refused admittance. In Little Hell the proselyting mission merely

[1] A Near North Side social worker pointed to the improvement resulting from the replacement of a filthy tenement block by a new building of the National Tea Company as the outstanding improvement in the two years her agency had been working to clean up Little Hell! The agency was little more than a spectator as, in the inevitable succession of the city's growth, the business and manufacturing district pushed relentlessly outward, wiping out old slums and creating new ones.

stirs up street fighting. On the "Rialto" the street meeting is met with indifference, amusement, or contempt.

A group of Moody students were holding a street meeting near "Bughouse Square." The preacher was constantly heckled. "I'll give God five dollars to strike me dead this minute." "If you believe in your God so much, let's see you drink a bottle of carbolic." "You're wasting your breath—go preach to the wall." When the preacher asked how many were ready to come to Jesus, several laughed or jeered, and others turned with groans and walked away.[1]

Throughout the Near North Side, then, community life, where it has not already disintegrated, is in process of disintegration. Community institutions are ceasing to function. The church, the school, the family, the occupational group, government, and the news have ceased to bear any direct relationship to local life. Behavior is individualized in the extreme. There is little or no public opinion. There is no common interest or cultural background. The greater part of the area is incapable of political action. What government

[1] K. Young, *A Sociological Study of a Disintegrated Neighborhood*, p. 84. The writer "staged" a series of street meetings with the help of a group of Moody students. The first meeting was held in Washington Square. John Lochman was haranguing from a soap box on the "petty cash register philosophy" of Henry Ford. He had a large crowd about him. When the Moody group sounded their cornet curious eyes were turned, but only a few men drifted over—"Let's go down here, you get some music." One man listened a moment, then turned away with a disgruntled "It's all the bunk." Another called to the leader, who was giving testimony, "You're nuts!" A third leered at the girls, and remarked in an aside, "I'd like to be janitor in the woman's building at Moody Institute." Soon the few who had been attracted drifted back to the crowds about the agitators.

The Moodyites were refused entrance to the Coal Scuttle, a bohemian hangout on Rush Street. A meeting was held in Tooker Alley, outside the Dill Pickle Club. The only response was the throwing of pennies from the windows. A fourth meeting, at the corner of the Erie Café, was ignored by the Clark Street crowds.

there is on the Near North Side is in the hands of the social agency and the police. But neither the social agency nor the police meet with any degree of success. Life is highly disorganized—lived without the law, and without the mores of the larger society. The Near North Side is a section of the old frontier transplanted to the heart of a modern city.

CHAPTER X

THE LOWER NORTH COMMUNITY COUNCIL

The Near North Side, we have seen, is an area of striking contrasts, contrasts calculated to catch the eye and to touch the imagination. Ten minutes' walk westward from the Lake Shore Drive takes one from America to Sicily, from the world of fashion to the slum. And while the Gold Coast as a whole might be oblivious to what lay behind it, individuals, through service on boards of trustees of settlements and social agencies, and in various other ways, were bound to come into contact with the slum, to be arrested by its desolation and squalor, and to take a sentimental interest in its sordid drama.

A few of these individuals, seeing the "other half" with the eyes of pity or romance, went to live in the slum. The Casa Maria, not far from "death corner," and the "House on Locust Street" are enterprises that were embarked upon a generation ago by well-to-do women from another world—"settlements," in the original meaning of the word, in that these women transferred their homes to the slum where they could live among those whom they longed to help. The goal of these early "settlements" was understanding rather than uplift.[1] Somewhat different in motive was Eli Bates House, founded nearly half a century ago by Unity Church in the

---

[1] The Casa Maria and the "House on Locust Street" were undertaken when Little Hell was Irish and Swedish. And because they were founded upon a sentimental interest in persons rather than on programs, their founders have been unable to adjust themselves to the Sicilian deluge. The Casa Maria has ceased to be a "settlement" and has become a boarding-house for working girls; while the "House on Locust Street" is about to be abandoned.

very shadow of the "gas house." An institutional settlement, it has striven through its organized activities to trans-
mute the attitudes and beliefs of the slum. In the past ten
years it has become one of the most fashionable charities in
Chicago, supported by the Gold Coast a dozen blocks to the
east.

There were other evidences of this sentimental interest
even more arresting than the settlement. The ward committee of the Woman's City Club, a decade or more ago,
conducted tours in Little Hell—instructive slumming parties
for society's socially minded during which large motor busses
brought the Social Register into fleeting and horrified contact with the "submerged tenth." At the same time an occasional scion of an old family was bringing back from Harvard or Princeton that first flush of enthusiasm for social
uplift which was soon to become a fashion, and later a profession. The great dining-room of one ancestral mansion was
opened to the dwellers in furnished rooms, the frequenters
of the "Rialto," and the denizens of Sicilian barber shops.
Working mothers sat beside débutantes about the candle-lit
table that had been the scene of many a memorable banquet.
But somehow the neighborliness that had been anticipated
as the result of this mingling did not materialize. Mothers
from the slum thought they were being patronized. Petty
politicians, unable to comprehend this startling phenomenon, thought their host must be intending to run for office,
and approached him for money in anticipation of their support. On the other hand, as the novelty of these unique
functions wore off, it became increasingly difficult to get
acceptances from the desired representatives of society. For
some years, now, the windows of the great dining-room have
been darkened.

The enthusiasm for social uplift, however, was sweeping the country at this time in the form of the community center movement. A group of Gold Coast women attended the first national conference on social centers in 1910, at Madison, Wisconsin. One of them writes of it:

> It was the deepest and most inspiring experience I have ever had with a group of people. Several hundred delegates and interested persons had come from every corner of the country—most of them with a new vision and enthusiasm for the possibility of neighborliness in the city. Some of us had caught the vision from the South Park Field House; others were fired by the experience of Edward Ward in the Rochester School centers. I remember little of the conference but its compelling enthusiasm. Woodrow Wilson spoke at one meeting. He said that the idea of the conference, if put into practice, would make America a true democracy. He urged the discussion of public problems by neighborhood groups as the most important step in political betterment. His interest was genuine and inspiring. Woodrow Wilson's idea dominated the conference. The Governor of Kansas and the regents of Kansas University were there. There was a group of newspaper men who wanted a better press. William Allen White spoke at the closing banquet. It was not like most closing banquets. It was a crusade consecration, and that not in any spirit of duty but in a joyful conviction that we had found the way into a new world. Tremblingly we stood on our feet and sang a Hymn to Brotherhood. A telegram had just been read from Charles Evans Hughes in which he had said: "I am more interested in what you are doing than in anything else in the world. You are witnessing the foundations of Democracy." As the last strains of the hymn died out a man near me turned to me and said: "This is the first time I have ever felt that I was in church."[1]

The community center movement amounted for a time almost to a religion. A number of community centers were started in the schools of the Near North Side as a part of the Chicago School Center Movement. The policy of the Board of Education was stated as follows:

[1] Document 65.

It will be observed that the policy adopted provides for the furnishing by the Board of Education of the building, lighted and heated, with the services of the engineer and the principal. The community itself is to carry forward such proper activities as it desires, and to provide the money to cover the expenses of operation and maintenance. Some of the community centers which have operated most successfully in the past have followed this policy which seems to be the true "community center" idea.[1]

Within a year all but one of these community centers on the Near North Side had failed.[2] It was not enough to open doors. There was no response from the community. Children came to the playgrounds. A few mothers came to the movies. But the men did not come. There was no evidence that people wanted to come together to discuss politics or local affairs. Neighborhoods did not support the centers. The doors were closed.[3]

Then came the war, and with it the Council of National Defense. The Twenty-first and Twenty-second ward organizations of the Chicago unit were particularly active. These wards corresponded roughly with the Near North Side. Wealthy women on the Gold Coast provided a budget. A Community Service Bureau was opened, with its own offices and a paid secretary. In the Twenty-first Ward a house-to-house canvass of thirty precincts was undertaken (these precincts including the southern part of the rooming-house district and the slum); a registration survey was made; mothers' meetings were held at public and parochial schools; food demonstrations were formed, groups of colored women having lessons in a "private" kitchen. There were com-

[1] Document 66.

[2] This one successful center, that at Kinzie School, was held together by two women, a remarkable worker and an interested woman on the Gold Coast.

[3] Document 67.

munity sings, community celebrations and demonstrations. Many needy families were helped. A Girls' Patriotic Service League was organized. A clipping bureau collected items of ward news. Volunteers from the Gold Coast did much of this work, society girls doing home visiting in the slum Patriotic propaganda took men and women from the neighborhood of the Lake Shore Drive into the foreign colonies. Out of this mingling, under the emotional stress of war, there arose an unusual amount of local feeling, of social tolerance, and of "neighborliness."[1]

After the war, when it was proposed that the local units of the National Council of Defense be perpetuated as community councils, the Twenty-first and Twenty-second ward organizations enthusiastically took up the idea, and the Lower North Community came into existence.[2] The office was maintained at the same address on Clark Street; a man who had done organization work for the Red Cross was secured as secretary; and it was anticipated that the large corps of volunteers which had worked under the ward organization of the Council of National Defense would continue enthusiastically to work for the Community Council.

The man who came, in the spring of 1919, as the first secretary of the Lower North Community Council had been fired with the enthusiasm aroused in many parts of the country by the social unit experiment in Cincinnati. He saw in the community councils the possibility of a greater organization of local life in the city. With a balance in the bank,

[1] See *Final Report of Woman's Committee State Council of Defense of Illinois and Woman's Committee Council of National Defense Illinois Division;* and Documents 68 and 69.

[2] The Lower North Community Council and the Stockyards Council (this latter an altogether different sort of organization) are the only councils which have survived.

turned over to the Community Council from the Council of National Defense, he launched upon an ambitious program.[1]

The plan was to organize from the bottom up—to make the council both communal and democratic. The immediate objective for membership was placed at five thousand. The direction of the activities of the Council was to be placed in the hands of an executive committee and delegated to sub-committees.[2] On these committees every language, race, and color, every shade of political and religious belief, every degree of economic and social position was to be represented. The work of the Community Council was to consist in the co-ordination of agencies and efforts devoted to the amelioration of conditions on the Near North Side, to the securing of needed improvements for the Near North Side, and, above

[1] The woman who had acted as secretary of the ward organization of the Council of National Defense had continued to act as temporary secretary of the Community Council, but she had declined to remain as permanent secretary, feeling that the future of the Community Council movement was far from assured.

[2] *Constitution for the Lower North Community Council.*

Name.—The name of this organization shall be the Lower North Community Council.

Object.—To improve the social, industrial, and living conditions of the 21st and 22nd wards through the co-operative efforts of individuals and organizations.

Membership.—Any resident of voting age in the 21st and 22nd wards may become a voting member of the council. Any non-resident of voting age with a business or other affiliation in the 21st and 22nd wards may become an associate member with advisory privileges. The annual dues shall be one dollar for voting and associate membership.

Administration.—The official bodies of the Council shall be the Executive Committee and Field-Work Committees. The Executive Committee shall be made up of the officers of the Council and the Chairman of the Field-Work Committees, and shall have the usual powers of an executive committee subject always to the control of a majority of voting members assembled.

The Officers shall consist of a chairman, vice-chairman, recording secretary, treasurer, and such other officers as the Community Council shall deem

all, to the building up of a spirit of neighborliness and a community of interest among the varied groups living on the Near North Side.

A few quotations from the minutes of the first annual meeting of the Community Council will make more clear the ideals and sentiment back of this program:

Mr. Chairman, Ladies and Gentlemen: Before the war our community life was made up largely of segregated groups. We took counsel together as Baptists, as Methodists, as business men, as members of labor unions, as members of women's clubs, to promote our particular interests. Even local politics, which should be of supreme importance to any community, was a matter of being a Republican, a Democrat, or a Socialist. Very seldom did we get together as a community.

During the war, however, our segregated groups were drawn together in a very striking way. They got on together harmoniously. They became a powerful chain of community organization and influence, which accomplished things that, before the war, would have seemed impossible to everyone of us. But not only was the impossible accomplished—more important, we discovered each other, we touched elbows, we found that our neighbors, though living lives different from our own, were pretty good folks after all; we found there was real pleasure in all getting together as a community.

Today we face the question of going back to the old life of segre-

---

necessary. There shall be the following Field-Work Committees: Spare Time Committee, Health Committee, Education Committee, Forum Committee, Industrial Committee, Housing Committee. Other field committees shall be appointed by the Executive Committee. Not over 50 per cent of the membership of the Field-Work Committees shall consist of the professional workers in the field covered by the committee. On each of these committees representation of the appropriate governmental bodies shall be included. The Executive Committee shall be elected by a two-third majority of the Council in April of each year and shall serve for one year.

Finance.—The collection of all money of the Council shall be in the hands of the Executive Committee, who shall determine and authorize all expenditures.

Meetings.—The annual meeting for the election of the Executive Committee and officers shall be held on the second Tuesday in April. Other meetings shall be held at such time as shall be fixed by the Executive Committee

gated groups. May I make a plea for the preservation of the kindliness of feeling, the neighborliness, the mutual interest, the pleasure in the touching of elbows that is our precious heritage from our wartime experience. May I make a plea for the realization, here in this city community, of the democracy that is our too nearly forgotten heritage from the American town meeting. Let us all continue to work together. [Long applause.][1]

A large number of committees immediately organized and set to work. A health committee began investigating sanitary conditions in the slum, attempting to organize blocks to clean up homes, streets, and alleys. A "pied piper" was hired by a member of this committee to rid the entire district of rats. A man was sent out on the streets of the slum with a bat and ball to search out groups of street gamins, gangs, and "athletic clubs," and to divert their interest from gang fights and gambling to organized play. A children's crusade for a cleaner and more sightly community found ten thousand children signing pledges to pick up papers and tin cans and keep their neighborhoods clean. A committee on housing also set to work in Little Hell. There were other committees on education, industry, spare time, a substitute for the saloon, music, community celebrations, a public forum, and the like. A community bulletin was printed weekly; a committee on membership began a drive to carry the membership of the Community Council into every group on the Near North Side. Italians, Persians, Germans, and Negroes served with Gold Coasters on these committees.[2]

[1] Remarks of the secretary of the Lower North Community Council at its first annual meeting; see Document 70, *Minutes of the First Annual Meeting of the Lower North Community Council*, December 8, 1919.

[2] The following plan of organization was published in Vol. I, No. 2, of the *Lower North Community Council Bulletin:*

[Footnote continued on page 208]

The emphasis, throughout, was upon the building up of neighborliness and fellow-feeling. Attempts were made to organize blocks after the pattern of the social unit plan. The Board of Education was asked to put a public reading-room on the Near North Side, with the expectation that it would prove a common meeting place. The music committee held community sings; stating that "nothing tends to break down the barriers of conventionality, social formality, and those intangible but none the less mighty differences which so-called class distinctions create, as does singing together.

I. *Voting council.*—Residents of the 21st and 22nd wards. Membership, $1.00 a year.
   A. Executive committee: chairman, vice-chairman, recording secretary, treasurer, chairmen of field-work committees.
      1. Field work committees:
         a) Health:
            Membership—resident physicians, nurses, midwives, and non-professional citizens.
         b) Education:
            Membership—school principals, teachers, Parent-Teachers Association, and non-professional citizens.
         c) Housing:
            Membership—real estate dealers, landlords, tenants, private residence owners.
         d) Industry:
            Membership—employers, employees, tradespeople, non-professional citizens.
         e) Forum:
            Membership—educators, business men, tradesmen, members of radical and conservative organizations.
         f) Spare time:
            1. Men's Athletic Council. Membership—athletic directors of parks, settlements, Y.M.C.A., churches, athletic clubs, non-professional citizens.
            2. Women's Athletic Council. Membership—athletic directors of parks, settlements, Y.W.C.A., churches, athletic clubs, non-professional citizens.

[Footnote continued on page 209]

Two men, no matter what may be their relative social positions cannot 'lift up their voices in song' together without becoming in large measure good fellows and friends."[1]

Community hikes were organized. There were great community celebrations at which leading citizens from the neighborhood of Astor Street welcomed newly naturalized Americans into the fellowship of the community. A civic forum was opened for the discussion of local issues, to which it was anticipated would come members of all the varied groups of the Near North Side to talk over together their common interests and problems. This forum was held, during the winter months, in the large auditorium of Lane Technical High School, and during the summer months out-of-doors in Lincoln Park. To start it off, prominent speakers were secured from outside the city, and crowds filled the auditorium to listen to them.

The office on Clark Street was turned into a center for dispensing information and advice. In the unsettled months after the war there was a constant stream of people in and out of the office. The day books of the Council afford an interesting picture of this neighborly service.

3. Music Council. Membership—musicians, choir leaders, directors of music schools and organizations, non-professional citizens.

4. Dramatic Council. Membership—teachers of dramatic expression, actors and actresses, pageant directors, non-professional citizens.

5. Dancing Council. Membership—dancing teachers, managers of dance halls, clubs leaders, non-professional citizens.

6. Substitute for the Saloon Council. Membership—former saloon keepers, business men and women, social workers, non-professional citizens.

7. Community Celebrations Council. Membership—directors of public parks, schools, business organizations.

[1] *Lower North Community Council Bulletin*, Vol. I, No. 3, February, 1920.

Mr. and Mrs. K——, colored, come in to ask for work. The secretary talks with them. She sends Mrs. K—— to the neighbor who wants a cleaning woman, gives Mr. K—— a card to the Illinois Free Employment Bureau, directs them both to Butler Community Center for colored people. It may be added, incidentally, that Mrs. K—— now has work every day, and Mr. K——, through the Hod Carriers' Union, has a job at a dollar an hour.

Then appears J—— G—— to get advice about being naturalized. She took out her first papers a couple of years ago, and lately she went on a six weeks' visit to Ireland. Someone at the Federal Building has informed her that, in consequence of this absence from the United States, the first papers are now worthless. Our secretary telephones the state's Immigration Association and the Naturalization Bureau and straightens out the tangle.

A lady who has returned to the city too late to register wants to know how she can vote.

A man enters to ask about dances and gymnasium classes in Seward Park.

A woman comes in great distress because her access to the alley has been barred. She keeps a cheap lodging-house and does not know how to arrange about having ashes and garbage removed. She is referred to the ward office of the Street Cleaning Department, and is promised also that the council will make special inquiries to help her out.

Next arrive ten small boys who form the Maple Square Athletic Club. They want the secretary to find them a "gym" where they can play basket-ball. She produces one by telephoning Miss Deer of the Lake Shore Playground.

It is four o'clock and the Executive Committee of the council arrive for their weekly meeting. They assemble at the rear of the office, but the secretary's work goes on. Another neighbor asks for help. The owner of a coal company wants her to investigate the case of one of his drivers, a resident of the Twenty-second Ward, who got into a fight, was arrested, and has totally disappeared. No record of him in police station or jail. The secretary promises prompt action.

Next appears Mrs. A—— M—— with a quadruple problem. She needs work. Something has gone wrong about her Red Cross allotments. Some time ago she entered a damage suit in regard to an injury to her first husband, who is now dead, and cannot grasp the reason it has not been settled. Now she has had trouble with her second husband, who has ordered her out of his house. This entails much telephoning. The secretary accomplishes something technical called "clearing registration." She gives Mrs. M—— a card to several households which have sought for cleaning-women. She refers her to the Red Cross and the Legal Aid, after phoning both organizations, and directs her to the Court of Domestic Relations in regard to her marital difficulties. Mrs. M—— departs hopefully, and the secretary, observing with a sigh that it is after five, proceeds to close up shop.[1]

This office was the visible symbol of the new neighborliness that was to weld the Near North Side into a community.

After the enthusiasm of organization passed, however, and the activities of the council had settled into a routine, it became evident that things were not working out just as had been anticipated. To begin with, the volunteers who had carried on the local work of the Council of National Defense drifted one after another into other things, until within a few months all the actual activities of the council were being carried on by paid workers. The professional men, who were to be the expert members of the various committees, grew impatient with common-sense points of view, lost interest, and dropped out. Moreover, the "community" did not respond as had been expected. The membership drive fell short of one thousand. The money in the bank was gone; the council was in debt; and subscriptions came in with disconcerting slowness. The "social block" experiments went to pieces. The attendance of the forum dwindled.

The first year the topics were left largely to the speaker and they were of a general nature. The attendance was very large. The second year we began to specialize. One week we would have a topic of gen-

[1] *Woman's City Club Bulletin*, January, 1921. See also the *Day Books of the Lower North Community Council.*

eral interest, and the next week a topic of local interest to the community. *Strange to state, the topic of local interest was always the one that fell flat. People were not interested in their local affairs. It was difficult to get them out for things of that kind. At one of the meetings I announced that one or two of the ward aldermen would speak, and a titter ran through the crowd and people began to leave. It has been impossible to get discussion of local issues and problems. The forum has become merely a lecture course. Even so, the attendance has fallen off greatly.* It has been suggested that we take the forum to the people, that we go out into the highways and by-ways with a soap box. I think this is what we must do if the people are to be reached. It is well enough for us to come out to these meetings. I am a bit doubtful if we will continue to come. The people from back west will not. They get the feeling that they are being patronized, that we feel we are a superior type coming out to uplift them. We will meet with inevitable failure if this feeling becomes established.[1]

People had practically ceased dropping into the office. It was admitted in 1921 that the affairs of the Lower North Community Council had reached a crisis, and a meeting was called to determine whether it would not be better to discontinue. There were there, however, a few men and women whose interest in the "community" remained. Their faith in the possibility of making neighbors of the Gold Coast and of Little Hell was gone; but they still felt the appeal of the drama of the slum. It was voted to continue the Lower North Community Council, but to change its policies. The secretary was allowed to resign to accept another position. The budget was cut in half. The efforts directed at the arousing of community feeling and neighborliness ceased. The *Lower North Community Council Bulletin* was discontinued. Community sings and celebrations were abandoned. A young woman from the Gold Coast became secretary,

[1] *Second Annual Report of the Chairman of the Forum Committee;* see also *Lower North Community Council Bulletin*, Vol. I, No. 9, August, 1920. Italics are the author's.

working on a part-time basis. For a period the Council drifted without well-defined policies, doing a hybrid sort of welfare work in the tenements or the slum, continuing its Monday night forums as meetings at the office, trying to discover its place in the district.

During 1922 the Lower North Community Council became involved in two local controversies. These controversies marked the turning-point in the history of the Council. From its experience with these controversies the Council derived a totally different conception of community organization. The controversies arose over attempts to put bath houses on the Oak Street beach, and the attempt of a group of property owners along the Lake Shore Drive to change the provision of the zoning ordinance.

The beach at the foot of Oak Street is small and has no bath houses to take care of the thousands who flock to it on hot summer days and nights from back in the rooming-house district and the slum. Conditions on the beach, sanitary and moral, had become a community scandal. In the summer of 1922 the Lower North Community Council tried to get the permission of the residents along the Lake Shore Drive for erection of bath houses and comfort stations to take care of the crowds. The Council worked in co-operation with the Lincoln Park Commissioners, who prepared the necessary factual data. But——and others flatly refused to allow it. And the influence of these residents proved greater than the combined influence of the Community Coun cil, the ward alderman, and the Lincoln Park Commission.

During the preliminary discussion of the zoning project and the actual work of the Zoning Commission the Lower North Community Council tried consistently to keep the people of the Near North Side intelligently informed as to what was going on. Members of the Council regularly attended meetings of the Zoning Commission. The Zoning Ordinance, when passed, provided that North Michigan Avenue, south of Oak Street, be given over to business, but that north of Oak Street the Drive should be reserved for residences. At preliminary hearings this provision, based on present usage, seemed to satisfy everyone.

But later the estates of ——, ——, and others, about a dozen all told, petitioned that the entire length of Lake Shore Drive be zoned for business, and they threatened to use their influence to defeat the whole ordinance unless their request was complied with. The Zoning Commission gave in before the threat. Not only the group of estates on the Drive, but also the North Central Business Men's Association, were behind the demand.

Leaders in the community saw in it, however, a blow at the welfare of the entire district. Had the Drive been so zoned it would have meant, not only that the residential desirability of the Drive itself would have been destroyed, but that the desirability of the side streets in the neighborhood would have been destroyed as well, and that the neighborhood would eventually have become such a one as that about South Michigan Avenue. The Community Council sent postals to all property owners in the eastern part of the community, the part directly concerned, advising them of the proposed change, that the final decision would be reached at the next hearing of the Zoning Commission, and urging them to attend. The critical meeting was attended by so many property owners that it had to be held in the council chambers. It was the beginning of a fight that went through five hearings of the Commission. Finally, through the efforts of the Community Council, the opposing factions were brought together. The —— estates found many of their intimate friends opposing them. Personal attitudes played an important part in the settlement. Additional forces enlisted by the Community Council were the alderman and the tax commissioner, who threatened to tax the Drive property on the same basis as the Loop property if the usage were changed. —— was finally won over, and a compromise was agreed upon whereby the nature of the neighborhood will not be materially changed and the Lake Shore Drive will become much such a street as Fifth Avenue.

We learned a great deal about community life from these experiences. We had already learned that in the city black and white, rich and poor, Protestant and Catholic, cannot be gotten to rub elbows and be neighbors as people do in small towns. The city just isn't like that. In the city people get together in groups on the basis of their differences, and these groups won't mingle. But if they are taken as they are, they can be manipulated. This means knowing the community, taking it as it is, finding out what groups are in it, who are the influential members of those groups, what are their interests, what are their attitudes toward each other. With this information, if issues or community crises arise, the Community Council can do something. But the old "be neighbors" stuff is a waste of time.[1]

As a result of these experiences the Lower North Community Council began to take a realistic rather than an idealistic attitude toward community life. Instead of setting up an ideal program of human relationships to be realized in the community, it began to take the community as it is, to try to analyze the forces at work in the community, the cross-currents of influence, the nuclei of action, and to try to learn how the forces and groups of the community could be manipulated.

The attitude of the Community Council toward the community changed slowly, of course. It is still far from objective, not to say mechanistic. Old attitudes remain, sentimental interests, vestiges of patronage. A great deal of "uplift" is still necessary to maintain the interest and good will of the contributors. But the tendency is markedly in the direction of a realistic approach to community life. And this realism is the most significant achievement in the whole field of community organization. To this realism has recently been added, through the interested influence of the University of Chicago, an experimental temper.

The history of Near North Side settlements and school centers, and of the Lower North Community Council, throws interesting sidelights upon the nature of local life in the city as revealed in the foregoing chapters. It demonstrates beyond the shadow of doubt the impossibility of converting local areas of the city into "villages" with the

Document 71.

neighborliness, face-to-face contacts, and emotional attitudes of the village of a generation ago. These various attempts at community organization have met with little response from local groups.

This lack of response seems due, for one thing, to a total
lack of any community of interest over local areas. It is
peculiarly significant that the moment the forums of the
Lower North Community Council turned from subjects of
general interest to local problems, the attendance at the
forum dropped to a mere handful, and this handful a group
of hobos and rooming-house dwellers who come night after
night because, as one of them said, "After all, it's something
to do." The only issue that can bring out a larger gathering
is an issue affecting property values—the Zoning Ordinance,
the proposals to widen the Lake Shore Drive and La Salle
Street, the traction ordinance—and these issues bring out
only people from the Gold Coast. The rest of the Near
North Side's population of ninety thousand persons either
remains totally indifferent, as does the lodging-house population, or expresses its interests through devious "political"
channels, as does the population of Little Sicily. It is impossible either to discover or create local issues that will
bring out a response from the so-called "community" as a
whole.

Even more significant in accounting for the failure of the
traditional type of community organization on the Near
North Side are the barriers of social distance—the lack of
understanding and the emotional attitudes that have grown
up about this lack of understanding—that exist between the
various local groups within the area. The Gold Coast, the
world of furnished rooms, the Rialto of the half-world, and
Little Hell are totally different worlds which altogether fail

to comprehend one another; which, from widely varying backgrounds of experience, have built up attitudes that tend inevitably to maintain their relationships on a secondary basis and to prevent any real mingling among them.

The efforts to bring about such a mingling have brought out interesting instances of these attitudinal barriers. The inability of the members of one social world to comprehend those of another was recently amusingly illustrated in the case of a man from the Gold Coast who decided to run for office in the ward. Before going campaigning in Little Sicily he got down an old hunting suit from the attic, collected some dust from behind a picture with which to soil his collar, and disarranged his clothes generally to give the appearance of being "one of them." A local judge, within the year, sharply rebuked a Sicilian for being unable to speak English after seven years' residence in this country. A settlement worker interpreted. "Well," exclaimed the judge, "you speak Italian? You must have lived in Italy a long time. Lord! It would take me twenty years to learn that lingo!" The vestryman of a wealthy church protested violently against preaching to the Sicilians in their own language. "Every one of them can speak English as well as you or I!" "How do you know?" asked the Italian pastor. "Know? I can tell it by looking at them!" When a girl from the Gold Coast who was playing the piano for a class at Eli Bates House was spoken to on the street by a Sicilian who had seen her about the settlement there was talk on the Gold Coast of kidnaping and the Black Hand.

In all these efforts at organization in the "community" there has been a considerable element of patronage. The people of Little Hell have been quick to sense this. Even during the war it proved difficult to find common meeting places because many of the women of the Gold Coast found it distasteful to go into the slum; and the women of the slum felt they were being patronized when they were asked to the mansions on the Lake Shore Drive.[1] There is still a note of uplift about the work of the Lower North Community Council. And unless it had this note, unless givers could feel that they were uplifting the slum mother speaking her broken English, and the little ragamuffin on the street, no money could be raised for its work.

The subjects discussed at the forum are now carefully censored because of the violent prejudices brought out by such subjects as "Why starve in the midst of plenty?" once debated there. The Gold Coast is suspicious of the economic doctrines of the forum clientèle and of the whole world of furnished rooms and the slum from which they come. Everyone west of State Street is a "red." The epithet "red" can damn anyone, and very nearly start a panic, in the neighborhood of the Lake Shore Drive. At a forum meeting of the Lower North Community Council not long ago the chairman of the educational committee got up to report upon the securing of a continuation school for the district. She was greeted with applause by the audience, composed of people from the rooming-houses, "Dill Picklers," and "reds" from "Bughouse Square." But when she closed her remarks with the comment that "the continuation school will make children much more valuable to their employers" there was a stony silence as she sat down. This local "ethnocentrism" often amounts to a downright provincialism. A prominent Chicagoan, a resident of the Gold Coast, protested to the Chicago Plan Commission against the widening of the Lake Lake Shore Drive and the Esplanade. When asked his

[1] Document 71.

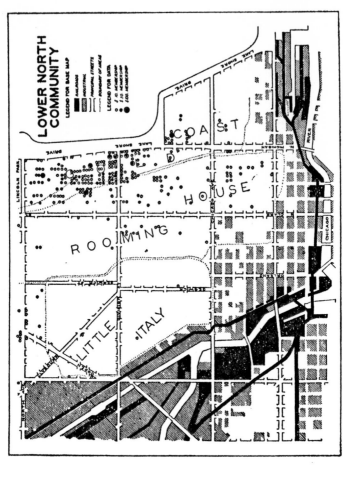

THE LOWER NORTH COMMUNITY COUNCIL.—The Lower North Community Council set out to make a little town out of the Near North Side, to make "neighbors" out of its residents. It started a campaign for five thousand members representing every element of the area. But the area did not respond. And the map of the membership of the Lower North Community Council shows it to be merely a local social agency, supported by the "Gold Coast."

reason, he replied, "I am near-sighted, and if the Drive is widened I won't be able to see the lake from my library windows." The outlook of the Gold Coast is bounded by State Street; it tends to make itself the measure of all things. A few years ago, when Thompson was running for re-election, one of its matrons remarked, "Why, Thompson simply can't win. *Everybody* I talk to is against him." But Thompson won. The Gold Coast was similarly astonished, more recently, when Small was re-elected governor. It was interesting to find that the persons on the Gold Coast who wrote documents on the "social ritual" invariably compared themselves with the Wilson Avenue district which they drive through on their way to Lake Forest—never to the part of their own "community" lying west of State Street.

The "other half," of course, is equally unable to comprehend the Gold Coast. We have already remarked that the young "Gold Coaster" who gave the open houses to the ward was frequently approached for favors and money. The residents of the "Rialto" and of Little Hell could not be convinced that he was not trying to work up a political following. Similarly, when the representatives of the various foreign groups who were on the committees of the Lower North Community Council found the Council's program was non-political, they soon lost interest and became suspicious that the council was merely another bit of patronage and uplift.

The Lower North Community Council is today merely a social agency. Its program is determined, not in a "community" council, but by an executive committee composed largely of people who live on the Gold Coast. Its work is done by a paid secretary and paid social workers. The money for carrying on its work is contributed in part by "wealthy members" on the Gold Coast; the remainder is raised by a benefit which is one of the smartest affairs of the social season.[1] It is a community council, in the traditional meaning of the words, only in name. It is nearer to a local council of social agencies. While it has worked out, from its experience, a technique that is a significant contribution to the community organization movement, it is at the same time a living monument to the neighborly type of social relations that were a part of the life of the village, but which have been engulfed in the expansion of the modern city.

[1] The story of the financing of the Lower North Community Council is an interesting one. The original plan was that it should be financed by five thousand one-dollar memberships. When this plan failed, a finance committee was appointed. It raised most of the budget on the Gold Coast, but it raised a considerable budget. Gradually members of the finance committee lost interest. Soon the executive committee found itself forced to raise the budget among friends of its members. Finally, in 1925, the executive committee was faced by the alternatives of greatly cutting down the council's program, of contributing a large part of the budget itself, or of giving a benefit.

It was decided to give a benefit. The benefit was a dance at the Casino. The invitation list was taken from the lists of Bachelors and Benedicts and the Twelfth Night Ball. The dance was one of the season's most exclusive affairs. Columns were devoted to it by society editors. Its list was ranked with that of the dinner given earlier in the season for the Prince of Wales as the criterion of social position. Similarly Eli Bates House must have a benefit performance of the Chauve Souris or the Music Box Revue, to which tickets are sold at ten dollars each, and at which all society is seen, to get up enough interest in Little Sicily to carry on settlement work. The story of the financing of settlements and "community" organizations in the inner areas of the city is a significant comment on the nature of local life in these areas.

CHAPTER XI

THE CITY AND THE COMMUNITY

The story of the Lower North Community Council is repeated again and again in the history of the community organization movement, a history identical with that of every projected social reform. The man with the muckrake lays bare the facts, and demands immediate administrative reform. The social worker eagerly steps in. Then a group of philosophically minded individuals become interested in the problem, feeling that if only they could draw up some sort of program people could be induced to act upon it and an ideal social order could be realized. Such a program was the keynote of the Madison Conference. Eduard C. Lindeman closes his recent book on the community with "A Twentieth-Century Confession of Faith." Miss Follett organizes *The New State* about a mystical, idealized conception of community.

But frequently, all too frequently, the realization of those programs meets with obstacles. Human nature offers some opposition; traditions and institutions offer more; and the very physical configuration of the "community" is unyielding to change. It becomes apparent that the life of a local area has a natural organization which must be taken into account. It becomes necessary to inquire into the nature of the community; to discover how the community acts, how it sets up standards, defines aims and ends, gets things done; and to analyze what has been the effect of the growth of the city upon the life of local areas, what changes in the community have come with the industrial city.

THE NATURE OF COMMUNITY

The word "community" is variously used and loosely defined. Rural districts are referred to as communities. Towns and villages are termed communities. Local areas within the city are "communities." We hear of the "community of Chicago," of the "American community," and of the "world community." We read of economic communities, of political communities, and of cultural communities. In all these usages, with the exception of that of "cultural communities," "community" would seem to imply some sort of community of interest among the members of a group, thought of with reference to their spatial distribution. The concept "cultural community" has a different content. The cultural community is defined primarily in terms of the common experiences of the group, and only secondarily in terms of its interests. It is with this content that the word "community" is used by the sociologist.

There is a noticeable tendency among those working in the research field to restrict still further the use of the term to designate a local area, spatially distinct from adjoining areas, such as the village or the "local community" of the city, over which are distributed a group of persons having a common background of experience. The actual study of communities, of so-called "communities," and of attempts at "community" organization has given us a clearer conception of what community is. An area does not become a community merely by virtue of having distributed over it a number of people and institutions, or by these people having certain interests in common. Still less does it become a community by virtue of being an administrative political unit. An area becomes a community only through the common experiences of the people who live in it, resulting in their becoming a cultural group, with traditions, sentiments and attitudes, and memories in common—a focus of belief, feeling, and action. A community, then, is a local area over which people are using the same language, conforming to the same mores, feeling more or less the same sentiments, and acting upon the same attitudes. Such is the community, mechanistically defined.[1]

The example *par excellence* of the community is the village; and it is the village type of life that community organizers have tried to recreate in the city. The village is a homogeneous, relatively undifferentiated social group. Its population is relatively one in social and economic status. There are few contrasts between the accepted and the outlandish. Every social situation has been defined for generations, and the person is made to conform to the traditional behavior patterns. Persons respond to situations with common attitudes. Where the person cannot meet the situation for himself, the community meets it for him. In a crisis the group acts as one.

The best analysis of the community and its control has been given us by W. I. Thomas, in *The Polish Peasant in Europe and America*, and in *The Unadjusted Girl:*

> The child is always born into a group of people among whom all the general types of situation which may arise have been defined and corresponding rules of conduct developed, and where he has not the slightest chance of making his definitions and following his wishes without interference.

> The family is the smallest social unit, and the primary agency through which the community defines behavior. As soon as the child has free motion and begins to pull, tease, pry, meddle, and prowl, the parents begin to define the situation through speech and other signs

[1] As opposed to the wishful definition of community organizers in terms of proximity, or of hypothetically common interests and needs.

and pressures: "Be quiet," "Sit up straight," "Blow your nose," "Wash your face," "Mind your mother," "Be kind to sister," etc. His wishes and activities begin to be inhibited, and gradually, by definitions within the family, by playmates in the school, in the Sunday school, in the community, through reading, by formal instruction, by informal signs of approval and disapproval, the growing member learns the code of society.

In addition to the family we have the community as a defining agency. Originally the community was practically the whole world of its members. It was composed of families interrelated by blood and marriage, and was not so large that all the members could not come together; it was a face-to-face group. I asked a Polish peasant what was the extent of *okolica*, or neighborhood—how far it reached. "It reaches," he said, "as far as the report of a man reaches—as far as a man is talked about." The community regulates the behavior of its members largely by talking about them. Gossip is a mode of defining a situation in a given case, and of attaching praise and blame. It is one of the means by which the status of the individual and of his family is fixed.

The community also, particularly in connection with gossip, knows how to attach opprobrium to persons and actions by using epithets which are at the same time brief and emotional definitions of the situation. "Bastard," "whore," "traitor," "coward," "skunk," "scab," "snob," "kike," etc., are such epithets. In *Faust* the community said of Margaret, "She stinks." The people are here employing a device known in psychology as the "conditioned reflex." If, for example, you place before a child (say six months old) an agreeable object, a kitten, and at the same time pinch the child, and if this is repeated several times, the child will immediately cry at the sight of the kitten; or if a dead rat were always served beside a man's plate of soup he would eventually have a disgust for soup when served separately. If the word "stinks" is associated on people's tongues with Margaret, Margaret will never again smell sweet. Winks, shrugs, nudges, sneers, haughtiness, coldness, "giving the once over," are also language defining situations and painfully felt as unfavorable recognition. In this whole connection fear is used by the group to produce the desired attitudes in its members. Praise is used also, but sparingly. And the whole body of habits and emotions is so much a community product that disapproval or separation is unbearable. This set of habits and reactions developed socially, under family, church, and community influence, may become almost as definite as the mechanistic adjustments the psychologists call instinct. Indeed, the "folkways" become equivalent in force to the instincts, and even displace them.[1]

No community, of course, is successful in defining situations so completely that the wishes of its members are absolutely regulated. There are occasions when a recalcitrant member, opposing his wishes to the will of the group, gets temporarily out of hand. The whole community then steps in to discipline him. In the European peasant village this community action involves a minimum of deliberation, consisting rather in an interaction of primary attitudes—immediate, concrete, and emotional—that amounts almost to crowd behavior.

In front of the volost administration building there stands a crowd of some 150 men. This means that a volost meeting has been called to consider the verdict of the Kusmin rural commune "regarding the handing over to the [state] authorities of the peasant Gregori Siedov, caught red-handed and convicted of horse-stealing." Siedov had already been held for judicial inquiry; the evidence against him was irrefutable and he would undoubtedly be sentenced to the penitentiary. In view of this I endeavor to explain that the verdict in regard to his exile is wholly superfluous and will only cause a deal of trouble; and that at the termination of the sentence of imprisonment of Siedov the commune will unfailingly be asked whether it wants him back or prefers that he be exiled. Then, I said, in any event it would be necessary to formulate a verdict in regard to the "non-reception" of Siedov, while at this stage all the trouble was premature and could lead to nothing. But the meeting did not believe my words, did not trust the court, and wanted to settle the matter right then and there; the general hatred of horse-thieves was too keen. . . . .

The decisive moment has arrived; the head-man "drives" all the judges-elect to one side; the crowd stands with a gloomy air, trying

[1] Adapted from W. I. Thomas, *The Unadjusted Girl*, pp. 42–59.

not to look at Siedov and his wife, who are crawling before the mir on their knees. "Old men, whoever pities Gregori, will remain in his place, and whoever does not forgive him will step to the right," cries the head man. The crowd wavered and rocked, but remained dead still on the spot; no one dared to be the first to take the fatal step. Gregori feverishly ran over the faces of his judges with his eyes, trying to read in these faces pity for him. His wife wept bitterly, her face close to the ground; beside her, finger in mouth and on the point of screaming, stood a three-year-old youngster (at home Gregori had four more children). . . . . But straightway one peasant steps out of the crowd; two years before someone had stolen a horse from him. "Why should we pity him? Did he pity us?" says the old man, and stooping goes over to the right side. "That is true; bad grass must be torn from the field," says another one from the crowd, and follows the old man. The beginning had been made. At first individually and then in whole groups the judges-elect proceeded to go over to the right. The man condemned by public opinion ran his head into the ground, beat his breast with his fists, seized those who passed him by their coat-tails, crying: "Ivan Timofeich, Uncle Leksander, Vasinka, dear kinsman! Wait, kinsmen, let me say a word. . . . . Petrushenka!" But, without stopping and with stern faces, the members of the mir dodged the unfortunates, who were crawling at their feet. . . . . At last the wailing of Gregori stopped; around him for the space of three sazen the place was empty; there was no one to implore. All the judges-elect, with the exception of one, an uncle of the man to be exiled, had gone over to the right. The woman cried sorrowfully, while Gregori stood motionless on his knees, his head lowered, stupidly looking at the ground.[1]

Absolute unanimity of opinion is the essential of community action. If a member of the group persists in holding out against the common will every resource of the community is mobilized to force his conforming, every emotional attitude arising out of the common experience of the group is appealed to.

[1] "V Volostnikh Pisaryakh" ("A Village Secretary"), p. 283, quoted in W. I. Thomas, *The Unadjusted Girl*, pp. 47–48.

It sometimes happens that all except one may agree, but the motion is never carried if that one refuses to agree to it. In such cases all endeavor to talk over and persuade the stiff-necked one. Often they even call to their aid his wife, his children, his relatives, his father-in-law, and his mother, that they may prevail upon him to say yes. Then all assail him and say to him from time to time: "Come now, God he.p you, agree with us too, that this may take place as we wish it, that the house may not be cast into disorder, that we may not be talked about by the people, that the neighbors may not hear of it, that the world may not make sport of us." It seldom occurs in such cases than unanimity is not attained.[1]

If the community is an Anglo-Saxon village, the rebel may be disciplined, not by the community as a whole, but by the elders of the community church, by the village council, or by the town meeting. In any case the result is the same. The rebel confesses, repents, acknowledges the code, and is reincorporated into the community; or he is cast out. The solidarity of the community is preserved. To all intents and purposes the village has no social problems.

All communal action in village communities is of this type, whether the question be over a violation of the mores or a settlement of land. In the American village, as in the Polish village, it consists in a "mass meeting" which the whole countryside attends. In the American village there is some pretense of parliamentary procedure. The Polish village acts more nearly as a crowd.

Communities of the type of the peasant village of Europe, or the early American town, are not found in the modern city. Yet in the outlying areas of the city there are local groups conforming to our conception of a cultural community, local groups having a common body of experience and attitudes, and capable of common action. We have seen

[1] F. S. Krauss, *Sitte und Brauch der Südslaven*, p. 103, quoted in W. I. Thomas, *The Unadjusted Girl*.

how a Rogers Park becomes aroused over the encroachment of clandestine vice, or a Hyde Park becomes aroused over delinquency, how mass meetings are held and community programs are adopted. But such instances of community action are rare enough to deserve columns on the first page of the metropolitan press. As a glimpse of the life of the Gold Coast, of Little Hell, of Towertown, or of the world of furnished rooms so vividly shows, local areas of the city are vastly different from the village, and over great areas of the city the last vestiges of the community are disappearing. The problem of local action and community is bound up with the growth of the city.

The nature of the changes in local life in the city has already been indicated in the concrete materials on the life of local groups within the Near North Side. A discussion of the processes involved in the growth of the city cannot fail, however, to throw these changes into relief.

THE GROWTH OF THE CITY

The most obvious fact about the growth of cities is the aggregation of population by which it is accompanied. It is customary to measure the growth of the city in terms of its area and the number of its people. Weber and Bücher have given an excellent discussion of this aspect of the city's growth.[1] Obviously this very aggregation involves consequences of significance for community life. But those who attempted to deal with the growth of the city, particularly those who attempted to predict the nature and direction of its growth—the realtor, the planning commission, the utilities company—soon discovered the city to be more than an aggregation; they discovered the city to be an organization displaying certain typical processes in its growth.

[1] Weber. *The Growth of Cities;* and Bücher, *Industrial Revolution.*

While the community organizer has been ignoring these processes, or working against them, the realtor and the utility expert, the city planning commission, and more recently the student of society in the university, have been seeking an understanding of them which would give some measure of control over the city's growth.

The most overt of the processes exhibited by the city's growth is that of expansion.

The expansion of the city from the standpoint of the city plan, zoning, and regional surveys is thought of almost wholly in terms of its physical growth. . . . . No study of expansion as a process has yet been made, although the materials for such a study and intimations of different aspects of the process are contained in city planning, zoning, and regional surveys. The typical processes of the expansion of the city can best be illustrated, perhaps, by a series of concentric circles, which may be numbered to designate both the successive zones of urban extension and the types of areas differentiated in the process of expansion.

Such a chart represents an ideal construction of the tendencies of any town or city to expand radially from its central business district—on the map, the Loop.[1] Encircling the downtown area there is normally an area in transition, which is being invaded by business and light manufacture (II). A third area (III) is inhabited by the workers in industries who have escaped from the area of deterioration (II), but who desire to live within easy access of their work. Beyond this zone

[1] This conception is perhaps implicit in some of the literature of the "muckrake," e.g., in Lincoln Steffen's *The Shame of the Cities*. But the first notable approximation to a natural history of the city was a small book by a real estate man, Richard M. Hurd, entitled *Principles of City Land Values* (1903). In attempting to generalize the fluctuations of land values in the city, Hurd found it necessary to describe certain processes typical of city growth, to treat of the city's growth in generalized terms. The surveys made by the Bell Telephone Company, and other public utilities, to predict the city's growth in anticipation of extension for future service, and the Plan for the Study of New York and its Environs, as well as the Chicago Regional Planning Association, are other attempts to analyze and manipulate the natural processes involved in the growth of the city.

is the "residential area (IV) of high-class apartment buildings or of exclusive "restricted" districts of single family dwellings. Still farther, out beyond the city limits, is the commuters' zone—suburban areas, or satellite cities—within a thirty- to sixty-minute ride of the central business district.

This chart brings out clearly the main fact of expansion, namely, the tendency of each inner zone to extend its area by the invasion of the next outer zone. This aspect of expansion may be called *succession*, a process which has been studied in detail in plant ecology. If this chart is applied to Chicago, all four of these zones were in its early history included in the circumference of the inner zone, the present business district. The present boundaries of the area of deterioration were not many years ago those of the zone now inhabited by independent wage-earners, and within the memories of thousands of Chicagoans contained the residences of the "best families."

Besides extension and succession, the general process of expansion in urban growth involves the antagonistic and yet complementary processes of concentration and decentralization. In all cities there is the natural tendency for local and outside transportation to converge in the central business district. In the downtown section of every large city we expect to find the department stores, the skyscraper office buildings, the railroad stations, the great hotels, the theaters, the art museum, and the city hall. Quite naturally, almost inevitably, the economic, cultural, and political life centers here. The relation of centralization to other processes of city life may be roughly gauged by the fact that over half a million people daily enter and leave Chicago's Loop. More recently sub-business centers have grown up in outlying zones. These "satellite loops" do not, it seems, represent the "hoped for" revival of the neighborhood, but rather a telescoping of several local communities into a larger economic unity. The Chicago of yesterday, an agglomeration of country towns and immigrant colonies, is undergoing a process of reorganization into a centralized decentralized system of local communities coalescing into sub-business areas visibly or invisibly dominated by the central business district.[1]

---

[1] E. W. Burgess, "The Growth of the City," in R. E. Park and E. W. Burgess, *The City*, pp. 50–51.

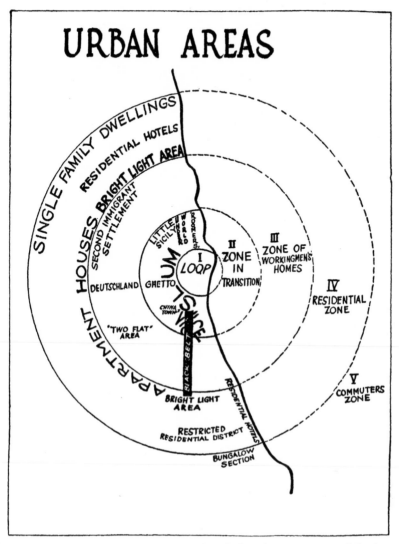

URBAN AREAS

SINGLE FAMILY DWELLINGS

RESIDENTIAL HOTELS

BRIGHT LIGHT AREA

SECOND IMMIGRANT SETTLEMENT

APARTMENT HOUSES

LITTLE SICILY

UNDER WORLD

ROOMERS

II ZONE IN TRANSITION

III ZONE OF WORKINGMEN'S HOMES

I LOOP

SLUM

RESTRICTED

DEUTSCHLAND

GHETTO

CHINA TOWN

IV RESIDENTIAL ZONE

"TWO FLAT" AREA

BLACK BELT

V COMMUTERS ZONE

BRIGHT LIGHT AREA

RESIDENTIAL HOTELS

RESTRICTED RESIDENTIAL DISTRICT

BUNGALOW SECTION

THE ANATOMY OF THE CITY.—The above chart discloses the gross anatomy of the city, the typical zones into which every city segregates as it expands. The chart shows, further, the segregation of typical cultural areas of Chicago within these zones (chart after Burgess).

THE STRUCTURE OF THE CITY

Such is a generalized description of the processes of *expansion, succession,* and *"centralized decentralization"* displayed in the growth of every city. It is a description, moreover, of the gross anatomy of the city. The concentric circles, or zones, represent the typical structure of a modern commercial and industrial city. Of course, no city quite conforms to this ideal scheme. Physical barriers such as rivers, lakes, rises of land, and the like may modify the growth and structure of the city, as is strikingly demonstrated in the cases of New York, Pittsburgh, and Seattle. Railroads, with their belts of industry cut through this generalized scheme, breaking the city up into sections. And lines of local transportation, along the more traveled of which grow up retail business streets, further modify the structure of the city.

The structure of the individual city, then, while always exhibiting the generalized zones described before, is built about this framework of transportation, business organization and industry, park and boulevard systems, and topographical features. All these tend to break up the city into numerous smaller areas, which we may call *natural areas,* in that they are unplanned, natural product of the city's growth. Railroad and industrial belts, park and boulevard systems, lakes and rivers, act as boundaries of these natural areas; while their centers are usually the intersection of two or more business streets. By virtue of proximity to industry, business, transportation, or natural advantages, each area acquires a physical individuality of its own, accurately reflected in land values and rents.[1]

[1] These natural areas, which are usually "trade areas," are not to be confused with communities. They are the result of the economic rather than of the cultural process. Communities may or may not conform to natural

Within the limits of these broader zones and of these natural areas, competition, economic and cultural, segregates the population.[1] There is no phenomenon more characteristic of city life, as contrasted with the life of the rural community or the village, than that of segregation. The village is relatively undifferentiated; its population is relatively of one economic and social class; the business area is the general store; the characteristic areas within the village are confined to a few shacks along the railroad, or to a "darky town." But the sharp contrasts of the city, emphasized as they are by segregation over given areas, are familiar to everyone: the great central business district, with its towering buildings and thronged streets; the railroads lined with smoking industries; slums and foreign colonies; the "bright light area" and the "red light district"; bleak areas of deteriorated dwellings, small businesses and "furnished rooms"; mile after mile of apartment houses;

areas, and natural areas may exist without corresponding communities, as the Near North Side clearly illustrates. Natural areas, moreover, are not always so well defined as this ideal scheme might seem to indicate. In a city like Chicago, where natural barriers are few, a natural area may be defined almost wholly in terms of land values, as is the case of the area occupied by the Gold Coast on the Near North Side.

Zoning ordinances may create natural areas by forming "barriers" to movements of population. However, a study of the relationship of zoning ordinances to the physical structure of the city, in the cases of Chicago and Cleveland, for example, indicates that zoning ordinances tend merely to add a legal definition to pre-existing natural areas. The Gold Coast has been guaranteed for another decade, at least, against the press of business and the rooming-house, by the recent zoning ordinance of Chicago.

[1] The modern city, industrial or commercial, like the plant or animal community, is largely an ecological product; that is, the rate and direction of the city's growth, the distribution of city features, the segregation of communities within the city, are by-products of the economic process—in which land values, rents, and wages are fixed—and the unintended result of competition.

outlying districts of single homes and dormitory sub-urbs. Nor is this segregation accidental. It is the result of competition and the economic processes which fix the utility and value of the land, determine the rent the land will derive, and consequently prescribe more or less rigor-ously the usage to which the land will be put.

Physical geography, natural advantages, and the means of trans-portation determine in advance the general outlines of the urban plan. As the city increases in population, the subtler influences of sympathy, rivalry, and economic necessity tend to control the distribution of population. Business and manufacturing seek advantageous locations and draw around them a certain portion of the population. There spring up fashionable residence quarters, from which the poorer classes are excluded because of the increased value of the land. Then there grow up slums which are inhabited by great numbers of the poorer classes who are unable to defend themselves from association with the derelict and vicious. Every great city has its racial colonies, like the Chinatowns of San Francisco and New York, the Little Sicily of Chicago, and various other less pronounced types. In addition to these, most cities have their segregated vice districts, like that which recently existed in Chicago, and their rendezvous for criminals of all sorts. Every large city has its occupational suburbs, like the stock-yards of Chicago, and its residence suburbs, like Brookline, in Boston, each of which has the size and the character of a complete separate town, village, or city, except that its population is a selected one. Un-doubtedly the most remarkable of these cities within cities, of which the most interesting characteristics is that they are composed of persons of the same race, or of persons of different races but of the same social class, is East London, with a population of two million laborers.

In the course of time every section and quarter of the city takes on something of the character and qualities of its inhabitants. Each separate part of the city is inevitably stained with the peculiar senti-ments of its population.[1]

[1] Adapted from Robert E. Park, "Suggestions for the Study of Behavior in the Urban Environment," *The City*, pp. 6, 12.

Through this process of segregation each natural area in the city takes on a color which sets it off from adjoining areas, and the city becomes a mosaic of neighborhoods, "communities," and little cultural worlds. But these areas are not distributed throughout the city at random. The striking contrasts and the heterogeneity which these numerous segregated areas of the city present, resolve, upon analysis, into the more generalized zones which we have already discussed. Segregated areas of a given type, wherever they may be located in a given city with respect to other such areas, invariably fall, in every city, within one of these larger and well-defined zones. And this follows from the fact that, important as cultural factors are in the ultimate segregation, the broad outlines of segregation within the city are fixed within the economic process. Because of the character that attaches to these segregated areas, lends them a certain identity, and tends to set them off from one another, it has been customary to look upon these areas as communities. But other processes which are a part with the growth of the city run counter to these tendencies, and have made many of these local areas within the city anything but communities.

PHYSICAL CHANGE AND SOCIAL CHANGE

The very march of the city, as commerce and industry push out from its center, encroaching upon residential neighborhoods, turning the population back upon itself, results in a physical instability and change which has significant implications for local life. We have seen how commerce and industry are constantly expanding, at once creating and reorganizing the slum; how the slum eats its way into adjacent areas, converting apartments into tenements and rooming-houses, wiping out whole communities before it; how apartment areas push their way into outlying residential areas which, giving way in turn, sprawl out into the country. The history of the Near North Side has shown that no area or group can long withstand the pressure of this relentless succession, fashionable residential districts giving way as rapidly as slums.[1]

Fashionable residential streets have become the heart of the rooming-house district; rooming-houses have become tenements; tenements have been reclaimed for studios and shops. Group has succeeded group; the world of fashion has become the world of furnished rooms, and into this world have come the slatternly residents of the slum. The Irish Kilgubbin has become the Swedish Smoky Hollow; the Swedish Smoky Hollow, a Little Sicily; and now Little Sicily becomes a Negro quarter.

As the physical growth of the city carries before it the little cultural worlds, the local groups, which make up its population, it wipes out the physical symbols of their identity. The town has its old church, in which everyone has been christened, married, and buried for generations. In the town cemetry are the graves of its heroes; the town finds there its history graven in stone, and each family finds there symbols that are the basis of emotional bonds of solidarity. The homes of the town's founders and notables

---

[1] A generation is as long a period as any area has been able to maintain itself as a fashionable residence area. In the slum, both on the Near West Side and on the Near North Side, the Irish, Swedes, Germans, and Italians have maintained their original communities not more than a generation (see *Hull House Maps*).

On the Near North Side during the writer's two years of residence there has been a startlingly rapid physical change which has completely altered the outward aspect of many neighborhoods and presages further cultural succession.

stand as visible symbols of the past, and are pointed to each succeeding generation. About these and other symbols gather the traditions, rituals, and sentiments that make up the community's history and are the core of its self-consciousness and solidarity. They are visible and permanent symbols which serve as the physical basis of the community's continuity. But local groups in the city have no such symbols. As the succession of the city pushes the groups farther and farther from its center, these physical symbols are abandoned and destroyed. The physical basis of local cultural unity ceases to exist, and with it many of the local group's unifying and controlling traditions.[1]

We have already seen that the same competitive process which has made of the city a mosaic of cultural units, and which has resulted in the succession of these cultural units over given local areas, has also resulted in a grosser segregation which has taken business and industry outside the community and has located it in well-defined belts or zones. Now practically the entire population of the city goes outside the community, often eight and ten miles outside the community, every day of the year, to a diversity of occupations concentrated in the Loop or in outlying manufacturing districts.[2] There are no longer common economic activities

[1] The Swedish colony which formerly centered at the corner of Elm and Sedgewick streets, where stood its original church, has in fifty years moved four times, each time building a new church and making an attempt to maintain itself as a distinct community. But it has repeatedly been invaded by migrations of other national groups. Its last move has taken it beyond Cicero Avenue on the Northwest Side. Even here it is finding difficulty in maintaining its identity. The present community has no history. The younger generation is drifting away, as it has tended to do each time the colony has moved (see Document 72).

[2] On the Near North Side, for example, the entire population of the world of furnished rooms, such part of the population of the Gold Coast as has occupation, and practically the entire population of the slum, go to work outside the community.

carried on by the community as such; men who live side by side no longer spend the hours of the day working at tasks that bring them together. Economic activities, which were in the village a source of much of the community's common body of experience, serve in the city community, more often than not, to draw men apart, to give them separate interests and points of view.

In like fashion recreation has ceased to be a spontaneous communal activity, and has become a commercialized affair segregated in the Loop or in a few so-called "bright light" areas. Whereas the hours of leisure brought together the members of the village community in a group of common activities, these same leisure hours now disperse them in a diversity of activities and areas without the community.[1] The fact that occupational and recreational activities have been taken outside the community has important consequences for local life. A common group of activities out of which may grow a common body of experience and a common set of traditions and attitudes is the *sine qua non* of community life and collective action. Without this common group of activities, the community of tradition and attitudes of the local group in the city rapidly disintegrates.[2]

[1] In Little Sicily, a case in point, the village festa is abandoned by the younger generation in favor of the pool hall and the movie.

[2] Clubs, theaters, department stores, restaurants, the metropolitan press, have developed at the expense of local life and sentiment. These great Loop enterprises undermined like enterprises in local areas; the competition of the Loop proved too much for local business. All manner of activities were then brought from surrounding local areas into the Loop. This process was at its height between 1890 and 1915, being coincident with the growth of the metropolitan press and the Sunday newspaper.

Then during the war period a number of things began to happen. There were signs on the "L" platforms, advising people to "Trade in your own neighborhood." "Satellite" loops, like those at Cottage Grove Avenue and Sixty-Third Street, Wilson Avenue, and Sheridan Road, or Milwaukee Ave-

Another aspect of the growth of the city equally significant in its consequences for local life is the increasingly detailed division of labor which it entails. The outstanding economic phenomenon of the industrial society and the great city is this ever more minute and more rigidly defined division of labor. In Chicago, according to the 1920 census, approximately 1,000,000 persons gainfully employed reported 509 occupations, and the 1,000 and more men and women in *Who's Who* gave 116 different vocations.[1]

This division of labor, resulting in occupational differentiation, combined with the segregation of commerce and industry which has taken economic activities outside the community, has produced an organization of sentiment and interest along occupational rather than along local lines. Every occupation, in the life of the city, tends to assume the character of a profession. The discipline required for success in specialized vocations and the associations which it enforces emphasize this tendency.

---

nue and Ashland Avenue, sprang up. A number of local newspapers came into existence. Outlying areas began to compete with the Loop.

People interested in community organization immediately saw in all this a revival of local life and of local interest, and predicted a growth of political and social life about these local business centers. But their predictions have not been borne out. These satellite loops, while they have developed somewhat at the expense of the Loop, have developed more at the expense of surrounding neighborhoods. The "neighborhood" store turns out to be a chain store; the local newspaper a syndicate advertising sheet. The satellite loop is a purely economic phenomenon, representing the telescoping of a number of communities into an economic unit. It is not the longed-for and often heralded revival of community life in local areas.

[1] E. W. Burgess, "The Growth of the City," in R. E. Park, and E. W. Burgess, *The City*, p. 57.

A person's occupational activities, over a period of time, influence his social attitudes and give him an occupational attitude toward life. After observing men at work in many parts of the world, Whiting Williams concludes: "We tend to live our way into our thinking, more than to think our way into our living."

An occupation is a standardized, repeated, and persistent type of activity. It is a habitual way of acting, or a complex set of ways of doing, according to which persons make a living. Any type of doing concentrates attention upon certain objects and processes or values. The seeking of these values produces attitudes, or tendencies to act. Each occupation has its own peculiar problems, its own demands upon the attention of its representatives, and its peculiar influence upon the latter's mental development and social attitudes. Doing a thing or a set of things according to certain routines every day, in season and out, tends to create mental and emotional patterns.

Business activity yields money profits, which become a chief value for business men, with its correlative monetary attitudes of life that characterize business men and often unconsciously influence their thinking. Missionary activity bears fruit in "converts" who become "values," and a convert-hunting attitude of life develops. In politics, "votes" are perhaps the chief "values" that are sought; they create a vote-hunting attitude.

Occupational attitudes and values become conventional and more or less fixed. Each occupation has its own type of social interstimulation. People who are working at the same tasks come together to exchange ideas. They have much in common, and "shop talk" is a daily phenomenon. By daily meeting of the same type as one's self, who are doing about the same type as one's self, who are doing about the same things in a similar way, one's tendency to develop, not only occupational attitudes, but an occupational complex, is magnified. Each occupation has its own organizations and institutions through which occupational attitudes and values become crystallized. Occupational journals cater to the occupational minds of their respective constituents. Each boasts the occupational values it represents until its readers become steeped in an occupational tradition. Occupational attitudes and values become fixed in group heritages. Children are trained in these traditional lines of thinking from earliest infancy. Table talk and family conversation have their occupational stimuli.

Each occupation tends to develop its own heritages, slogans, beliefs, or even superstitions.

It would seem that two persons might start with about the same inherited predispositions, the same mental equipment, and by choosing different occupations—for example, one a money-making occupation, and another a service occupation such as missionary work—at the end of twenty-five years have become "successful" but have drifted so far apart in occupational and social attitudes as to have almost nothing in common.

Occupational attitudes create class cleavages and other social divisions. Occupational values often come to be rated so high that occupational groups seek social and political power. Business organizations seek to control legislation; organized labor enters politics; and even professional groups lobby, sometimes in questionable ways, for occupationally desirable laws.[1]

The following document, an interview with the senior member of one of Chicago's largest law firms, a highly specialized and widely recognized expert in his profession, whose home is on an exclusive residential street on the Near North Side, illustrates this process and its significance for local life.

Really, I could not name, off-hand, half a dozen men in the legal profession who live on the North Side. I know a good many lawyers, of course—but even among them I know only those who are in the same line of work that I am in, the carrying on of preliminary negotiations between groups to determine problems of policy.

The city law organization is a very specialized affair, a legal "department store." For example, there are twenty men in this office, each a specialist, in a particular department of the law—taxation, corporations, deeds, the criminal law, the arguing of appealed cases,

[1] Adapted from E. S. Bogardus, "The Occupational Attitude," *Journal of Applied Sociology*, VIII (January–February, 1924), 170–77. J. M. Williams, in his *Principles of Social Psychology*, gives a discussion of the operation of occupational attitudes in American life; and Thorstein Veblin, *The Theory of the Leisure Class*, is the classic discussion of the class attitudes of the wealthy.

etc.—and knowing as little, perhaps, as the layman about other departments of the law. And the specialization extends even farther.
There are many departments of the law which require a very specialized knowledge, but in which there is not enough call for opinion to
make it practicable for us to keep a specialist in them in our office.
But there are men in the city who perhaps handle all such cases that
arise in Chicago, and we can get these men here within twenty minutes
when we need them. For instance, we were recently asked to handle
an injunction. Such cases are rare, and there is no one in the office
familiar with the procedure. But there is one man in Chicago who
does nothing but handle injunctions, and we employed him to handle
the case. It results from this specialization that the lawyer's contacts
in his profession are much narrower than might be supposed.

The professional man, and especially the lawyer, travels a great
deal. The office here handles business in twenty states, and I am in
New York, Philadelphia, and Washington as much as I am in Chicago.
My professional interests are thus widely dispersed. Socially, too, I
have as many interests in these cities and in the suburbs of Chicago,
such as Lake Forest, as on the Lower North Side. There is, furthermore, no neighborliness among those who live on the North Side. I
live in a twenty-apartment hotel, and of the others who live in it I
have a speaking acquaintance with but five, and know but one. I do
not think there is any local attachment or feeling on the part of those
who live there—naturally there would not be. People live on the
Lake Shore Drive simply because it is the most expensive place in
the city to live.[1]

As a result of this process, the older organization of the
community, based on family ties and local associations, is
being replaced by an organization based upon vocational
interests and attitudes. This vocational organization cuts
across local areas; defines itself spatially as city-wide; and
takes much of the person's life out of the local community.
It is only the retail merchants and realtors, among these
vocational groupings, that tend to organize on the basis of

[1] Document 73.

locality. Their organization is only for the performance of certain economic services, and has little relation to the other persons in the community. While it is not accurate to state the contrast between city and village as one between secondary and primary relationships, yet it is true that there is an increasingly large number of secondary relationships involved in the life of the city, and that primary contacts in the city tend to depend increasingly upon occupational interest rather than upon contiguity of residence. The person's sentiments, like his economic activities and interests, tend to find their object outside the community.

THE RISE OF SOCIAL DISTANCE

The segregation of the city's population into local areas characterized by sharply differentiated cultural traits, and the rise of occupational groups, have been accompanied by another process which we may designate *the building up of social distances.*

The concept of "distance" as applied to human as distinguished from spatial relations has come into use among sociologists in an attempt to reduce to something like measurable terms the grades and degrees of understanding and intimacy which characterize personal and social relationships generally.

We are clearly conscious, in all our personal relationships, of degree of intimacy. A is "closer" to B than C—and *the degree of this intimacy measures the influence which each has over the other.* It is not only true that we have a sense of distance toward individuals with whom we come in contact, but we have much the same feeling with regard to classes and races. Moreover, this sense of distance with reference to whole groups of persons, this "race" and "class" consciousness, frequently interferes with, modifies, and qualifies personal relations. There is always some sort of social ritual that keeps servants at the "proper distance." The Negro or the Chinaman is "all right in his place." The importance of these personal, racial, and class reserves, which so invariably and inevitably spring up to complicate and, in some measure, to fix and conventionalize our spontaneous human relations, is that they get themselves expressed in all our formal social and even our political relationships.[1]

In the village community where everyone knows everyone else, where everyone calls everyone else by his first name and knows all about him, where attitudes and sentiments are held in common, there are few personal, class, or racial distinctions. The village community is practically without social distances. But various factors in the life of the city tend to create them.

For one thing, there is a wide diversity of cultural backgrounds among the city population. A large part of Chicago's population, with its many nationalities and languages, has come from a variety of sources outside the city, from a diversity of urban, village, and rural cultures.[2] According to their backgrounds, these persons and groups react very differently in identical situations. And they fail to understand each other's reactions. They look upon each other as "common" or "snobbish" or "queer" or "foreign" or "outlandish" or "red." The segregation of city life emphasizes these differences. Persons of like background tend to live in local groups and to have a minimum of contacts with persons unlike themselves. The outward manifestations of culture accompanying this segregation emphasize differences in attitudes, tradition, and point of view. The city becomes a mosaic of worlds which are totally incomprehensible to one another. As we have seen, the Gold Coast and Little Sicily are as far apart as though separated by the

[1] Adapted from R. E. Park, "The Concept of Social Distance," *Journal of Applied Sociology*, VII (July, August, 1924), 339–44.

[2] In Chicago you always ask "Where do you come from?" An "old settlers" picnic draws 1,200 people from a population of 3,000,000.

Atlantic. So far as local issues get into politics at all, they represent conflicts between these diverse worlds.[1]

Attitudes built upon occupational experience, particularly as occupational groups achieve self-consciousness and definition in the heightened competition of city life, tend to set up similar barriers to understanding, to be likewise the measure of social distances.

COMMUNITY MENTALITIES

Moreover, the minute division of labor in the city, working with the segregation so characteristic of city life, has had an important effect upon community action through a differentiation of community mentalities. The division of labor has made group action more and more a matter of techniques; that is, the possibility of group action comes increasingly to require that within the group there should be "experts" and "specialists" capable of directing this action. But as men become experts and specialists, and as their incomes increase, they tend to segregate in the more desirable and fashionable residential districts. Thus, the persons in *Who's Who* whose residences are in Chicago are segregated along the Gold Coast, in the neighborhood of the University, and in the city's fashionable suburbs. The result of this segregation is that, whereas formerly communities were more or less alike in mentality and adaptability, there are today marked differences among communities in these respects.

[1] How isolated the segregated foreign colony may be from the rest of the city is interestingly revealed by an anecdote related by Jacob Kahn, editor of the *Vorwärts*. A Jewish family that had lived several years on the East Side of New York wrote to the *Vorwärts* about a young man who had been rooming with them. Some money had disappeared, and they suspected him of taking it. They felt sure that if the editor published their letter and the young man read it he would return the money. They did not want to speak directly to him for fear he might leave. And they did not want to lose him, for "he is such a nice young man; he tells us all about America."

NORTH SIDE RESIDENTS IN *Who's Who*.—Each spot represents the residence of a Near North Sider whose name appears in *Who's Who*. The map illustrates strikingly the differentiation of "community" mentalities that takes place as the successful and expert segregate in the wealthy and fashionable residential districts, and the concentration of the Near North Side's intellectual and professional leaders along the "Gold Coast."

There are communities such as the Gold Coast which are capable of acting effectively in any situation, so far as mentality is concerned; and there are communities within the slum practically incapable of effecting group action because, as a result of this segregation, they are, in no very metaphorical sense, feebleminded.

MOBILITY AND THE INDIVIDUATION OF BEHAVIOR

Hand in hand with the industrialization of the city and the differentiation of occupation and interest which has accompanied it, has come an increasing mobility of the city's population as over against that of the population of the town. One of the most striking characteristics of city life, it is inextricably bound up with the economic relationships of the city—division of labor, and segregation of commerce and industry on the one hand, which takes the person outside the local community, and increasing facilities for transportation and communication on the other hand which make this movement progressively easier. Under mobility we include both the range and the frequency of the person's physical movements and the number of contacts and stimulations which the person experiences.

The elements entering into mobility may be classified under two main heads: (1) the state of mutability of the person, and (2) the number and kind of contacts of stimulations in his environment. The mutability of city populations varies with sex and age composition, the degree of detachment of the person from the family and from other groups. All these factors may be expressed numerically. The new stimulations to which a population responds can be measured in terms of change of movement or of increasing contacts. Statistics on the movement of urban population may only measure routine, but an increase at a higher ratio than the increase of population measures mobility. In 1860 the horse car lines of New York City carried about 50,000,000 passengers; in 1890 the trolley cars (and a few surviving horse cars) transported about 500,000,000; in 1921, the elevated, sub-way, surface, and electric and steam suburban lines carried a total of more than 2,500,000,000 passengers. In Chicago the total annual rides per capita on the surface and elevated lines were 164 in 1890, 215 in 1900, 320 in 1910, and 339 in 1921. In addition, the rides per capita on steam and electric suburban lines almost doubled between 1916 (23) and 1921 (41), and the increasing use of the automobile must not be overlooked. For example, the number of automobiles in Illinois increased from 131,140 in 1915 to 833,920 in 1923.

Mobility may be measured, not only by these changes of move-ment, but also by increase of contacts. While the increase of popula-tion of Chicago in 1912–22 was less than 25 per cent (23.6 per cent), the increase of letters delivered to Chicagoans was double that (49.6 per cent; from 693,084,196 to 1,039,007,854). In 1912 New York had 8.8 telephones; in 1922, 16.9 telephones; ten years later, 19.5 tele-phones per 100 inhabitants. In the same decade the figures for Chicago increased from 12.3 to 21.6 per 100 population. But increase in the use of the telephone is probably more significant than increase in the number of telephones. The number of telephone calls in Chicago in-creased from 606,131,928 in 1914 to 944,010,586 in 1922, an increase of 55.7 per cent, while the population increased only 13.4 per cent.

Land values, since they reflect movement, afford one of the most sensitive indexes of mobility. The highest land values in Chicago are at the point of greatest mobility in the city, at the corner of State and Madison streets in the Loop. A traffic count showed that at the rush period 31,000 people an hour, or 210,000 men and women in sixteen and one-half hours, passed the southwest corner. For over ten years, land values in the Loop have been stationary, but in the same time they have doubled, quadrupled, and even sextupled in the strategic corners of the "satellite" loops, an accurate index of the changes which have occurred. Our investigations so far seem to indicate that varia-tions in land values, especially where correlated with differences in rents, offer perhaps the best single measure of mobility, and so of all the changes taking place in the expansion and growth of the city.[1]

[1] E. W. Burgess, "The Growth of the City," in R. E. Park, and E. W. Burgess, *The City*, pp. 59–61.

The Near North Side illustrates how mobility touches the most diverse areas and communities, from the world of furnished rooms, the Gold Coast, and the "Rialto," even to Little Sicily in the slum. In any case, mobility results in a dissolution of public opinion and a decay of social solidarity. Whether this dissolution of opinion and decay of solidarity results in conflict or mere social atomization depends upon whether the mobility is chiefly a matter of stimulation or of physical movement.

Little Sicily affords an example of the first, a dissolution of opinion and decay of solidarity leading to social conflict. We have seen how the second generation going outside the colony to work and attending schools representing a different culture comes to live in two social worlds which define the same social situations in contradictory terms. Dr. W. I. Thomas' description of this process in the Polish village, as the second generation, through seasonal occupation in German cities, diverges from the mores of the first generation, applies equally well to Chicago's Little Sicily.

This type of disorganization of the community in which the process starts with the young generation is essentially and primarily a dissolution of social opinion. The community begins by losing the uniformity of social attitudes which made common appreciation and common action possible: the introduction of new values breaks it into two or more camps with different centers of interest, different standards of appreciation, and divergent tendencies of action. If the process continues, social opinion degenerates into gossip; public interest centers on matters of curiosity instead of those of social importance, and, except in the condemnation of the most radical crimes, no unanimity can be reached; there comes a more or less marked decay of social solidarity, both because divergence of appreciation and action breeds hostility and because most of the forms in which solidarity used to manifest itself are no longer adequately enforced by social opinion and rely only on individual moral feeling or desire for response.[1]

The result in Little Sicily, as in the Polish village, is an active conflict between generations. In Little Sicily, moreover, the second generation, unable to participate either in the colony or in the larger American life about it, tends to create a world of its own, characterized by ganging, disorder, and behavior characterized as delinquent by the community. Nor is this result of mobility confined to foreign colonies within the slum. Because of the conflict of cultures, it is more marked in a ghetto or a Little Sicily. But a similar contact with divergent standards, due to the increasing mobility of city life, affects the unanimity of opinion and social solidarity of outlying native communities.[2] Unlike the village, the local area within the city is not spatially isolated. Cultural areas merge. There is movement between them. Isolation is broken down and interstimulation leading to variant behavior is inevitable.

In the world of furnished rooms, on the other hand, an exaggerated physical mobility leads practically to an atomization of social relationships. Where the modal length of residence in an area is well under four months at a given address, as it is in the rooming-house district on the Near North Side, the cultural life of the area literally goes to pieces. People do not know anyone else in the neighborhood. There is no group life; people are lonely. Their wishes are often unsatisfied. Life organizations disintegrate. There is no public opinion. There is not even gossip. And in this situation individuation of personal behavior is extreme.

[1] W. I. Thomas, *The Polish Peasant in Europe and America*, III, 80.

[2] Indeed, the conflict between generations is almost as marked upon the Gold Coast as it is in Little Hell.

Physical movement is not confined to the population of the rooming-house districts, however. Eighty-thousand Chicago people "move" the first day of May.[1] Family areas change, if less rapidly, yet constantly. The following item appeared recently in the *Chicago Herald and Examiner:*

NINE FAMILIES LIVE IN A BLOCK TOTAL OF 257 YEARS

For a total of 257 years, nine families in the same block on North Harvey Avenue in Oak Park have been borrowing each others' lawn mowers, rakes, and umbrellas, without the slightest semblance of an argument or a neighborly fight.

Moving van men, viewing that condition, occasionally gnash their teeth, for in all that time nary a one has moved out of the homes they chose when Oak Park looked like a prairie.

Frank Kuntzer, 516 North Harvey Avenue, has lived there for thirty-six years; James Benson, of 532, is next, with thirty-four years residence, ...

That a family should live as long as a generation in one community, even in an outlying suburb, is news for the sensation-seeking metropolitan press!

It is the exaggerated physical mobility of the city which has made possible its vice districts and its bright-light areas. In these areas of high physical mobility public opinion has ceased to exist. There is no protest from the people who live along North Clark Street against noise, all-night cabarets, or disorderly hotels. This is the mark of complete disorganization of local life, for when there is no protest against the radical violation of the mores the last vestige of community has disappeared. In such areas vice rapidly segregates. Transporation makes them accessible from all parts of the city. People are able to get out from under the restraining mores of their own communities into these areas where there are neither mores nor public opinion.

[1] *Chicago Tribune*, May 2, 1925.

This makes it possible for individuals to pass quickly and easily from one moral milieu to another and encourages the fascinating but dangerous experiment of living at the same time in several different, contiguous, perhaps, but widely separated worlds. All this tends to give to city life a superficial and adventitious character; it tends to complicate social relationships and to produce new and divergent types. It introduces at the same time an element of chance and adventure, which adds to the stimulus of city life and gives it for young and fresh nerves a peculiar attractiveness. The lure of great cities is perhaps a consequence of stimulations which act directly upon the reflexes. As a type of human behavior it may be explained, like the attraction of the flame for the moth, as a sort of tropism.[1]

Life in these areas, with their accelerated change, their divergent behavior patterns, their element of chance resembles that of the frontier town of a generation ago. Indeed, mobility has made the areas of the inner city the frontiers of today.

The very march of the city, then, has destroyed the physical continuity of local life, the physical symbols about which local sentiment and tradition becomes organized. The economic differentiation of the city, with its attendant segregation of commerce and industry, has taken out of local areas many of the activities which formerly gave rise to a common body of experience among those who live in these areas. The ever more minute division of labor, with differentiation of occupations and professions, has resulted in an organization of sentiment and interest upon occupational lines rather than upon contiguity of residence. The mobility of the city has broken down the isolation of the local community, admitting divergent elements of experience, divergent standards and values, divergent definitions of

[1] R. E. Park, "Suggestions for the Study of Behavior in the Urban Environment," in R. E. Park and E. W. Burgess, *The City*, pp. 40-41.

social situations. At the same time it has resulted in a rate of movement that makes strangers of neighbors.

A large part of the city's population lives much as do people in a great hotel, meeting but not knowing one another.[1] The result is a dissolution of social solidarity and public opinion. Face-to-face and intimate relationships in local areas are replaced by casual, transitory, disinterested contacts. There arises an extreme individuation of personal behavior that makes of the local area within the city something vastly different from the town or village community. There is within it no common body of experience and tradition, no unanimity of interest, sentiment, and attitude which can serve as a basis of collective action. Local groups do not act. They cannot act. Local life breaks down.

[1] A new Manhattan apartment building, in advertising in the *New York Times*, observed, "It is not necessary for prospective tenants to dress poorly when they call. Our prices are fixed and are the same for all." The astonishing anonymity of city life is revealed in a recent news dispatch from Philadelphia to the effect that the police are seeking a young woman who has been impersonating accused wives for a Philadelphia "divorce mill"!

CHAPTER XII

REFORM, REALISM, AND CITY LIFE

The breakdown of local life within the city would seem to be the inevitable result of city growth. This breakdown of local life has brought with it a host of "problems"—as the life of the Near North Side, teeming across the preceding pages, so strikingly has shown. A generation ago the problems of the city began to attract the attention of the reformer. Pulpits thundered against the city's shame; crusaders marched against its brothels; the muckrake .turned up corruption in politics and industry; evangelists called upon the city to repent, turn from sin, and be saved. Reform was the cry of the day. The city suddenly became self-conscious. While reformers were storming, with typically American gusto, spasmodic attempts began to be made to control the city's problems. The resulting political and social experiments throw further light upon the nature of life in the areas of the inner city, and point to a new politics and a new conception of action and control in the city of the future.

THE DECAY OF PARLIAMENTARISM

The change in the nature of social life that has come with the city first attracted attention by the change that it brought in the nature of politics. Parliamentary government, under which elections are supposed to be based upon real issues, and carried out to decide those issues, grew out of a condition of small communities, primary contacts, face-to-face associations. It is theoretically the government of the United States today. But while it was adapted to the needs of the thirteen seaboard colonies of 1790, it is not adapted to the needs of an industrial nation of large cities.[1]

The thirteen colonies were in the north largely farming communities about small towns; and in the south, great rural estates. There were few cities, and these were small. The largest, New York, had a population of but 29,906;[2] and the average community was a township having under 1,000 people. The members of these communities lived their lives in contact at practically all points. In relation to his neighbors, the New Englander might be on Monday the postmaster or merchant, on Saturday the justice, and on Sunday the deacon in the church. Associations were largely face-to-face, attitudes were primary—immediate, concrete, and emotional. The community was organized more largely about sentiment than interests, and it was relatively isolated from other communities.

The politics of the day revolved about the town meeting. Political issues grew out of the everyday life of the community. These issues were real issues—political parties stood for real differences in opinion, real conflicts in interest, actual currents in community life. A parliamentary system of government was well adapted to the political needs of the day. So it remained for two generations.

But in the three decades following the Civil War, the character of American life was completely changed. These

---

[1] Webster defines parliamentarism as "the parliamentary system of government"; and goes on to define parliament as a "meeting or assembly for consultation and deliberation; as a legislative body; a national legislature. . . . ." It is in this sense that the word is here used—to denote a system of government, irrespective of particular party system and name, in which issues growing out of community life are debated and legislated upon by a representative deliberative body.

[2] Leonard, *History of the City of New York*, p. 303.

decades witnessed a period of rapid national and industrial expansion. Factory communities began to blacken the skies from their smoking chimneys; a network of railroads and telegraphs bound communities more closely together; and great industrial and commercial cities sprang up, completely altering the nature of social life. New York's population increased from 805,658 to 3,100,000 during these decades, and its area to 359 square miles.[1] Boston, Philadelphia, Pittsburgh, and Chicago were drawing great populations to labor in their factories and mills, or to work in their warehouses and marts of commerce.

This industrial expansion brought with it problems entirely new to American life, problems with which parliamentarism was not prepared to cope. These were the days of the "captain of industry," of "concessions," and shortly of the "trust." At the same time the growth of the city, with its mobility and anonymity, its organization along lines of interest rather than sentiment, its specialization, its breaking down of local life, greatly changed the nature of political life. The old issues, which continued each four years to be written into doctrinaire party platforms, were no longer real issues—indeed, the host of social questions that came with the industrial society, and which were the real if imperfectly recognized issues of the day, were rarely acknowledged as political issues. People were no longer divided upon the formal political issues. Party struggles were no longer based upon constitutional questions. Party organizations were indifferent to social questions. Politics narrowed down to struggle for office and the booty of office. It was the day of the "spoils system" of the "ring" and the "machine." The "boss" became a power in local politics,

---

[1] Leonard, *loc. cit.*, p. 403.

and the "lobby" in national politics. The pursuit of "honest graft" was added to the professions.

There was a gradually growing realization of the inefficiency of this new party régime. A few ministers thundered against it from their pulpits; reformers began to raise a hue and cry. And in 1871 came the first of the sensational attacks by the *New York Times* upon the Tweed Ring. It was an unheard of thing for a paper to attack a member of its own party, however crooked, as all the issues of the world were supposed to be bound up in party solidarity and supremacy. The *Times* was the first paper to break with that tradition. The *Times* did not realize that Tammany Hall was the inevitable product of parliamentarism and party government in great cities. But it did realize that parliamentarism was not functioning as it was intended. And the *Times* campaign against Tweed, from 1871 to 1876, gave a tremendous impetus to the reform movement, and to the re-evaluation of our political institutions. It was a first objective, uninterpreted presentation of fact, and brought results where denunciation from the editorial column and the pulpit had failed.

THE MAN WITH THE MUCKRAKE

Following the *Times* exposé, there came a series of investigations and journalistic reports that covered every phase of political and social life in the city. It was the era of "the man with the muckrake" and of the "yellow press." In 1890 Jacob Riis wrote his *How the Other Half Lives*. It was largely descriptive, with many photographs picturing conditions of the life of the slum. Incidentally, Riis did more than anyone else to make "slumming" a popular sport. He made the city *interesting;* threw a romantic glamor over its life. Riis showed the city to Roosevelt when the latter was police commissioner of New York, got him interested in social problems, and convinced him that publicity was the only real solution of its problems.

Parkhurst began his sensational vice crusade in New York in 1893. Pulpits had thundered against vice before. Societies had been organized to suppress it. But Parkhurst was the first to turn upon vice the pitiless light of publicity, to get the facts, and retail them Sunday after Sunday. His crusade, sensational in its attempt to connect vice with political corruption, created a tremendous stir. Parkhurst wanted to *get* the *system*, which his investigation showed to pervade wide areas and high places. "Our object is, not to convict criminals, but to convince the public." Here a new note was struck—a change of attitude toward the accepted institution, instead of an arraignment of its functioning, and the resultant turnover in New York was a beginning of legislation on the basis of intelligent popular opinion instead of party doctrine.

Steffens published *The Shame of the Cities* in 1904. He maintained that with his knowledge of New York he could go to any city and quickly gauge conditions; that conditions in New York were not due to the failure of one institution peculiar to that city, but were due to a general condition incident to the growth of cities. This was the first recognition of the fact that the city has a natural history, and that the social conditions turned up by the muckrake were the product of this history.

Meantime the magazines had turned to the literature of exposure; the *American* published its sensational stories on Lawson and Wall Street; and Ida Tarbel, in *McClure's*, was painting in lurid colors the story of Standard Oil. The same

years saw the meteoric rise of the yellow press. The newspaper ceased to work on the principle that readers were
mainly interested in reading about themselves—records of
"weddings, funerals, lodge meetings, oyster suppers, and all
the small patter of the small town." The metropolitan press
began to search out the drab episodes of city life for the
romantic and the picturesque, to give dramatic accounts of
vice and crime, to take an interest in the movements of per-
sonages of a more or less mythical high society. The yellow
press grew up in an attempt to capture for the newspaper a
public whose only literature was the family story paper or
the cheap novel. The problem was to write the news in such a
way that it would appeal to the fundamental passions. The
formula was: love and romance for women; sports and
politics for men.[1] The result was not only enormously to
increase the circulation of the newspaper, but to cast the
glamor of romance over the life of the great city, to get
people to reading and thinking about its problems.

Upton Sinclair's *The Jungle*, published in 1906, marked
the high point of muckraking, the literature of exposure, the
yellow press. It was in 1906 that Roosevelt coined the
word "muckrake," and contemptuously applied it to the
attempt of the press to commercialize public taste for the
sensational, rather than to attempt reform by creating a real
interest in social problems. And people were getting "fed
up" on sensationalism; public interest began to flag. The
net result of the era of muckraking upon the life of the city
was negligible. It created a tremendous stir; public interest
was aroused; reforms were proposed; yet little happened.
But muckraking and yellow journalism, in addition to adver-

[1] Robert E. Park, "The Natural History of the Newspaper," *American
Journal of Sociology*, XXIX (November, 1923), pp. 273–89.

tising the breakdown of parliamentary government in the
city and making the city and its problems interesting, had
created a faith in publicity, a realistic tradition, which was
to play a leading rôle in the development of a new politics.

THE RISE OF SOCIAL POLITICS

Related to the literature of exposure was the organized
charities movement. The problems of the city became interesting and talked of. Naturally, to those who had the time
and the wherewithal to do, the "other half," the "submerged
tenth," was most interesting; and this interest went deeper
than that manifested in slumming parties on the East Side.
Settlements were established in the slums, and many societies and organizations came into existence to meet the needs,
and deal with the problems, of the poor, the unfortunate,
the down and out.

With the establishment of organized charities in this
country we had the beginning of a specialization to meet the
needs of a large and growing city life. The general problem
of "the other half" turned out to be a complex of related but
individual problems. At first the relationship was not clearly seen, and between 1870 and 1880 there grew up a host of
small charity organizations, each attempting to deal with
its own problem, and largely disregarding what other organizations were doing. But soon these organizations began to
run into one another, to tread upon one another's toes.
There was much duplication of work. An increased multi-
plication and specialization to avoid this led to a situation
in which cases were passed endlessly along from one organization to another. It gradually dawned upon social workers
that the special problems with which they were working
were, in fact, very intimately related, and that the many

organizations belonged together. The idea of a clearing house through which the large number of organizations working on specific problems could be correlated was taken up. We began to hear of Associated Charities, of Federated Charities, of United Charities.[1]

Those interested in social problems soon saw that the problem went deeper than relief. On the basis of the knowledge and information pooled in the uniting of charity organizations, and with the aid of experts familiar with various problems through the work of these organizations, legislative programs were drawn up; the social problems of the large city and the industrial society at last had a political formulation.

Out of this effort grew the social survey movement. To get social legislation, the people must be interested in social problems; and to interest the people in social problems, publicity must be given to social facts. It is significant, perhaps, that in the same year, 1906, the popularity of the literature of exposure began to wane, the social survey came into existence with the publication of the Pittsburgh survey.

The survey took up the task just where "the man with the muckrake" was compelled to lay it down. It began in a more serious, sober, and thoroughgoing way, and with a less sensational appeal, to reassemble and publish the facts. Investigation by committees, commissions, and experts replaced the muckraking reporter; the survey publicity-display replaced the yellow journal. The social survey dealt with the same problems as did the organized social agencies; it got from these agencies its expert investigators and much

[1] The first "Associated Charities" came into existence in Buffalo in 1876. For a history of the Charities movement, see A. G. Warner, *American Charities* (3d ed., revised by M. R. Coolidge, 1919).

of its information; it aimed to put across the social policies formulated by these agencies. But what was perhaps the most characteristic feature of the survey, its attempt to put over the facts to the community, and to secure by publicity the action of the community on the basis of these facts, went directly back to the realistic tradition and faith in publicity that had grown out of the literature of exposure and the yellow press.[1]

Social problems, then, were beginning to find political expression, but in a politics vastly different from "party politics," and which we may call "social politics," the methods and policies of dealing with what we call *social* problems, as opposed to constitutional problems. It is not a struggle based upon party doctrine, as was parliamentarism, but an attempt to secure legislation on a basis of fact. We find issues derided irrespective of party; and non-partisan leagues, and the like, growing up in the attempt to play parties over against one another on social questions.[2]

Since the Civil War, party distinctions have largely broken down, and the attitude of the people toward politics has changed. In Congress the committee system has displaced the parliamentary debate. The newspaper has taken over the parliamentary function of discussion. In printing the news it enables the public to make up its mind on the basis of fact as issues arise, instead of on the basis of party doctrine, an opinion less definite, perhaps, but more intelligent. And the survey hangs together with this whole move-

---

[1] Shelby Harrison's introduction to the published findings of the Springfield Survey contains an interesting statement of the point of view of the social survey.

[2] The cry of the day was "Keep it out of politics—don't let reform legislation go on the rocks by becoming a political issue," and philanthropy and reform turned, as big business already had, to publicity and the lobby.

ment, which we have termed "social politics," in that it is a device for securing intelligent community action on the basis of facts objectively ascertained.

The rise of social politics has great significance from the standpoint of community life. The great mass of social legislation is passed by states and cities. It is largely formulated by the expert representatives of city-wide or state-wide social agencies. It is not democracy in the old sense. Those who formulate the legislation and put it across are not members of the communities most affected. Moreover, social agencies tend more and more to a system of interlocking directorates, where a *small* number of experts control, to all intents and purposes, the policies of these agencies and of social legislation. Plainly, social politics is a movement away from the local urban community and in the direction of the standardization characteristic of other aspects of city life.

BACK TO THE COMMUNITY

But at the same time that the rise of social politics was tending to take social legislation out of the realm of the local community, and to put it into the hands of the expert, there was growing up another movement intended to revitalize the political life of the community. This movement, too, was related to the organization of charities. For social agencies, in their treatment of cases through the clearing house, come to see the interrelations of these cases and their dependence upon a common social situation. Out of this insight grew the concept of the community, and the belief that social problems arose out of the breakdown of community life in the city. And, beginning with the settlements, there came a succession of attempts at organizing the community.

Those who were interested in community organization felt the changes in local life that had come with the growth of the industrial city. They looked back to the day of towns and rural communities as to a golden age of social life. They felt that if something could be done to "awaken" the local community in the city, to restore to it the neighborliness and friendliness of the town, its problems would take care of themselves. And attempts were made to go into the areas which had become eddies and backwaters in the stream of city life and to arouse in them a spirit of neighborliness and an interest in their own problems and the problems of the city as a whole.

The first agency to go into these disorganized areas, which were broadly termed the "slum," was the settlement. The first American settlement, established in 1886, on the Lower East Side of New York, was the Neighborhood Guild; Hull House in Chicago, the College Settlement in New York, and South End House in Boston soon followed, until today there are settlements in every large city.

Robert A. Woods, then head resident of South End House, expressed as follows, in an early paper, his idea of what the settlement was attempting to do:

The settlements are able to take neighborhoods in cities, and by patience bring back to them much of the healthy village life, so that the people shall again know and care for one another. They will impart a softer touch to what social powers now act there, and they will bring streams from the higher sources of civilization to refresh and arouse the people so that they shall no more go back to the narrowness and gloom, and perhaps the brutality, of their old existence.[1]

Miss Jane Addams, of Hull House, expressed much the same conception of the function of the settlement, and settle-

[1] *Philanthropy and Social Progress*, 1893; "The University Settlement Idea," quoted by John Daniels in *America via the Neighborhood*.

ments generally seem to have conceived of their rôle as that of stirring to life those areas of the city which, chiefly through poverty, were unable to do for themselves. But settlements have always been much after the pattern of a mission, largely institutional in character, directed by people of a different social world. Their work has consisted in kindergartens, boys' clubs, mothers' clubs, and the like, and their activities have not been distributed throughout the community. Moreover, in America the settlement has usually been placed in an immigrant community, a community unadapted, perhaps, but far from unorganized. The settlement has always been something of a riddle to the community, rarely has enlisted the active participation of any considerable numbers of the community, and never has succeeded in restoring to the really disorganized areas of the city the neighborhood sentiment, and the unanimity of interest, of the town.[1]

In contrast with the institutionalized nature of the settlement's approach to the problems of the community is the effort of another group of agencies to promote community of interest and action upon the basis of local units. To this group belong neighborhood and improvement associations, to some degree charity organization societies, Community Service Incorporated, community councils, the block unit experiments as carried out in New York, and the experiments of the National Social Unit Organization. There is no suggestion of "uplift" in their work; no handing down to the less favored from the more favored. They all

[1] Despite these facts the settlement has played an exceedingly important rôle in city life in calling the attention of the larger "community" to the problems of its submerged areas, in interesting it in these problems, in enlisting its imagination. The settlement has been the greatest single factor in interpreting the slum to the rest of the city.

recognize, implicitly and explicitly, the breakdown of parliamentarism, and aim to make good its defects. The political unit and the local group no longer coincide. The interests and problems of the local community find no political expression, and nothing is done about them. There must be some extra-political organization in the local community to meet its problems. And the community council, or the social unit, seeks to organize the local groups in a given area to meet the problems of that area.

We have already followed the fortunes of one such experiment in the Lower North Community Council. Another, and perhaps the most widely advertised of these experiments in community organization, was that of the social unit in Cincinnati. A typical city area was selected for the experiment, the so-called Mohawk-Brighton district:

This district, located in the "West End" of Cincinnati, presented conditions which were fairly typical of the city as a whole. Divided by Dayton Street (the old "Fifth Avenue" of this part of Cincinnati), and with the Lafayette-Bloom school at its geographical center, it presented many of the aspects of a small town, having its schools, its churches, its library, its factories, its stores, its old mansions, its working class section, and its mixture of population—Greek, Roumanian, Austrian, and German-American, with the latter predominating.

The population was largely native born, however, and fairly homogeneous, and the area was more or less a cultural unit. It was not an extremely disorganized or "slum" area. It had not been selected as a "social laboratory," but had selected itself, so to speak, by petition for organization. It had, to begin with, the response of a fair proportion of its population, and most of the civic and social agencies in Cincinnati were behind it.[1]

[1] *Bulletin of the National Social Unit Organization, No. 3*, "Creation and Purpose of the Cincinnati Social Unit Organization," p. 11.

The social-unit experiment aimed at the revitalization of democracy in the life of city areas—defining democracy as "the organization of the people through which they come together for the purpose of satifying their common needs and desires." It recognized that in the life of large areas of the city parliamentarism was not functioning.

> Because the areas electing popular representatives at present are so large, such representatives, however honest or able they may be, are not able, as society is now organized, to keep continuously, sympathetically, completely, and intelligently in touch with their constituents—knowing personally each man, woman, and child within their precincts, being sensitive to their needs, wishes, opinions, and desires, and being held responsible by them at all times to express what they think. Nor for the same reason can the people readily follow and check up the records of these representatives. Hence popular control over representatives is too frequently merely nominal. Some way must be found by which to bring the representative much closer to the people than is now the rule, and to convert him (or her) into a social worker whose chief objective and main pursuit is to study the needs of his constituents, and to help him to satisfy those needs.[1]

The social-unit experiment sought to accomplish this through block representatives to keep in touch with these needs, a relating of the expert to the people in satisfying these needs, a democratic organization of all persons and groups in the district, and the re-establishment in this city area of the neighborliness and sentiment characteristic of the town.

> *The Social Unit Organization aims to restore the advantages of village life to city people.* For that reason it has divided the Mohawk-Brighton District into small blocks of about 500 people each. *The plan is to make each of these blocks a tiny village where folks will come to know one another and to be interested in having their neighbors happy and contented.* In a country village there is usually some one woman who is a

---

[1] *Bulletin of the National Social Unit Organization, No. 1,* "The Social Unit Experiment," pp. 19–20

sort of village mother to whom folks go in times of trouble, who knows everyone, and is always busy getting people to help those in need. Taking her as an example, the Social Unit Organization is planning in each tiny block village to have a block worker, or block mother, who will know when anyone needs help of any kind and will see that this help is given by the right agency. This village mother is to be chosen by the people of her block. . . . . As the people get interested in their blocks, they may decide to give them real names, just as small villages are given names by the people who live in them. The thirty-one block mothers together will form a Citizens' Council. The work of this Citizens' Council will be to learn what the needs of every part of the Mohawk-Brighton District are, and to see that plans are worked out for meeting these needs. In doing this, it will use the knowledge of the different skilled groups in the community.[1]

After a trial of three years, the Cincinnati social-unit experiment was abandoned. Unfortunately, we have no analysis of its failure, no adequate discussion of the forces involved. But it might have been predicted at the inception of the experiment, by one familiar with the natural history of the city, that it was bound to fail. Any attempt at community organization must fail which disregards inevitable trends in the growth of the city. And in attempting to restore to local urban areas the neighborliness, sentiment, and face-to-face associations of the town, it is attempted to disregard these trends, which are clearly in the opposite direction—toward secondary contacts in local areas, toward anonymity in these areas, toward the organization of persons upon the basis of interest rather than of sentiment—as the preceding chapters have shown.

The professional man's interests are organized about specialized problems that lie, for the most part, outside the community. He is too busy to devote much time to talking

---

[1] *Bulletin of the National Social Unit Organization, No. 4,* "Description of the Unit Plan," p. 6. Italics are the writer's.

over local problems with people who do not share or understand his viewpoint. Men of wealth and influence, if there are any in the community, are tied up to city-wide movements and organizations. Social barriers exist between various economic and cultural groups. While the experiment is new and novel, social distance and difference of interest may be forgotten. But soon the professional man becomes irritated and bored with the layman who cannot see his technical point of view. The unionist becomes suspicious of the motives of those who contribute money. The woman whose name is found in the Blue Book shrinks from rubbing elbows with her sister from the slum. Social distances, conflicting interests, the lack of any common bond of sentiment, become apparent. And the community organization falls to pieces.

It is to be regretted that the failure of the social-unit experiment in Cincinnati was complicated by a political controversy, the opposition of the mayor of the city. He saw in the social-unit plan the possibility of a new political organization which might be completely subversive of party politics. And his branding of the social unit as socialistic, even bolshevistic, hastened its collapse. But the division of opinion which followed this controversy demonstrated that professional interest is stronger than local sentiment, and that the people who live in a given local area in the city have little in common, either of sentiment or interest, that is enduring. And moreover, the failure of the Lower North Community Council and of scores of other similar attempts to convert city areas into little "towns" tends greatly to discount the significance of the political controversy in the failure of the Cincinnati experiment.

The community organization movement, then, is bound

up with the rise of the industrial society and the growth of the city. Parliamentary government does not function in the city as it did in the town. The real issues of city life are not written into political platforms. Politics becomes a game, and the problems of local areas of the city find no political expression. As a consequence, a new social politics has grown up, consisting in the preparation of legislation by experts of social agencies, and passed on a city-wide basis. The tendency of social politics is to take legislation out of the local community entirely. The realization of this has led to various efforts to restore to the local area in the city something of the nature of the small town, with the expectation that it would then take an interest in its peculiar and local problems, and that much of the disorganization of local city areas would be done away with. But these attempts to reorganize the community on the basis of neighborliness and local sentiment invariably fail, and the failure seems to lie in the inevitable trends of city life. The areas where the need for community organization is most apparent are areas in which the very nature of city life makes community organization impossible.

REFORM AND REALISM

The sequence of events we have just sketched—the decay of parliamentarism, muckraking and the rise of the yellow press, the "uplift," the settlement, attempts at community organization, and the emergence of a social politics—is more than an additional interesting comment upon the nature of local life in the city. It is typical of prevailing attitudes toward the problems of the city. Periodically we witness sensational exposés of some aspect of the city's life— political corruption, festering slums, sweatshop exploitation, vice, crime. The cry goes up from press and pulpit for reform. Militant organizations spring up over night. Repressive legislation is proposed and too frequently enacted. The sentimental and idealistic device some new form of "uplift" which makes more work for the police. Then public interest flags. Little is actually accomplished. Yet the next exposé of city life creates the same demand for reform. The explanation of this characteristic attitude toward the city's problems is not far to seek.

Reform and the "uplift" are the inevitable result of the conflict of urban and rural cultures. The life of the city has tended toward the disintegration of the old rural patterns of life, to changes in long-accepted institutions, to the emergence of new standards of conduct and of divergent types of personal behavior, a process we have watched in the world of furnished rooms. But the city has never been a cultural unity. The types of behavior that are most typical of the city are found largely within the city's inner areas. The city has wrought less fundamental changes in the life of its outlying areas. In these outlying areas are found communities less touched by mobility and culturally more stable. The population of these communities is largely of rural origin; the culture of these communities is traditionally "American" and rural in its background. Reform and the "uplift" are the crystallization of the resulting conflict of cultures as the stable communities of the outer areas of the city have attempted to control the divergent behavior of the inner city and to impose upon it the standards and ideals of their essentially rural culture.[1] The reformer has played

[1] Most of Chicago's well-known reformers live, for example, in Winnetka! These reformers are often enough highly civilized cosmopolites. But they cling to the stern mores of an older and essentially rural generation.

a colorful rôle in the growth of the American city. He has been a fanatic who has waged an uncompromising war on reality. He has been a sentimentalist and romantic who has thought all things possible. He has been an idealist who has failed to sense his own futility—"If wishes were horses, beggars might ride"; but wishes are not horses, and beggars shuffle the sidewalks of the "Rialto of the Half-World." The sentiment and idealism back of reform is, however, one of the most precious things in our life. The life of the city would be intolerable and its future hopeless without the dreams of the reformers. But their dreams are hopeless while they remain unrelated to the realities of life. While reformers were vainly attempting to stem the tides of city life, however, realtors, engineers of public utilities, city-planning and zoning commissions, students in universities, and others interested in predicting the future of the city were discovering much about the nature of these tides, about the ways in which the city grows. Especially significant have been the studies of the American Bell Telephone Company, and other utilities, for the purposes of extension in anticipation of future service, the studies of the Russell Sage Foundation for the Regional Plan of New York, and the research into city life of the Community Research Fund of the Laura Spelman Rockefeller Memorial. The aim of all these studies has been the understanding of the city.[1]

In the preceding chapters we have attempted to give, in all its intimate detail and dramatic contrast, a cross-section

[1] Park and Burgess, *The City;* Burgess, *The Urban Community;* Anderson, *The Hobo;* Thrasher, *The Gang;* Mowrer, *Family Disorganization;* Cavan, *Suicide;* Gosnell, *A Study of Non-Voting;* and Wirth, *The Ghetto,* contain much of the material on city life accumulated by the Community Research Fund in Chicago. The Russell Sage Foundation will mail a list of its publications upon request.

of life as it is lived in a great city of today. We have attempted, further, to trace the tendencies which give to this
cross-section of city life its particular form and color, to
describe the processes which give the city its physical configuration and its characteristic types of cultural life and
behavior. In short, we have attempted to bring together the
results of studies of city growth into an intelligible and
realistic conception of the city's life.

It becomes clear that a fundamental change is taking
place in the nature of local life in the city. Over large areas
of the city, "community" is scarcely more than a geographical expression. The community is gradually disappearing. And its disappearance is the result of the fundamental processes of the city's growth—mobility, centralization, succession, and the consequent breakdown of culture
and public opinion within local areas, the rise of social
distances, and the organization of sentiment and interest on
the basis of vocational activity rather than contiguity of
residence. The "problems" of the city that have aroused
the reformer are largely the result of this breakdown of community life.

It has been attempted to control these problems by re-
viving the community. But this attempt to run counter to
the trends of city life has proved futile. Local areas in the
city cannot act. The old democracy, control of local problems by popular discussion and vote, is gone. We have tried
to control these problems by legislation. But the effectiveness of legislation rests ultimately upon community opinion,
and this attempt has hardly been more successful. We are
just beginning to realize that the city may be taught to act
as a whole, not through the old politics which with the
passing of the community has come to mean little more than

exploitation by politicians, but through recognizing the trends of city growth and evolving new technique to utilize them.

Already interesting experiments are being carried on in the attempt to meet the governmental problems that have come with the growth of the city. Municipal voters' leagues have arisen in the effort to get the populations of cities to consider the administrative problems of the city as a whole. Proportional representation makes the city more nearly articulate. The advocates of "pluralism" recognizing that an organization of sentiment and interest about vocational and other groups is succeeding that based on local areas, would base the vote on membership in social groups rather than on residence. The commission and city manager forms of government, realizing that city government is becoming increasingly a matter of business administration rather than of crystallization and definition of opinion, attempt, with the aid of bureaus of municipal research, to introduce into city government the standardization and scientific management already found in industry.

Even more interesting, and perhaps more significant, is the city and regional plan. The city plan grew out of the dreams of idealists impatient with the city that was. They found, though, that the city resisted their arbitrary attempts to translate their dreams into steel, brick, and concrete. There was a period of disillusionment. But just as the interest in the city plan began to flag, it was given fresh impetus by the realization on the part of practical men that the growth of the city, left uncontrolled, was involving city governments and public utilities in a maze of well-nigh unsolvable problems. Zoning commissions began to try to control the city's physical structure and growth. They, too, found the city resistant; but, finding it resistant, they turned to the study of the city in the effort to understand its resistance. Out of these studies has arisen a new city plan, a plan that is possible because it is based upon a recognition of the natural process of the city's growth, a plan that is the dream not of an ideal, but of a real, city. The city plan may ultimately involve the entire region about the city, as does the Regional Plan of New York. The significance of the city plan is twofold. It tends toward an increasingly realistic conception of city life. But beyond this, as city plan commissions resort to publicity to arouse public interest, the plan begins to give the city a conception of itself—a self-awareness, a sense of its history and rôle, a vision of its future—in short, a personality. And only when the city has achieved self-consciousness, only when the mosaic of cultural worlds which compose it come to think of themselves, not as over against one another, but as related to a vision of the city as a whole, can the city adequately act.

Meanwhile, "social politics," the rise of which at the opening of the century we have already noted, is playing an increasingly significant rôle in the city's life. In "social politics" the social problems which have arisen with the decline of the community, and which have been ignored by the older politics, are at last finding expression. "Social politics," however, while recognizing the decline of the community, has not been fully aware of the potentialities of the public that has replaced it. The realistic tradition and faith in publicity that grew out of the era of the muckrake and the yellow press have been left to the exploitation of the tabloid and the demagogue. "Social politics" has endeavored to solve the city's problem by legislation that too frequently found no sanction in public opinion. Moreover, this legisla-

274 THE GOLD COAST AND THE SLUM

tion has too often reflected the attitude of reform, the conflict between rural and urban culture. However, "social politics"—expert social legislation on a city- and state-wide basis—will play an increasingly significant rôle in the city's life as the realist displaces the reformer and as social legislation is related more intimately to public opinion.

The attempt to control the city's problems by giving the city a voice and teaching it to act as a whole leads to reevaluation of the city's human resources. The old democracy exalted "the man in the street," "the doorbell vote," "the will of the people." But the realistic attitude toward the city and its problems attaches a new importance to good will, vision, leadership, and wealth. And these resources, we have seen, tend, in the competition and selection of city life, to become segregated on the city's Park Avenue or Gold Coast. Thus the persons whose names appear in the *Social Register* assume a new rôle in the city's life. Pageantry, display, froth, will always be part of the life of society, will always give the Gold Coast its color. Yet the Gold Coast is the only element in the city's life that sees the city as a whole, dreams dreams for it as a whole. The literature of society shows how its imagination plays with the city as a living thing—while to little Sicily or the world of furnished rooms the city is merely part of the landscape. Moreover, the Gold Coast has the wealth to realize these dreams. It has the "good will" necessary to realize them; it has the leadership necessary to establish them, for, as we have seen, in the differentiation of "community" mentalities that takes place in the city's life, the Gold Coast comes to have a concentration of the city's expert ability and leadership, as shown by the map facing page 244 of the residences of persons whose names appear in *Who's Who*. Finally, the Gold Coast has, as no other group, a sense of its rôle in the life of the city, and of its responsibility for the future of the city.

Nothing could make more real the rôle of the Gold Coast in the life of the city than a recent autobiography, *Growing Up with a City*, by Louise de Koven Bowen. No name is more intimately bound up with the civic and social life of Chicago than is hers. It looms large in the story of Hull House, the United Charities, the Juvenile Court, the Juvenile Protective Association, the Visiting Nurse Association, the Chicago Council of Social Agencies, the Committee of Fifteen, the Birth Control League, the Woman's City Club, the Chicago Equal Suffrage Association, and many other organizations.[1] As she describes her connection with these various civic and social enterprises, across her pages pass the names of many other residents of Chicago's Gold Coast who have played and are playing equally significant rôles in the city's life. The accompanying map, showing the concentration of the directors and trustees of Chicago's social agencies on the Gold Coast and along the North Shore, gives some conception of the intimate relationship of the good will, wealth, and leadership of the Gold Coast to the life of Chicago.

Mrs. Bowen's Astor Street home, like many other Gold Coast homes, has been the birthplace of many a plan that has left its imprint on Chicago's life.

I have lived for thirty-two years in my house on this street; it has been used at various times for all kinds of meetings, from suffrage gatherings, where we were urging women to join the suffrage ranks, to neighborhood meetings where we made appeals for the betterment of conditions in the ward.

We have had many dinners where some scheme of benefit to the city or county has been hatched out behind closed doors. The meetings have been held here in order not to have anyone know about them.

[1] Louise de Koven Bowen, *Growing Up with a City*, pp. 22 23.

I remember when my friend, Mr. Alexander A. McCormick, was made president of the county board, he told me that he was most anxious to appoint good people as heads of the various county departments, such as the warden of the hospital, the head of the social service department, etc., and that if we could suggest good people he would appoint them. I immediately called together about twenty-five people, heads of settlements, men interested in civic affairs, social workers, etc., and we sat all one evening trying to think of good men and women for the various county positions. . . . . There were other dinners on the question of education where matters were coming up on the school board which demanded immediate action by citizens.

Some of these plans which we formed at these dinners or meetings were sprung at large meetings held later, and I have heard people say that they wondered where the plan originated, but no one ever gave it away.[1]

[1] Louise de Koven Bowen, *Growing Up with a City*, pp. 215–17. "I was connected with so many organizations and had so many meetings and speeches to make that I hardly had any time to myself. One day in the fall of 1924 I noticed that my mail was a large one, and, just for curiosity, as I opened every letter, I had my secretary take down the contents of it. I found that in this one mail I had seventy requests either to make contributions, to buy, to sell, or to attend meetings. The following list at least illustrates the growing complexity of life in a modern city. I was asked: to buy stock in a certain trust company; to entertain a prominent woman; to attend a church dancing party; to go into business in a cleaning and dyeing company; to attend a course of lectures on the theater; to buy bonds of a foreign company; to visit and give to a prominent hospital; to go to a series of concerts; to build a new hospital; to join the Big Tree League of California; to subscribe to a public health magazine; to write a letter of condolence to the family of a public official; to found a school of music; to subscribe to a monthly review of music; to join an association of railroad owners; to go on a trip around the world; to subscribe to a journal of health; to buy lingerie of a new firm; to use my name in an advertisement for political purposes; to advance some money for a worthy cause; to vote the straight Republican ticket; to join a music association; to patronize a certain beauty parlor; to buy my Christmas presents at a certain jewelry store; to vote the Democratic ticket; to patronize a certain chiropodist; to give a subscription for a settlement; to attend a series of lectures on wood prints; to attend a luncheon on social service; to send my autograph for certain purposes; to become a subscriber to an eastern paper; to go on a cruise on the Seven Seas; to join

The residents of the Gold Coast have grown up with the city, have watched it lift its towers, have been a part of its pulsing life, as has no other element of the city's population. Consequently their roots are deep in the city; they identify themselves with its life; their imaginations play with its future. Mrs. Bowen's grandfather lived within the stockade of old Fort Dearborn; her mother was born within its stockade. Tales of early Chicago were a part of her nursery lore: "I became so familiar with the stories of these early days that it is most difficult to disentangle them from my actual experiences." How intimately she identifies herself with the city's life, how deep her roots go into that life, how her imagination plays with the city as a living thing, is revealed as she writes:

----

a certain Chicago club; to invest my funds in a disreputable concern; to make an investment in a certain company; to send my signature for business purposes; to patronize a bucket shop; to give a subscription to the Salvation Army; to attend an exhibition at the Drake Hotel; to put all my savings in a magazine of fashion; to be chairman of a large committee about to be formed; to buy a book on etiquette; to buy my Christmas linens of a New York firm; to attend two public luncheons; to send a check to a children's charity; to send a check for a Presbyterian church; to visit a famous hotel in the South; to buy my diamonds at a New York jeweler's; to purchase my linens at a New York linen store; to buy my opera coats at a certain store; to buy my tea gowns at a certain store; to send my old clothes to a re-sale shop; to give to a Presbyterian home; to buy old carpets at a certain shop; to attend a luncheon and hear a celebrated speaker; to buy clothing for myself and family at a certain store; to use my name on a Republican advertisement; to vote for Governor Small on the ground of his good service; to become vice-president of a large political club; to give a talk over the radio; to preside at a political meeting; to hold a meeting concerning a matter of public policy; to patronize a detective agency; to accept as a gift a suit of underwear and a pair of silk stockings; to give my opinion on some candidates for re-election; to support a string quartette; to buy some old prints; to endorse three separate candidates for the same office for election; to order some photographs."

As I close this book I am looking from the window of my office in the London Guaranty Building, on the very site of Fort Dearborn. I look from one window up the Chicago River, past the new Wacker Drive, once South Water Street, where my grandfather was a commission merchant.

Not far along this drive was once a little hotel kept by my great-uncle, where travelers were made welcome and given the best the little inn could afford.

A short distance south of the Wacker Drive, my father sat in the office of his bank and made his first loans to the merchants who were even then building their grain elevators and establishing a center for the meat industry of the world.

I look out another window across the sparkling waters of Lake Michigan and up Michigan Boulevard where the great Wrigley Building stands, and the beautiful Tribune structure lifts its tower toward heaven.

I also look at the Kirk Building, where stood the home of the first white man in Chicago, John Kinzie, my grandfather's best friend, whose daughter was my mother's bridesmaid. Mr. Kinzie had to abandon his house several times because of Indian depredations. The site of his old home is now fairly humming with industrial activities.

The boulevard I overlook is one of the busiest thoroughfares in the world. Thousands of cars pass every hour over the fine bridge which spans the river and gives access to two street levels. It is almost on the very spot where my grandmother used to pull herself across the river on a ferryboat drawn by a rope. On the north side of this river she used to pick blueberries, ready to fly any moment if she heard an Indian approaching.

The noise of the motors, the whistling of the tugs on the river, the traffic policeman's warning, the roar of the crowd, penetrate to my office, and I marvel at the great changes which have been wrought within three generations and even in my own lifetime.

Chicago—the little outpost in the wilderness where deer drank from the river, wolves howled at night, and Indians lurked in the shadows.

Chicago—peopled by indomitable early settlers with energy, courage, and perseverance, and, above all, with vision. They saw the great advantages of a situation at the foot of the Great Lakes, surrounded by the fertile corn and wheat fields of the West, and they laid the foundation of what is soon to be, not only one of the largest, but one of the most beautiful, cities in the world.[1]

In the light of these facts the life of the Gold Coast assumes a new interest and significance. In spite of the fact that the average man, getting his impressions from the Sunday rotogravure section, seeing only its externals, pictures the Gold Coast as ostentatious, snobbish, condescending, the existence of such an aristocracy, with its wealth, leisure, morale, and interest in the city, is in the long run a controlling factor in the city's destiny. No other group of citizens is competent to do what the Gold Coast is doing for the life of the city. The *Social Register*, the "social ritual," the effort of society to keep track of itself, to maintain its integrity and solidarity, to distinguish among those who are "in" and those who are "out," is something more than snobbery. For the effectiveness of the Gold Coast's leadership, the fulfilment of its rôle in the life of the city, depends upon the maintaining of this solidarity. The Gold Coast plays a more vital rôle in the life of Chicago than does Park Avenue in the life of New York because it has been more successful in preserving its solidarity.

Great changes are impending in the life of the city. What the city's future will be, it is hard to predict. But a study of the areas of the inner city cannot but give us a clearer and more realistic appreciation of the character of the city's life and the city's problems, a more accurate evaluation of the rôles that various groups have played and are playing in controlling the city's destiny. And it seems probable that the rôle of the Gold Coast will be more significant than that of the street meeting in Bughouse Square, the discussions in the garrets of Towertown, or the political club over the shop of Romano the barber.

[1] *Loc. cit.*, pp. 224–26.

INDEX

Abbott, Edith, 71

Addams, Jane, 262

Aggregation of population, 208. *See also* City

Alson, E. W., 30

Anatomy of the city, 231

Anderson, Nels, 106, 108, 111, 115, 270

Anonymity, 73, 75, 80, 82, 86, 91, 98, 99, 100, 104, 116, *248–50*. *See also* City

Beggars, panhandlers, street fakers, 110 ff. *See also* Rialto of the Half-World

Board of Education, 188, 202–3

Bogardus, Emory, 240

Bohemia. *See* Towertown

Bowen, Louise De Koven, 10, 275–80

Breckinridge, S., 71

Brown, L. Guy, 111

Bughouse Square, 114. *See also* Rialto of the Half-World

Burgess, E. W., 230, 233, 238, 250, 270

Centralization and decentralization, 230. *See also* City

Chatfield-Taylor, H. C., 1, 22, 39, 41, 45

Chicago: early immigration, 18; founding of, 17; frontier town, 18; hobo capital, 105; incorporated as a city, 18; river industries, 19, 25; "wobbly" capital, 114

Church: changing community and the, *182 ff.;* Fourth Presbyterian, 185; Gold Coast, 184–85; missions, 107, 153; Moody Bible Institute,

198; Negro, 183; Plymouth Congregational, 186; Sicilian, 177–78, 183–85

City: aggregation of population, 208; anatomy of, 231; anonymity of, 80, 248, 251; centralization, 230; city plan, 228–29, 270–73; decentralization, 230; democracy in, 274, 279; differentiation of community mentalities, 244; diversity of vocational interest, 237–42; division of labor, 237; ecology of, 69, 155, *232;* expansion, 1, 3, 4, 28–29, 33, 41, 42, *229;* individuation of behavior in, 245 ff.; mobility of, 43, 44, 67, 68, 71–73, 126, 145, 148, 176, *245–49;* muckraking, 255–57; municipal voters' leagues, 272; natural areas, 231; natural barriers, 6, 41, *231;* natural history of, 229, *256;* problems of, 254; politics in, 193–94, 198, 252–58, 268, 273–74; realistic attitude toward problems of, 254; reform in, 221, 268–70; rôle of various groups in life of, 274 ff.; segregation in, 20, 64, *232–36;* settlements, 261–63; social distances in, 12, 13, 15, 45, 126, 151, 153, 216–19, *242–44;* social survey of, 259; succession, 4, 34–36, 41, 43, 70, 102, 127, 147–50, 160–61, *230–36;* typical zones of, 229–30; zoning, 272–73

City planning, 228–29, 270–73

Clark Street. *See* Rialto of the Half-World

Committee of Fifteen, 117, 119. *See also* Vice

Community: action, 225–28; board of education and community center movement, 188, 202, 203; church and community life, 182–86, 198, 235; common experience as basis of, 237; community organi-

281

zation movement, 261–67; disintegration of, and social disorganization, 16; family and community, 188–89;little more than a geographical expression in city, 16; Lower North Community Council, 200 ff.; mentalities, 244; merchants' associations and community life, 189–91; mobility and the community, 247–52; natural organization of, 221; nature of, 222–28; Near North Side, 182; newspaper and local life, 191; opinion regulates behavior of members, 223–28; police, government by, 195–99; school and community, 154, 164, 187–88; social agencies and community life, 195–99, 200–201, 220; suburban, 227–28; succession and community life, 235–36; village, 182–83, 223–27; vocational interests and community life, 236–42

Community organization movement: Cincinnati experiment, 264–67; community councils, 264; Lower North Community Council, 200 ff.; rise of, 261; settlements and, 262–63; social unit plan of, 263

Crime: black hand, 170–73; cabaret and liquor vending, 116–18; dance halls, 120–21; disorganization of second generation immigrant, 153–58; dope peddling, 123, 135–36; gangs, 156, 174; mafia, 164, 170–73; prostitution, 120; slum, 156–58; vice, 114–23; underworld, 118–19, 137–38

Crime Commission, 156

Cultural conflict, 152–58, 176. See also Disorganization

Currey, J. S., 22

Dance halls, 120–21. See also Rialto of Half-World

Daniels, John, 141

Day, Helen A., 164

Death Corner, 170–71. See also Little Hell

Delinquency. See Crime, Disorganization, Slum, Little Hell

Democracy, old and new, 274, 279. See also Politics

Dill Pickle Club, 89–91, 96, 101

Disorganization, personal and social: beggars and panhandlers, 110–12; black hand, 170–73; cabarets and vice, 116–18; conflict of cultures, 152–58, 176; crime, 156–58; dance halls, 120–21; drink and drugs, 123, 135–36; economic failure, 130–32; family disorganization, 153–54, 175–76, 188–89; gang and delinquency, 154–56, 174, 192; government by police and social agency, 195–99; human derelicts, 122 ff.; mafia, 164, 170–73; pauperism, 152; physical inadequacy, 110, 130–32; political disorganization, 193 ff., see also Politics; prostitution, 120 ff.; rooming-house life,80ff.; sex, 96, 99, 100, 109, 112; shut in personalities, 84, 85; suicide,83;Towertown an escape from conventions of more stable communities, 91, 98, 99, 104; underworld, 137–38; unstable personalities, 92, 96, 97, 98, 132 ff.; vice, 114, 115, 118, 121, 123

Division of labor, 237 ff.

Dope, 123, 135, 136. See also Crime

Ecology of the city, 6, 19, 25, 41, 69, 122, 123, 128, 141, 154–55, 231

Economic inadequacy, 129 ff. See also Slum

Eli Bates House, 50, 178, 200–201

Expansion, a process of city growth, 229

Family disorganization, 153–54, 175–76, 188–89. See also Disorganization and Cultural Conflict

Fergus, Robert, 21, 27

"Five hundred dancing men," 56. See Gold Coast

Forbes, Genevieve, 92

Foreign colonies. See Slum

Fourth Presbyterian Church, 50, 80, *183 ff.*

Free love, 99. *See* Towertown

Gang: criminal gangs, 174; delinquency and the gang, 156; ecology of the gang, 154–55; gang and community, 191–92. *See also* Slum

Germans, 4, 19, 20, 22, 25, 127, *150*

Gold Coast, 7, *45 ff.;* ability segregated on, 47; apartments break up community life of, 66; as it appears to the slum, 15; assemblies, 50; churches, 50, 184–85; clubs, 50, 192–93; community life, 63 ff.; diversity of interests, 67–68; ethnocentrism of, 219; "five hundred dancing men," 56; Friday Club, 62; "hall-room boys," 56; hotels, 50; Lake Shore Drive becomes the fashionable place to live, 39–40; "little brothers to the rich," 56; Lower North Community Council, 200 ff.; mobility, 67–68; North Michigan Avenue, 7, 41–42; rôle in philanthropic and civic movements, 61–62; segregation, 64; social climber, 51 ff.; social distance, 45, 217–19; social game, 49–56; social position, 49–51; *Social Register,* 47–50; social ritual, 57 ff.; social secretary, 55, 56; society (defined, 45, 46; class-consciousness, 63, 64; growth of city breaks up old society, 47–48, highly localized, 64, 65; old society based on family almost a clan, 47; resolves itself into sets and cliques, 65; society in early Chicago, 3, the sixties, 20, the eighties, 26 ff.); solidarity of caste rather than of contiguity, 68; wealth segregated on, 47

Gold Coast Book Store, 108

Government. *See* Politics

Greeks, 4, 12, *145–47*

Hall, Norman, 49

"Hall-room boys," 56. *See* Gold Coast

Harrison, Shelby, 260

Hayner, Norman S., 119

Hobo, 106 ff. *See* Rialto of Half-World

Homosexual, 96, 100. *See* Towertown

Hungarians, 149–51

Hurd, Richard M., 229

Immigrant areas. *See* Slum

Immigrant Protective League, 143

Immigration, five great waves of, 19

Individuality of behavior. *See* Disorganization

Irish, 4, 30 ff., 35, 127

Isolation, 78 ff. *See also* Rooming-house

Juvenile Protective Association, 116, 119, 121

Kirkland, Caroline, 21, 27

Lake Shore Drive, 7. *See also* Gold Coast

Laura Spelman Rockefeller Memorial, 270

Levitt, Marie, 171, 173

Little Hell characterized, 5, 31, *159 ff.;* Death Corner, 170; Eli Bates House, 178; gangs and crime, 174; history of, 160; invaded by the Sicilian, 160–61; nationality composition, 161; physical aspect, 159; Sicilian (American law and life, 173–74; black hand, 171–73; church, 163, 167–68, 177–78; community, 164, 167, 180; disorganization of second generation, 176–77; economic status, 174; family life, 162–63, 167–69, 175–76; Little Sicily an Old World village, 164–70; mafia, 164, 170–73; mobility and conflict of cultures, 176; Old World traits, 162–64, 164–70; political attitudes, 162, 175, 177–80; settlement and the, 178); succession, 160–61

Little Sicily. *See* Little Hell

Loop, 1, 2, 229–30

Lower North Community Council, *200 ff.;* a local council of social agencies, 219; activities of, 207–11; council of national defense, 203–4; difficulties encountered, 211–13; financing of, 220; Madison conference on school centers, 202; origin of, 204; program of, 205–9; realistic attitude toward local life, 213–15; school center movement, 202; social distances revealed, 216–19

Mencken, H. L., 88

Mentalities of city communities, 244

Merchants' associations, 189–91

Miller, H. A., 141, 164, 171

Mission, 107, 153. *See* Rialto of Half-World and Church

Mobility: cause of cultural conflict, 247–48; defined, *245–46;* Little Hell, 176; local opinion dissolved by, 247–49; measurement of, 43, 44, 245–46; on Rialto of Half-World, 122; rooming-house, 71–73; slum, 145, 148; social life atomized by, 248–49. *See also* City

Mowrer, Ernest, 270

Muckraking, 255 ff. *See* Newspaper and Politics

Municipal voters leagues, 272. *See* Politics

Nationality groups. *See* Population

Natural area, 231. *See* City and Ecology

Natural history of the city, 229, 256

Near North Side, an area of contrasts, 4 ff.; an area in transition, 17 ff.; becomes an area of the inner city, 32; building, no residence built in past ten years, 128; characterized, 44–45; Chicago fire wipes out, 23; history of, 17 ff.; nationality composition of population, *see* Population; population declining, 43; transportation, 3, 6, 18, 19, 25

Negro, 4, 38, 127, 147–49

Nesbit, Florence, 143

Newspaper: local life and, 191; muckraking and the yellow press, 256 ff.; parliamentary function of debate taken over by, 260; publicity, creates faith in, 258; social politics and, 258 ff.; *Times* exposé of Tweed ring, 255. *See also* Politics

Pal Re-sale Shop, 125

Park, R. E., 141, 164, 171, 230, 233, 238, 243, 250, 257, 270

Parliamentary government in the city, 252 ff. *See also* Politics

Pawnshop, 107, 122 ff. *See also* Rialto of Half-World

Persians, 4, 12, 38, 142–45

Physical inadequacy, 110, 130, 132. *See* Disorganization and Slum

Pluralism, 272. *See* Politics

Police, government by, 195–99. *See also* Politics and Social Agency

Politics: becomes a game, 254–55; and the city plan, 228–29, 270–73; community organization movement, 261–67; democracy old and new, 274, 279; effect of the city's growth on, 254; and local problems, 193–94, 198; muckraking, 255; municipal voters' leagues, 272; *New York Times'* exposé of Tweed, 255; occupational attitudes and local life, 238–42, 272; parliamentary government fails in city, 252 ff., 268; police, government by, 195, 197, 199; realistic attitude toward city's problems, 270 ff.; reform (breakdown of local life, 252; conflict of rural and urban cultures, 269; futility of much, 270; rôle of reformer, 269–70; typical history of, 221); rôles of various groups in, 279; settlements, 261–63; Sicilian political attitudes, 162, 175, 177–80; social agency, government by, 195–99; social politics, and community life,

261; nature of, 260; public opinion and, 273–74; related to organized charities movement, 258; rise of, 258; rôle of Gold Coast in, 274 ff.; social questions lack political expression, 198, 254; social survey, 259; yellow press creates a faith in publicity, 251–58; zoning, 272–73

Population: of Near North Side (in 1866, 19; in 1884, 25; at time of Fair, 32; in 1910, 37; in 1920, 45; today, 4); German, 4, 19, 20, 22, 25, 127, 150; Greek, 4, 12, 145–47; Hungarian, 149–51; immigration, 19; Irish, 4, 30 ff., 35, 127; Little Hell, 161; Negro, 4, 38, 127, 147–49; Persian, 4, 12, 38, 142–45; rooming-house, 70, 71; Sicilian, 4, 34, 35, 38, 127, 159 ff.; slum, 128; succession of nationalities, 34, 35, 127, 150, 160–61; Swedish, 4, 25, 30, 35, 127, 150

Prostitution, 120. See Crime, Disorganization, Rialto of Half-World, and Vice

Rauber, E. L., 75

Realism and city life, 270 ff. See Politics.

Reform, 252 ff. See Politics.

Rialto of the Half-World, 105 ff.; barber shop the local news bureau, 107; beggars, panhandlers, 110–12; Bughouse Square, 114; business, 42; cabarets, 116–18; Gold Coast Book Store, 108; dance halls, 120–21; dope, 123; "flops," 106; history, 28; hobo, 106 ff.; main street to the slum, 10; missions, 107; night life, 115 ff.; pawnbroker, character of, 124–25; pawnshop, 107, 122 ff.; prostitutes no longer a caste, 120; prostitution and the cabaret, 120; psychopathic personalities, 114; physically handicapped, 110; rialto types, 105; sex and status, 109, 112; squawker, 110; street fakers, 112; underworld, 118, 119; vice, 114–23; "wobbly" agitators, 114–15

Riis, Jacob, 255

Robinson, H. N., 148

Rooming-house district, 8 ff., 69 ff.; anonymity of, 73, 75, 82; as a social situation, 72–74; boarding-house contrasted with rooming-house, 73; charity girl, life-story of, 76 ff.; community lacking, 82; disorganization, 37, 80, 81; ecology of, 69; history of the typical, 69, 71; individuation of behavior, 86; isolation, 82; location of, 8; loneliness in, 78; mobility of, 71, 72, 82; political indifference of, 82; population of, 7, 71; phantasy as compensation for wish thwarting, 84, 85; shut-in personalities, 84, 85; social control breaks down, 82; social groups lacking, 82; social relationships, 82; suicide, 83; wishes thwarted, 82, 83

Russell Sage Foundation, 270

Schools: board of education and community center movement, 188, 202–3; community life and the, 187–88; conflict of cultures and the, 154; Gold Coast, 188; Jenner, 164

Segregation: as a social process, 232–34; early segregation by nationality and cultural status, 20 ff.; Gold Coast an illustration of, 64; rooming-house district, 70, 71. See also City

Shaw, Clifford, 157

Sicilian. See Little Hell and Population

Sinclair, Upton, 257

Slum, 10 ff.; area of disintegration and disorganization, 128; as it appears to the world at large through the news, 14; attitudes accommodate the person to, 132, 134–53; characteristic patterns of life, 151; Clark Street, Main Street to, 10; conflict of cultures, 153–54; contacts with conventional world through law and social agency, 152; cosmopolitan, 157; created by expansion of Loop, 4, 128–29; crime, 156–58; delinquency, 156; drink and dope, 135–36; economic failures, 130–32; family, 153–54; gang, 155–56; German colony, 149–51; Greek colony, 145–47; history of, 21 ff.; inadequate personalities, 132 ff.; immigrant colonies (areas of first settlement, 128; characterized, 139–41; disorganization of second generation, 153–58; ghetto the pattern of, 140; isolation of, 141; reason for location in slum, 141); interpenetration of cultures and breakdown of social control, 152; location of, 9; lodging area, 70, 129; man's world, 139; missions, 153; Negro colony, 147–49; Persian colony, 142–45; physical aspect of, 128; physical inadequacy, 130, 132; population, 128; segregation of sediment of society, 129; social agency a legitimate graft, 152; social distances reduced to a minimum, 151; sociological meaning of, 151; Swedish colony, 149–51; types of human derelict, 129 ff., 132; tenement town, 129; underworld, 137–38. See also Little Hell, Rialto of Half-World, and Social Agency

Social agencies: charity organization movement, 258–59; church, 182 ff.; community organization, 261–67; Eli Bates House, 200–201; financing of, 220; government by, 195–99; legitimate graft to resident of the slum, 152; Lower North Community Council, 200 ff.; missions, 107, 153; settlements, 200–201, 262–63; United Charities, Lower North District, 5, 130, 132, 174–75

Social climber, 51 ff. See Gold Coast

Social control and the community, 223–28

Social distance: cultural isolation the problem of the city, 15; defined, 242; distances among cultural areas or Near North Side, 13, 126, 153; isolation beneath cul-

tural contrasts of city's life, 12 ff.; life of city atomized by, 45; little in village, 253; revealed by attempt of Lower North Community Council to organize the Near North Side, 216–19; rise of in city, 243–44. See also City.

Social game, 49–56. See Gold Coast

Social politics. See Politics

Social position, 50, 51. See Gold Coast

Social Register, 47–50. See Gold Coast

Social ritual, 57 ff. See Gold Coast

Social secretary, 55, 56. See Gold Coast

Social survey, 259. See Politics

Society. See Gold Coast

Squawker, 110 ff. See Rialto of Half-World

Steffens, Lincoln, 229, 256

Streeterville, 32, 41

Succession: as a process, 230–35; city's streets can be read like the geological record in the rock, 4; effect on community life, 235–36; expansion of the Loop, 1, 3, 4, 128–29; industry takes over the slum, 43; of nationalities, 34, 35, 127, 147–49, 150, 160–61; rooming-house district, 35, 36, 41, 70; the "village" passes, 102. See also City

Suicide, 83. See Rooming-house

Swedes, 4, 25, 30, 35, 127, 150

Tarbell, Ida, 257

Thomas, W. I., 223, 225, 227, 247, 248

Thrasher, Frederick M., 156, 270

Towertown, 87 ff.; bohemia, 92–96; commercialization of bohemian reputation, 101; contrasted with Greenwich Village and the Latin Quarter, 91; Dill Pickle Club, 89, 90, 91, 96, 101; expansion of Loop obliterating, 102; flavor of art, 88, 89; free love, 99; homosexuals, 96, 100; hunger for new experience, 90; location, 12, 87; radicalism, 90; poseurs and dilettantes, 92; region of escape from conventions of more stable communities, 98, 99; rôle in the city's life, 104; student life, 90; Three Arts Club, 90; personalities, 97, 98; a woman's bohemia, 91

Trotter, 69, 74

Underworld. *See* Slum, Little Hell, Rialto of the Half-World

United Charities, Lower North District, 5, 130, 132, 174–75

Urban League, 148

Van Rensselaer, Mrs. John King, 48, 49

Veblen, Thorstein, 240

Vice, 114–23. *See also* Disorganization and Crime

Village communities, 182–83, 223–27

"Village," the. *See* Towertown

Vocational attitudes and community life, 236–42. *See also* City

Warner, A. G., 259

Williams, J. M., 240

Wirth, L., 270

Wolfe, A. B., 71, 73

Woods, R. A., 262

Yellow press, 257 ff. *See* Newspaper and Politics

Young, Kimbal, 129, 198

Zoning, 272, 73. *See* Politics

Please remember that this is a library book,
and that it belongs only temporarily to each
person who uses it. Be considerate. Do
not write in this, or any, library book.

DATE DUE
